Published by
Orders: Please con
www.ar
First published 2015
ISBN: 978-0-9573179-7-0
Copyright © Antony Stagg

All rights reserved.
Apart from any permitted use under UK copyright law,
no part of this publication may be reproduced or transmitted
in any form or by any means, electronic or mechanical,
including photocopying, recording, or any information,
storage or retrieval system, without permission in
writing from the publisher or under license from
the Copyright Licensing Agency Limited.
Further details of such licenses
(for reprographic reproduction)
may be obtained from the
Copyright Licensing Agency Ltd,
Saffron House, 6-10 Kirby Street, London EC1N 8TS.

Editing
We write for you
http://wewriteforyou.co.uk/

Wrate's Editing Services
www.wrateseditingservices.co.uk

Typeset by www.colourbox.net

Printed in Great Britain by Bell & Bain Ltd,
303 Burnfield Road, Thornliebank,
Glasgow G46 7UQ.

Special thanks to my Mum and Dad

Also raising awareness for Stick 'n' Step,
a charity helping children with cerebral palsy.
www.sticknstep.org

**Note to reader:
please read, it's important.**

All the stories in this book are true.
They are emotional, graphic,
inspirational, and they cover a number
of adversities, including: cancer, alcohol
addiction, extreme car accidents,
ill health, amputation and many more…
The best way to read this book is from
the beginning. That way you will
understand how it came to be and what
has evolved as a result of the journey.

Contents

Introduction

You know something is wrong when you experience the flutter of butterflies in your stomach. Overwhelmingly happy and blindly in love, I'd chosen the rustic and romantic setting of the south of France to propose to my girlfriend. Searching for quaint little places in the fortified town of Carcassonne, I was eager to find somewhere impressive. On the list in my mind was a restaurant housed in a medieval stone building. It had a roaring fire and ivy draped from the walls. What failed to cross my mind is the fact that I would never make it there…

My last working act on December 18 2012 was to rush to catch a train in the cold winter sun. Looking down at my phone I read a text message from my girlfriend. 'Can we talk?' it read. Instantaneously, I knew. This was not good. I felt my intestines gurgling and turning inside me, as if they were about to explode on the pavement beneath my feet.

The 30-minute journey back home, where my girlfriend was waiting for me, seemed to take hours. When we finally sat down to talk, I thought how sudden her change of heart was. We had sat and planned for Christmas. She knew about everything apart from the ring.

I did my best to remain calm and tried to understand her uneasiness. Things like this do happen, I reasoned, people do change their minds. Maybe it was too soon for us to tie the knot. After all, we'd only been together for a year. But this was different; like nothing I'd experienced in previous relationships. There was a knowing and I trusted my intuition - it had never failed me before.

The following days passed by painfully. My happy perspective on life became blurred; my rose tinted view of the world morphed into a blunt and negative self-evaluation of the past few months in other areas of my life as I searched for reasons for her sudden U-turn.

I drove to the local shops and wished there was an eject button in the driver's seat of the car to beam me to a far and distant land. Every time I scanned through the radio stations, a Christmas song belted out through the speakers. Mariah Carey's *All I want for Christmas is you*. *Bye Mariah* I thought as I switched stations to hear Slade's *Merry Xmas Everybody*. I used to love that song, but not today.

Just a few months earlier, in March 2012, I'd taken the plunge to work on my business full time. I'd left a safe, secure job to create a company that helped young unemployed people in North West England get back into employment and training.

The leap was rewarding and challenging, and, after many setbacks and obstacles, my business partner and I successfully got 21 out of the 30 people we worked with into jobs or training schemes. This was amazing, especially considering our target was 10.

Despite our passion and hunger, and praise from MPs and local councillors, our funding dried up, which meant that we could no longer continue our business. I felt angry and disillusioned. It had worked for Christ's sake. How could the funding be discontinued? The hopes and aspirations of young people were so low down on the list of priorities that they straddled the curb. It also appeared that I would need to use my own techniques to begin a job search myself!

I began exploring others ideas: writing books, working online. I spent hours and hours seeking new opportunities. My girlfriend and I were still together, but her declaration that she wasn't ready to take our relationship to the next level had made things awkward between us. I still felt the same about her, but something wasn't right.

I'd planned to crouch down on one knee on December 21 2012. It was a date in history that many people fretted over, as it signified the end of the Mayan calendar. A date of doom, it was the end of the world according to prophets from the past (or at least, that's the way we interpreted it). Trust me to pick such a date!

Then came another shock. My nan, who had lived literally 300 metres away from me for nearly all my life, was taken into hospital. My attention diverted to the past. As a 10 year old, I would skateboard from the top of her road towards her house, allowing the momentum and sharp slope to carry me along at speed. Ice cream and lemonade in a tall glass awaited me, along with endless supplies of chocolate biscuits.

Nan was the matriarch of the family, a woman who radiated warmth and wisdom. Perhaps her astuteness was gained from all the years she had spent working as a nurse at Mossley Hill Hospital in Liverpool; a job she loved.

She was a living great, great grandmother, with so many grandchildren it's impossible for me to come up with a number. It was a sudden and emotional piece of news so close to Christmas.

When December 21 2012 arrived, I wished I had a remote control so that I could fast forward it. I was like a child who looks forward to attending a birthday party, ready for fun and excitement, only to feel the complete desolation of realising they'd got the date wrong.

Feeling foolish, I sat in an environment of apathy with my girlfriend. We were in a bar called Que Pasa. Situated in Lark Lane, Liverpool, the place normally had a nice feel, but not today. The small tea lights flickering gently on the compact pine tables did nothing to stir any romantic feelings. In fact, we didn't make it past looking at the menu before an argument ensued. At one point, someone opened a large glass door and the icy wet air from outside slapped me in the face. What's going on? I thought. This is not right. I still felt shocked and embarrassed over my girlfriend's decision, and so empty when I visualised the vacant seats on the plane to France.

Vacant was the word to describe the following day. On December 22, a different shade of heartbreak was delivered. Later in the evening, my dad rang me to inform me of my nan's passing.

She'd only been taken in as a precaution. How could this have happened? I am usually OK with death. After all, it happens to everyone and my nan had lived a full life and was in her 80s. But the shock of her passing, coupled with the timing of it, became too much. I felt for my mum, too. She'd lost a parent and the two of them had been very close.

I'd never appreciated how grim Christmas could be before. Instead of having fun, I chose to stay away from the festivities. I didn't feel like celebrating after having just lost my grandmother and having my relationship butchered by the sudden decision of my girlfriend. I sat with my family on Christmas Day shuffling food around my plate without even attempting to be sociable. I just wanted to be on my own.

To make matters worse, all the presents that my girlfriend and I had bought for each other sat unopened under the tree; she was employed by an airline and was working on both Christmas Eve and Christmas Day.

Alone on the evening of Christmas Day, I sat in darkness watching repeats on TV. I toyed with escaping to Australia to see one of my friends. If worse came to worst, the warmth of the sun could cheer me up and I could start a new life.

However, once my girlfriend returned home, a weird, uneasy truce grew between us as I tried to paper over the cracks. Scratching my head I thought, what cracks? How has this happened? The last year has been amazing.

Even though it was a shaky foundation, my thoughts turned to the funeral. Will my mum hold up? Will everyone be OK? Grief wasn't a new emotion for us. Over the past couple of years we'd lost two family members far too young to cancer.

The funeral was to be held in Woolton, a small suburb of Liverpool. It's where I grew up, and it was literally a two-minute walk from my girlfriend's place, where we lived together.

It's a small village, a tiny dot on the global map, but it's a place with a huge history. The church bells of St Peter's bellow out night and day from their elevated position, as if keeping watch on the streets of sandstone terraced houses below. Another church, St Mary's, stands right next door to it. People new to the area always get confused which one to attend, but it's always St Mary's for funerals and St Peter's for weddings.

St Peter's Church is famed for being the place where John Lennon and Paul McCartney first met. It's also the subconscious birthplace of the Beatles song Eleanor Rigby. The headstone of a woman by that name is amongst the graves.

Four days into January, I was standing in a graveyard. As well as giving us a chance to say goodbye to Nan, the funeral was about reflecting on her life, celebrating it and telling stories. However, throughout the day, my mind was scrambled. I could feel my girlfriend's uneasiness as she stood beside me. The following morning she told me that the relationship was no longer working. We were over.

Slumped on the couch, my jaw gaped open in shock as I tried to process what she'd just told me. In my anger, I threw the house keys at her, stormed out of the front door, rattled the garden gate open and walked to my parents' home through the same church grounds I'd been in the previous day.

Within a couple of days, I discovered there was someone else in my girlfriend's life. I felt a range of emotions, from anger to utter desolation. I felt like such a failure. Just a couple of weeks earlier I'd been on cloud nine. How could I now be sat in the gutter? What the fu*k was going on?

Standing at the side of a quiet road to escape my family's concern, I bent over retching. Still in shock, I stood there trying to be sick when all that was left was bile.

You're a joke, I thought. No wonder she's gone! I'd been pissing about with new ideas, had no car or consistent income.
Now I was going to have to move back to my childhood home.
I'd never faced heartbreak or real failure in my life before.

There was no manual that told you how to cope. And with that, escape became my dominant thought. Australia here I come. A new job and lifestyle. The clear Indian Ocean of Western Australia or the ice covered roads of Liverpool? I pursued Australia, hounding my friend to speak to his bosses about job possibilities. *Get me an interview, get me on that plane*, I thought.

Meanwhile, I wallowed in self-pity as I sat with a ring worth thousands of pounds. Having just sold my house a couple of months earlier, I'd only just managed to pay off my debts. I was back in my old single bed in a room full of blank magnolia walls. My two-year-old nephew slept in the adjacent room with my sister and would wake screaming in the middle of the night. What had I done to deserve this?

The ring sat on my bedside table. *This piece of shit has to go back*, I thought. So the following day I set off on the 45-minute journey to Knutsford in Cheshire, where I'd bought it. My dad came with me for support.

I jangled the bell on the jeweller's front door with a solemn face. The owner, who'd served me so many times before, peered at me over his glasses, as if stunned by my return. My body language stank of rejection and I decided to tell him only what he needed to know. I certainly wasn't going to tell him the full story.

'I need to get some money back on the ring,' I said.
Shocked, he didn't know what to say at first.

'I've not seen this in over 25 years,' he eventually replied.

Thanks, I feel real special now! I thought.

Handing it over, I thought it would release some anxiety, that somehow this would go away, but no, not at all. I might as well have flushed it down the toilet. It's funny how things are worth half as much as soon as you walk out of a shop.

Shuffling along the quaint high street, the soles of my shoes scraped along the pavement as if I was a prisoner tied to a heavy ball and chain. On the return journey home, Dad was on go slow. His short cuts took longer, which fuelled my anger and frustration and stretched the thin amount of patience I had left.

Back at my parents' house, I agonised over the decision to stick or twist on moving to Australia. There were still things to pay for, and trying to motivate myself became hard because I didn't have a regular pattern to my day.

Luckily, I landed a two-week contract working in a school. The money I'd earn from it would be enough to lift me out of my financial decline.

In the meantime, a job offer came through from Australia and I read the contract. It described a role I knew I wouldn't want to perform - recruiting people in the oil and gas industry. I'd escaped working for other people. Although being my own boss was tough, it felt good. Plus, there were too many loose ends. What if I could resurrect my relationship? Was I mad to even think that? Would I want to? What about the ocean and sunshine? A new lifestyle, rooftop terraces, beers in the sun and walks along the beach. Was I mad not to accept?

I drew on my previous experience. I'd been here before. Twice in the past I'd chosen to ignore my feelings when making decisions regarding career moves. Now for a third time my stomach churned.

The butterflies were back, but not in a good way – it was a signal not to go through with it.

But worse followed. Something happened which angered me. I didn't get paid for the work I'd been subcontracted to do at the school, and more rage erupted from my core. I was relying on that money! My calls and emails were never returned – it was a complete disgrace. I now didn't have enough money even to fly to Australia, let alone pay rent until my new employer paid me.

All I could think about was getting my own back. I was consumed with thoughts of revenge and destroying the people who felt not a tinge of remorse for what they had done to me. But in reality I couldn't do that, it's not me. I'm writing about it now only to describe how the journey started.

After much thought, I decided to stay put and try and get my business back on track. I had to earn fast, and turned to my friend and mentor, Alan McCarthy, to get me through this bumpy financial time. He is an amazing man. He possesses a genuine passion; a philanthropic desire to see people progress and grow. Short in stature and bullish in personality, he can smell bullshit the way a shark can smell a drop of blood in the ocean from miles away. It was these traits that would help me carve through the admin process I was about to encounter.

I began a new quest to secure some local government funding. This involved constant battles through the goo of bureaucracy. Each meeting seemed to extract my will from within. It took at least eight weeks to receive a yes, but then the race was on to deliver. Weeks of effort commenced. This involved designing a course, finding students and begging schools to let me train those students who hadn't responded well in the classroom. I wanted to prove again that with the right training and work experience, students could flourish. I wanted to show that we had a product capable of making a difference - and surely this time there would be no doubts...

We put every ounce of effort we had into creating this programme, yet there were so many hurdles to jump through. Administration, health and safety documentation, parents' meetings...the list was endless.

Despite this, my determination was fuelled by my desire to return to my own space. I wanted to rejoice in freedom again, and not be woken by crying babies in the middle of the night. This was just the opportunity I needed to wake up and eliminate this nightmare existence I'd found myself in.

By the time the four-week programme commenced, my adrenaline tank was nearly empty. Now the real work would begin, and managing a large group of the most challenging students takes its toll, even though it is immensely rewarding.

I felt a great sense of pride once the programme was complete. I continued to support the students by making visits to their parents' homes. This time, 13 out of the 15 students we worked with secured jobs or training. I felt buoyant; our hard work had paid off. But the next phase of meetings burst my bubble.

It was the same old story every time. No money and no urgency. The public sector was descending into chaos because so many people were losing their jobs. It was the same everywhere I went until it got to the point where I was becoming a nuisance. The situation became a carbon copy of the previous year's failing, but there was still a huge problem to be solved. Reading the newspapers everyday, I'd learn how huge companies commissioned to tackle unemployment were receiving millions of pounds. However, they only managed to place 3 in 10 people into employment. This was because they were big companies and had certain policies in place that were impossible for smaller organisations to adhere to.

It was now June 2013. I was disheartened that my passion to facilitate change wasn't shared by the idiots I had to deal with. The money in my bank account was dwindling fast so I borrowed money to survive. I felt ashamed to ask a girl out. *Who is going to want to go out with me?* I thought. I could picture the initial conversation.

'So, what do you do?'

'I help young people, but the business failed after it worked.'

'Where do you live?'

'With my mum and dad.'

'What car do you drive?'

'I don't.'

Sound like a great catch, don't I?

My confidence was like a sponge on a hot summer's day - bone dry - and I was unable to eek out just a little bit of hope. My exterior showed a brave face and a false smile that said 'leave me alone'.

I had a scattergun approach to my work, doing bits of recruitment, bits on YouTube, bits teaching students and bits of writing. People would ask me what I did and I didn't know what to say. I felt uncomfortable saying 'entrepreneur'. The little voice in my head would reply, 'fu*k off, not you mate'. So was I a teacher, trainer, business owner? I was like a badly glued model train. My wheels had come off and there was no fire in the engine, but I needed to get back on track; any track. I realised that I needed some inspiration. I wanted to understand how people recover from adversity. I was not naïve enough to think that I was the only person to have had a hard time of it. Millions of people have been through worse than me. People around the world experience relationship problems, death and financial challenges, it's life. My girlfriend and the other people who had caused me pain, just made decisions that affected me. It didn't stop my anger though. When you're in the eye of the storm, you don't really care about what's going on with others. Well, that's how I felt anyway.

Now over half way through the year, and out of the blue, a thought occurred. Write a book to help inspire others. For once I didn't hesitate and, in July 2013, I began.

Ben Donnelly – Redemption

Feeling optimistic and determined, I began to craft an outline of how I could achieve my vision. Deciding on 40 stories, each around four pages long, I decided I wanted to meet regular people; people who have overcome adversity and whose stories were not as accessible as, say, famous people's are. My desire was to record a broad cross section of experiences that could inspire others who were lost in a thick fog of negative emotion. However, it wasn't long before I poured cold water on the vision.

What would I say? How would I find these people? Why on Earth would they speak to me? Deep down the doubts began to rise, but equally a passion burned. I had to start somewhere and I did this with a phone call to Ben Donnelly.

Ben was my first ever customer back in 2010. I first met him at a presentation he delivered in 2009, and I knew right away that we would keep in contact. He had an amazing energy, and was so passionate, ambitious and positive. He gave people the opportunity to restart their lives and I knew there was a story behind his business – I just had find out what it was.

I borrowed my sister's tiny grey Nissan Duke, which was a huge benefit, even though at 6'3" tall, I resembled a man in a Wendy house. I was sipping a strawberry McDonald's milkshake as I drove into the industrial unit to meet Ben. It was unusually hot. Workers wearing high visibility vests stood outside, basking in the sunshine. Only the slightest breeze was enough to force dust through the pallets of old wood; this stung my eyes like the wisps of sand on a beach.

The building Ben worked from was a recycling centre. The size of an aircraft hanger, it was full of old plastics and other unwanted materials. Here, he had created a social enterprise to provide employment opportunities for people who had made some unwise decisions in the past.

Despite it being a long time since I had last seen him, Ben hadn't changed much. He still had the same broad smile, thin build and longish blonde hair brushed back over his head. In fact, he looked similar to Brad Pitt - a comment to please any bloke.

Chewing the fat, there was a lot to catch up on and we reflected for some time. Sitting forward in a leather chair, with my elbows resting against an office desk, the conversation turned to the motive behind my planned book. I told Ben about my nightmare over the last few months, which naturally led to him discussing his own story.

Ben Donnelly

Litter, dust and junk piled up high in the buildings that lay abandoned near my home in Wavertree, Liverpool. Life was cramped in the typical two-bed Edwardian terrace where I lived with my parents and brothers and sisters. My mum and dad had both experienced difficult childhoods and raising a young family during a time of high unemployment and deprivation was a significant challenge for them.

The stench and plumes of smoke from cigarettes poisoned the air inside my home. My first childhood memories, from around the age of five, are of the sounds of glasses clinking against tables and the smell of smouldering ash.

The smoke came from a congregation of my mum's friends. They huddled in a tiny room nattering away for hours upon hours. This meant one thing; alcohol. My dad was often absent because of the situation at home. The constant comings and goings encouraged him to stay in the pub and do his drinking there.

Alcohol nearly always induced volatility in my parents, which made them unpredictable. Violent and vicious arguments usually manifested, meaning plates, glasses and their contents splattered the walls. Having the honour of being the oldest child was far from a pleasurable experience as I'd be caught in the crossfire trying to quell the violence. The following day, however, my mum and dad would plod down the stairs as if nothing had happened. But this was alcohol and what it could do to people.

There were better times, and I remember my mum's cooking - she was and is fantastic in the kitchen. My friends loved coming over to sample her culinary talents and she never disappointed. She has a heart of gold and would always give her own food away to others, but it was the alcohol that killed the love. Booze seems to mask the true personality of a person, and it certainly destroys family values. Indeed, my home would be very different at times from the ones experienced by my friends.

I remember waking up one morning surrounded by a sea of broken glass. In our house, each door had a windowpane and all of them had been smashed. Greeted by an eerily silent atmosphere, I slowly descended the staircase careful not to slice my unprotected feet. Much of the glass lay hidden in the sunlight as if waiting for me to make a mistake. My natural reaction was to look around to see where my parents were, but the house was empty. Placing my head through the space in the front door where glass had once been, I thought, *where is everyone?*

Although this sort of experience represented normality to me as a child, it still played havoc with my mind. And instead of playing with toys, I plotted my future. In doing so, one aspect of it became absolutely certain - I didn't want a life like this. Unfortunately, however, that life came looking for me, and it found me in the end.

In primary school, aged no more than six, I was expelled for having a knife. I was also excluded from junior school, around the age of 10, for my out of control behaviour. I remember, even as a very young child, thinking: I need to get out. I was desperate to escape from the situation at home, but powerless to change anything.

My father was at work all day and I rarely saw him because of his commitments. This stirred a great anger within me. I used to punch walls and look at my shredded and bloodied knuckles desperate to be loved, and for the pain to go away. If anybody recognised the reality of life in our family, nobody did anything to help and my conduct attracted no understanding or support.

Throughout my formative years, I boiled with a hatred of drink and drugs because I saw what they could do. However, over time, I saw them as a potential ally.

Longing for attention and respect, I could see only one way to achieve both. At the age of 14, I started taking drugs and experimenting with anything I could lay my hands on.

Stumbling upon a tiny amount of my aunt's cannabis, I smuggled it into school. As soon as I had the opportunity at break time, I marched to a darkened area of the playground, using my coat as a makeshift tent to shroud me from the elements.

Lurking in darkness, I tried construct what I thought resembled a joint. The reality was that it resembled the nose of Gonzo from *The Muppets*. Although bemused by this lacklustre attempt, it fuelled my determination to keep trying and gain attention.

Hurting inside, with no one really to turn to, I was expelled again, this time from high school at the age of 16. I hadn't even completed my exams. Aged 17, I became a father. By 19 I was living in a new home with my girlfriend and owned a franchise in a milk delivery business.

I was 18 when I had my first real introduction to alcohol. Starting on Friday nights, I'd go on binges that would end in the early hours of Monday morning. Swaying up the stairs, my bashing and banging against the banister signalled my return home. This triggered vicious fights with my girlfriend. There'd be shouting and screaming and televisions would be thrown through windows; I became everything I despised. Only when the alcohol wore off did I comprehend the pain I'd caused.

The inevitable split with my girlfriend followed. Heartbroken, I tried to recover by reading all the self-help books I could find - but nothing worked. My life became a series of broken promises to my baby daughter. At times, I even failed to pick her up from school. It's only now that it kills me to think how she would have been left holding a teacher's hand, waiting patiently for me to arrive. I left her to face that awful feeling of abandonment as the last child to be collected.

My problem with alcohol escalated one year on Boxing Day. I still can't believe what I did. I was back at my childhood home and after drinking with my mum, I left, got into my car and drove off. The only memories I have are of waking up and feeling blood oozing down my face.

Recklessly turning a corner at high speed, I had lost control and careered into a lamppost. It was one of the old Victorian ones; tall and black like something out of Charles Dickens's *A Christmas Carol*. I was lucky to be alive because it was the only lamppost that wasn't cradled by a concrete base. Instead of dying, I merely shattered my face so badly that it had to be reconstructed.

Following this accident, life became a roller coaster. There were times when I was homeless, others times when I seemed to be progressing. I got a job working in recruitment and did fantastically well. I thought, *Yes! I am finally making something of my life*, and then I would push the self-destruct button again. I'd fall back into the black depths of alcohol, returning home in the early hours of Monday morning to get ready for work.

At this point, I was a functioning alcoholic, but it became increasingly clear to me that I couldn't continue like this. It was like putting diesel into a petrol engine. Much the way diesel can seep into and destroy an engine, alcohol and drugs were seeping into me: my blood, my heart and my brain. Yet I was the one who kept pouring this poison into my body.

The moment of change came when I was walking through a park one summer's day. Dressed smartly in new black shoes, a shirt and a tie, I was very much the corporate professional portraying an illusion. The only problem with this picture was the beads of sweat rolling down my face; I was drunk in the middle of a working day.

Switching my phone off, I sat by myself on a long green park bench, my chin tucked into my chest. The bench had been vandalised by people etching their names into it, as if to seek attention, which was really all that I wanted. As the moments passed I repeatedly screamed in my mind: You are a disgrace, look at you, you've done it again. Then I thought: *You are better off dead, you're a disgrace to your family. Your daughter does not need you now. And finally, Just kill yourself.*

My useless existence in this world required termination - and my mind focused on suicide. My idea was to use the fumes from my car exhaust, but when the time came, something broke, scuppering my plans. Another failure. I cursed myself, saying, 'You can't even get that right, you're useless.'

My whole life had been blighted by drink and drugs, and now I just needed to escape. It was this endless negative self-talk that drove me to despair, and I could see no alternative.

Since childhood, I had been the protector. Solving problems and diffusing arguments, I was always there to help people. On this occasion though, when my self-esteem was at the same level as a piece of rotten gum on the pavement, it was my sister who saved me. She found a 12-step fellowship, which she hoped would help me overcome my addiction to alcohol.

Mustering the courage to even attend a meeting was difficult. I got close to the front door a couple of times before deciding to back out. But when I finally did make it past the initial fear, I returned home and sobbed for hours because this was the first time I had experienced hope.

It would be a mistake to claim that the journey I embarked on that day was an easy one. Each tear that streamed down my face was a release. The memories and hateful aggressive thoughts that had clogged my mind began to change. For the first time a chink of light shone through the door of redemption. I just had to build the courage to push the door open.

Being brand new to the 12-step process, my moods oscillated between extremes of false happiness and bleak depression. The solution to avoiding bad times had always been drugs and alcohol. Therefore, it became an obsession, a craving that controlled my every waking thought.

Trying to suppress the urge to abuse drugs and alcohol became impossible. Temptation took charge one Sunday evening. My mobile phone lit up the darkness in my room as I frantically rang every conceivable number to purchase drugs, but no one answered. It was unheard of – nobody!

I beat myself up about this, but when I spoke to my sponsor he was supportive and said, 'you didn't and that's a big step'. His encouragement gave me the confidence to believe that I could beat this.

Following the 12 steps was tough. They say the darkest hour is always before dawn and for me it really was. I had been conditioned to function on drink and drugs. I had tormented myself with them, but the torment of trying to leave them behind seemed unendurable. I wanted so much to succeed and create a new life, but it was like being held down by a pack of lions that were biting away at me.

Salvation came in the warmth of other people; people who knew what it was like to be alone. They gifted me positive words of encouragement and faith and gradually, as I became mentally and physically stronger, my self-perception began to change. The overwhelming feelings of embarrassment, failure and worthlessness started to leave me and the cogs of hope began to turn slowly in a new direction. I met new people and ultimately, through my greatest despair, I met the woman who became the love of my life, Jen.

As my thirst for alcohol and drugs faded it was replaced with a new thirst for redemption. Increasingly, I felt a different future was possible. My desire was to focus on the positives and to do something with my life that would make a difference. Immediately my attention turned to repairing and rebuilding relationships with people I'd hurt – family members, teachers and women from the past whom I had behaved badly towards. Finally, a light shone at the end of a long dark tunnel and I made the move from being selfish to selfless.

I began my quest by creating a social enterprise. I worked with local probation services and assisted people who had suffered from alcohol and drug addiction. I wanted to help others rebuild their lives. This presented new challenges as I had no idea where to start, and I made numerous mistakes - as so many people do when they start a business. Still dogged with self-doubt at times, I'd look in the rear view mirror at my past life, seeing the abuse and the stupid things I'd done.

But I also recognised that this wasn't about me anymore; it was about other people, and about making a difference. No amount of mental or physical scars were going to stop me. I learned quickly that the most magical part of life is seeing people change and knowing you have been a part of their transformation.

I am now 35 years old. I was 28 when I finally got clean, and I have not touched alcohol or drugs since. Becoming free has changed my life. I enjoy an amazing relationship with my family, and I am part of my daughter's life.

Probably the most beautiful day was picking her up from college in my car. Our conversation turned to alcohol and drugs and we had an open and frank discussion.

'Isn't it great that we can talk like this?' she said. 'None of the other girls can speak to their dads the way I can speak to you.' I was overcome with emotion because all I ever really wanted was to be a great father.

In the last three years, I have helped more than a 1000 people into employment, from cities around the UK. Many have suffered from addictions and have previously been in prison. I have also supported a number of people from the 12-step fellowship by taking them through the same process, so that they can become free, create happy careers and raise families of their own.

Life for me is about contribution and positivity; it is about inspiring and making a difference. Many people around the world suffer with alcohol related sickness, and some don't even realise they have a problem. The same is true of drugs, but help and support is available and crucially, there are people who will give everything to pull others through.

By confronting and tackling the demons that lived in my mind, I have discovered a desire to live a better life. The lessons I've learned have led me to create a social enterprise with my fiancé, Jen. Together, we have created an abstinence recovery home for people who are suffering from addiction illnesses. I feel immensely proud about giving people a chance like the one I had.

I hope you - the person reading this - can learn from my experiences. I want you to know that even in the deepest, darkest place there is hope, help and happiness if you want it. Even though I left school with nothing, even though I got myself into the worst, intolerable mess and nearly destroyed myself, I kept pushing forward. Through whatever adversity you face, you do have the choice to create the life you want, and if I can do it, you can too.

Speechless is the only way to describe my state when the interview ended. It was as if Ben was waiting for this moment. He poured out his life story with such detail and emotion, and I was grateful because it takes an enormous amount of courage to discuss what he did.

As we said our goodbyes, I walked into the bright afternoon sunlight squinting and protecting my eyes. Unlocking the car was like opening an oven as a rush of hot air blasted against my face. Walking in circles around the vehicle while it cooled, my mind raced with thoughts of shock, redemption and inspiration.

Driving home, I reflected some more. I understood that you're not weak to seek help from those who have trodden the same path as you. Without question, you can lose your senses when facing a rough time, as I had. But you most definitely lose your senses with alcohol and addiction.

As I wrote up Ben's story, the emotion and shocking revelations left me inspired because it was an example of someone who had come through a more graphic and harrowing experience than my own. What Ben's story did for me is to shift my thoughts, allowing me to look from another perspective. Without question, there are many crazy actions committed when under the influence of alcohol. But Ben's willingness to change was the mark of a man, especially in being able to right his wrongs.

Reflecting on my habit of trying to do everything myself, and consequently staying stuck in the mud, I learned from rereading and listening to Ben's words that the quality and concern of good people provides the steel your backbone needs when you are down and out.

I also learned that there was no turning back on my journey. There was no way I'd let Ben down, or the other people who needed to read his words. There will be people across the globe living Ben's old life, and they need to know that they too can overcome adversity.

Tim Reddish – Champion

I was in a thoughtful frame of mind as I sat on the train to Sheffield. It was July 30, and I was excited to be starting this book, but fearful at the same time. After all I'm not a writer, and my biggest concern was finding people. How was I going to do this?

I stared out of the window at the fields and valleys of Lancashire and South Yorkshire and tried to answer the questions that flowed through my mind.

It didn't take long for my thought pattern to be interrupted. A woman was loudly discussing her relationship problems on her mobile phone, while a man moaned and grunted depressingly about work to his friend.

His moaning reminded me of what had happened with my business. Still angry by the red tape and a 'computer says no' attitude, I toyed with the idea of setting up a charity or social enterprise. This new line of investigation came after meeting with a man named Paul Reddish. In fact, he was the reason I was on my way to Sheffield.

Paul was achieving success with his own charity, and he'd worked hard to understand the complexities of funding applications. I called him to talk about my own progress and this book, asking if he knew anyone inspirational.
'Speak to my dad,' he said. 'He may be able to help.'

Arriving at the Holiday Inn, Sheffield, I walked from the July sunshine into the darkness of an old Victorian style building. Dimly lit with large chandeliers, it reminded me of walking into a cinema, such was the change in the light.

When I'd spoken to Paul's dad, Tim on the phone to arrange the venue, he'd mentioned introducing me to other inspirational candidates. This immediately showed his character; how humble he was, and how he was always thinking of others.

Walking nervously into the lobby and bar area, I turned to my right and saw a black Labrador lying on the floor underneath the brown leather chair that Tim sat on. After I'd introduced myself, we sat and chatted about sport, life and my reasons for writing this book. It was then that Tim started to reflect upon his own life, and I listened intently to his revelations.

Tim Reddish

The smouldering poker made a buzzing sound as it moved at speed towards me. I manoeuvred quickly to avoid a potential branding, and it plunged into the couch, letting off the horrible smell of burning material. Dumbfounded, I remember thinking, *what have I done?* But this was my life. I was a child living in a volatile and unpredictable world.

My father was a bus driver; an intense man frustrated by the daily grind of long, mind numbing hours spent working to support his family. He came through the door that day and saw the aftermath. Naturally looking for answers, his stare blazed in my direction as my mother pointed the finger of blame at me.

I lived in the gritty industrial city of Nottingham. Relative to many working-class families in Britain during the 50s and 60s, my childhood was unremarkable. By today's standards, my family would have been labelled dysfunctional.

Theoretically, Mum stayed home to raise her family, but she was fond of alcohol and would often disappear for the weekend. Understandably, this behaviour was a source of many problems within our household. Often arguments between my parents turned to violence. On a few occasions I got in the way and caught a punch or two.

My escape from this madness was sports and play. In the evenings and at weekends, I found refuge playing in the street with other local kids. Our inquisitive natures encouraged exploration and we would sift through harsh rusty metals, which we used to make homemade bikes.

The hangover from the Second World War lingered. There was high unemployment, miners' strikes and a double-digit inflation rate - growing up was tough.

Despite the bleak outlook, there was a job for me. Aged 12, I began my role as a butcher's boy, delivering meat to people's homes. Customers would pay me and I would cycle back excitedly to the shop in order to collect my wages. They didn't last long, though. Half of everything I earned went straight to my mum as a contribution to the household income.

Sport dominated my teenage years and at the age of 17, I met my soulmate, Val.

I was attending our football club presentation when a friend asked me if I would go out with his sister. At first I was apprehensive because we were friends and I worried that it might affect our relationship. However, when I met Val and we started chatting, it soon became clear that we shared similar values. That initial meeting was the starting point for nearly half a century of love together. We share our laughter and mutual joy with our children, Paul and Christopher.

Going back to our early life together, I was unable to obtain credit from the bank to pay for our wedding. I had never borrowed money in my life and didn't know how to, but my mother did. To this day, I don't know why she borrowed money in my name and didn't pay it back. Consequently, Val and I had to pick up the pieces and dig ourselves out of this hole. It was a very upsetting introduction to the world of adult responsibility.

During this period in my life, my early 20s, my career path changed drastically. A random visit from an old friend led to a new role as a swimming coach, teaching young people how to swim. Swimming was an escape from the stench of meat. This was replaced by the smell of chlorine and the sound of excited youngsters, which reverberated around the pool.

With a newfound stability in our marriage, we thought we'd overcome the challenges of our early lives. The adversities we encountered together forced us to become harder and impenetrable, otherwise we would break. We couldn't have known that I would face an even greater adversity, one that would test us for many years.

A chance meeting between Val and my cousin alerted her to the possibility that I might be losing my sight. My cousin mentioned a genetic eye condition that ran in the family called Retinitis Pigmentosa, which is caused by abnormalities of the photorecepters. Suddenly, Val saw my awkwardness and constant minor collisions in a new light. I can only imagine the horror and distress this caused her. A visit to a specialist on my 31st birthday confirmed our worst fears: The condition was diagnosed as degenerative and initially doctors were unsure of the timescales, or if I would completely lose my sight. The uncertainty of it all was dreadful. I thought constantly about what would happen to my job and family if I went blind.

My enthusiasm and commitment to swimming enabled me to attain the position of Facilities Manager at a local leisure centre. I put everything into this job and became involved in every aspect of the work, from plumbing to administration and management. I was so completely absorbed by the day-to-day demands of the post that I became even more fearful of revealing my news. How was I going to tell my employers that I was losing my sight? I was fraught with worry. How I would pay the bills? The job brought the security of a pension and a steady salary, essential for feeding our two young sons.

Things we had not taken much notice of before, such as the inherent untidiness of the kids, took on new significance. For example, Paul and Christopher would leave their things lying around the house and I would be constantly tripping over footballs and toys. In practical terms, life was tough and my personal thoughts raced at speed.

Fearful of the future, I focused my thoughts on the many possible outcomes. So many things we took for granted were under threat. What about my sons' lives? It's every father's dream to watch his children having fun. To see them participate in sports days in the summer, to witness the expression on their faces when they score a goal, and to catch sight of them running about with broad smiles on their faces. With the loss of my sight, I would never be able to see them play again.

Throughout the adversity, my employers were very supportive, which was an amazing relief. The uncertainty of becoming blind was the most difficult part as there was still a chance it may not happen. Doctors were still unsure of the final outcome. However, I wasn't. The process of losing my sight was very much like the sun's journey beneath the horizon each day. It was a gradual process until I hit the age of 38, when I lost my sight completely. What compounded the cruelty was the heartbreak of not knowing if our sons had inherited the condition. It took seven long, nerve-shredding years to discover that they were free – something that Val and I are immensely grateful for.

At the same time, I struggled with the reality of not being able to spend time with my wife the way we used to. We had always loved going to the cinema or playing pool together. So many experiences I valued seemed to have been snatched away.

I worried for Val, too. She was literally the other half of me and had been there since I was 17. Would she cope? With no real idea about how to manage practically, I had to completely retrain and learn how to use a cane, locate bus shelters and work with a guide dog. Confused and depressed, the prospects seemed bleak, although the security of work gave me hope.

I became absolutely clear that whatever the future held, I wanted to lead a life where I could continue to contribute by helping others. Unexpectedly, an opportunity to fulfil my ambition of 'making a difference' presented itself. However, there were considerable risks attached and pursuing it would make our financial situation even more precarious.

This opportunity came in the form of a fantastic job. The problem? It was a one-year contract, had no pension and paid less money than I was already earning. I think Val thought I'd gone mad.

Blind, I was now risking the security I had worked hard for to chase a job that might be over after 12 months. Nevertheless, understanding just how much this opportunity meant to me in terms of fulfilling my personal aspirations, my amazing wife encouraged me to apply.

My application was successful and in 1998, I took up the post of National Performance Co-ordinator for British Swimming. Although initially advertised as a year-long appointment, the actual duration of the post lasted from 1998 to 2013.

During this time, I held such roles as National Performance Director and Executive Director. This was a huge honour for me. I loved the challenge and I loved swimming. It proved to me that by taking a chance to pursue the things you love, and combining that with determination and passion, you can make it work.

In parallel to all these life developments, aged 35, I started swimming competitively. This turnaround from coach to competitor was a direct consequence of the encouragement I received from an inspirational swimmer from Liverpool called Margaret Kelly. Following her successful participation at the Seoul Olympic Games in 1988, she gave me her commemorative medal and said, 'I want you to go to Barcelona in 1992 and give me yours.'

This gesture gave me fantastic motivation, so in 1992 I began my pursuit of medals at the Paralympic Games in Barcelona. I won a silver and bronze in the butterfly and freestyle events. I subsequently represented Great Britain in all key European and world events, and I participated in the Paralympic Games in 1996 in Atlanta. In 2000, aged 45, I also took part in the ones in Sydney.

More than the medals and other accolades, I am most proud of the example I have been able to give to other sportsmen and women. One of the most fulfilling moments I have experienced came when one young Chinese swimmer, Yang Bosun, broke my world record in 2008. After his accomplishment, I had the opportunity to meet him. He politely told me how I had been an inspiration, giving him the confidence to compete. This was important to me and far outweighed winning a gold medal. Here was this special young man from the other side of the world, talking about me, a normal bloke from Nottingham, being an inspiration to him. This demonstrated the power of sport and the extent to which it can connect so many people, whatever their stage in life or the adversities they may face.

Another huge honour was to be asked to run for the elected position of Chair of the British Paralympic Association. I didn't have any money for marketing or big advertising campaigns, but I was committed to making things better. I thought, if I am going to go for this then I am going to be myself, state my beliefs and show people what I can do.

In 2008, following a very tight contest, luck and the votes were with me and I took over the reigns as Chair. Few people realise the amount of money that needs to be raised simply to get the Paralympics GB team competing in games. The costs are numerous and enormous. In addition to paying the salaries of those who are employed, we have to find in the region of 15 million pounds over a four-year cycle.

Excited rather than daunted by this sort of challenge, I have an incredible thirst for life and an insatiable appetite for making a difference. This sort of approach to life has manifested in my private life. One of my favourite pastimes is skiing, although pursuing the hobby initially was difficult. This is because people made judgements based on their perceptions of what I can and can't do. In the early days, I was told I could not take up this sport because I had lost my sight. My response was simple:

'I may not be able to see, but it's not going to stop me.'

Now I go on an annual skiing holiday to the Alps. I am directed by an instructor through a headset, but I still feel the speed, the adrenaline rush from anticipating obstacles, the crispness of the air and the warmth of the sunlight on my skin. I can ski just as well as many other people can.

The most important consequence of becoming blind is that I have not let it define who I am. I'm driven not to let anything stop me from living the life I create. While we all experience challenges in our lives, it is our response to those challenges that makes us who we are.

The most joy I experience arises out of contribution. I am currently working with Oxford University to assist in developing their retina technology, which may ultimately help blind people regain their sight.

Reflecting on my life, it's clear to me that it has always been characterised by overcoming obstacles and helping others to achieve their goals. Losing my sight may have changed the path I followed, but my aspirations and achievements were those I brought with me from my younger days. I hope that you are able to fulfil your greatest ambitions, whatever they may be, and I urge you not to let any physical or mental barriers stand in the way of you becoming the person you want to be. If I can do it, you can too.

Slumped in a dark leather chair, I scratched my head in awe and smiled. Changing career at 35 to become a swimmer. Winning and competing when most people retire from the sport aged 20-something, and for good measure becoming a skier. Oh and blind! Wow! And I thought I had encountered challenges.

As we finished the interview, Val, Tim's wife, joined us and we discussed in more detail the shock on people's faces when Tim skis. 'They tried to drown us with health and safety,' she said. 'No chance, we were doing it!'

With short dark hair, Val possessed the same granite determination as Tim, and I admired her ability to cope with such life changing circumstances. What a couple. They epitomise the values of marriage as they have stuck together through adversity because of the bond of love.

Thinking of my own situation, I asked Tim for some inspirational advice. He replied, 'Be clear, be responsible. Know exactly what it is you want and be 100 per cent accountable for making it happen.'

This made absolute sense and the advice articulated Tim's character. He was clear, helpful and ambitious.

Without question, I needed to be clear on the vision for the book and, more importantly, to be responsible for sharing the information I collected for it. The vision was to move people emotionally, to inspire.

Not long after our meeting, I had a chance to test the vision. I started a careers programme for 700 students at Archbishop Beck Catholic College in Liverpool. I told each class the story of Tim Reddish, and was careful to watch the faces of the students as I did so. Their mouths gaped open as they absorbed the information. Their silence was a good sign.

I wanted them to be inspired like me. I wanted them to understand that whatever career path they choose, they could achieve, if, like Tim, they were clear and accountable. I wanted them to empathise with Tim and to understand that all people have challenges but whatever they are, they can be overcome.

A few weeks later, I stood waiting outside the large and imposing green coloured school gates on Cedar Road, Liverpool.

Waiting for a taxi at 3pm was not a good idea. The sound of the school bell belted out and waves of laughing and joking children filtered like an army of ants from the available exits.

Then my ears came alive. I overheard a male student saying to his friend, 'there's that fella (meaning me) who motivated us today with a boss (good) story.'

This proved to me the part that stories play in helping people believe. It proved to me that the book was achieving its purpose.

Thank you, Tim.

Terry Nelson – Warrior

Fresh home from Sheffield, July closed and August opened for business. Reading my emails, I saw an invite to a breakfast meeting hosted at a local college. The event was with the shadow education minister and was being hosted by Frank McKenna.

Frank owned his own business organising political and networking events, as well as hosting his own radio talk show. He had kindly let me loose on air to discuss education a few months earlier. Tall, with dark hair, Frank was always dressed in a suit and possessed bags of enthusiasm. I told him about this book and my quest for stories. He didn't require any time to think.

'Terry Nelson!' he said. 'I'll send you his details.'

Just a week later, I sat nervously in Costa Coffee on the Albert Dock. It was a gorgeous summer's morning, one of those few days when a stroll along the waterfront is pleasant. Warm air brushed against my face instead of the usual brutal winds that roar in from the River Mersey.

Sitting in silence waiting for Terry, I took a slurp of coffee and my mind wandered to the past. What was my ex-girlfriend doing? Was she OK? Then some angry thoughts rapidly extinguished any glimmer of compassion.

Sometimes, no matter what inspiration I tasted, there was a flaw in me. I suppose it's called being human. We're emotional beings and negative thoughts from the past sometimes like to invade. Call them weaknesses, call them what you will; sometimes emotions are difficult to shrug off. They are like the automatic doors I sat facing, which were so sensitive that the floating of a feather had triggered them to jerk backwards and forwards. However, they performed their proper purpose only a few seconds later as Terry entered wearing a beige suit jacket and shorts, which exposed his prosthetic leg. The first thought that leapt into my mind was: *military accident*.

Terry was tanned and his blonde hair was combed forward. It was hard to tell his age. He was maybe in his late 40s or early 50s, but one thing was for sure - he was someone special.

Also there was Lisa, Terry's assistant. Tall, with dark hair, she was as equally full of enthusiasm and intrigue about my writing project as Terry was.

Terry learned forward, pressing in his hearing aid and listening to me talk until the natural time came for him to discuss his own experiences.

Terry Nelson

Nothing could beat the atmosphere of Saturday afternoons, the smell of hot food and the sound of the fans talking as they walked up and down the terraced streets wearing their red and white scarves.

Everybody would be speculating about who would be in the team that day. I would watch in amazement as the areas around the stadium swelled with people as kick off became closer. Thousands of fans sang songs. The sound carried on the cold crisp air from what was Anfield, the home of Liverpool Football Club.

My only ambition was to play professional football for my beloved Liverpool. At the age of 15, my dream came true when I joined the Liverpool 'A' team. I was playing just below the standard of my heroes, but I was moving ever closer to them, knowing within that I had something.

I was talented, determined and single minded, and I seemed to have a promising future ahead. However, one thing conspired against me, and ultimately it ruined my career.

I joined Liverpool in the late 70s, a period when the club was dominating domestically and had its sights set on Europe. Back then, football philosophy was very different from how it is today.

In earlier decades, if a player sustained an injury, there was no rest; he just carried on. If a player allowed his injury to affect the necessary self-discipline associated with practice and performance, he was regarded as weak and would never be considered for the first team.

Understanding this only too well, I carried on training regardless of a groin injury, and continued to play in every match, although my injury was clearly visible to the studious fans.

Known for my work ethic and passion, it got to the point where I was limping through the heavy, mud-laden pitches that reminded me of the trenches. I'll never forget the squelch of football boots running across fields without the trace of a blade of grass.

But this was my dream. I was a local boy who could see the stadium from my school window. It was so close I could nearly touch it. However, the dream turned into a nightmare and I left Liverpool with my shoulders hunched, my head bowed and my soul left in a muddy heap as the gates of the stadium clattered together and shut the door on my career. My body would not heal from the groin injury that plagued my career and ultimately ended it. Football left me a bruised young man. My ego and self-worth had been sucked out of me. Initially, to cope, I helped my brother Dean train for the paratroopers and was so happy when he was accepted.

Happiness, however, was a destination far, far away from me. My lifestyle for the following two years consisted of partying, drinking and feeling sorry for myself. My brother lived in a completely opposite world. When he came home on leave he told me tales about his adventures around the world. He looked the picture of health: tanned, fit and full of energy. I'd think, *wow, look at him*. That's when I also thought, *Terry, stop wasting your life*. I was disgusted at what I'd become.

The defeat of leaving football had affected me deeply, and I became determined not to let that happen again. I began to train hard for the paratroopers myself, and visualised spending time with Dean and travelling to places such as Belize and Jamaica.

The training was rigorous and tough, but I rediscovered my passion for exercise and fitness and was eventually accepted into the paratroopers - or so I thought. The final part of the selection process was the medical that revealed some devastating news - news that would send me down a path of turmoil and anguish that no person should ever have to face.

'Terry, we have found protein in your water,' the doctor said. 'There will be no more training for a military career.'

I didn't know what protein in my water meant, but the gaunt look on the doctor's face as he avoided eye contact told me that this was serious. The reality was that I had kidney disease, but

I couldn't accept it.

After a few seconds, all the emotion from my previous experiences came to the surface. I let out a screeching howl; I didn't believe it was possible for any human being to make such a noise. A combination of anger, despair and frustration made me sound more wolf-like than human. 'NOT AGAIN, NOT AGAIN,' I screamed. In my mind, the dialogue raged: It can't be happening, they have made a mistake. I jump out of planes, carry bricks on my back for miles…

My dream of playing professional football in front of all the Liverpool fans, making my family proud, living nearly every young man's dream had been taken away from me through injury and I was determined not to be revisited by the pain and mental distress of that experience. In desperation and total denial, I tricked my way into the marines by substituting a friend's urine sample for mine.

It was only while on the Royal Marine's training course in Devon that I discovered how ill I was. I had been one of the best trainee paratroopers and was consistently in the top three for all tests. I expected to replicate my achievements, but I was barely able to hold on to the thickly knotted rope as it dangled from the sky. Hunched over like a weak old man on his deathbed, I discovered the truth. Without a kidney transplant, I was going to die.

I am still moved to tears by the unbelievable sacrifices others make, which are born simply out of compassion. There are so many people who contribute to helping and serving others without a moment's hesitation, and the person who did that for me was my brother, Dean. Without a thought for himself, he agreed to give me one of his kidneys. He gave up his military career to save me, forfeiting all those adventures, his friends and his entire way of life.

He is a huge presence; a scar snakes from his face and slithers down his neck, making him an intimidating force. His gift to me necessitated a change of employment and he ultimately became a male nurse. He now works with kidney transplant patients.

He made a huge commitment and I was indebted to him. I felt I had to repay him for the second chance he had given me. My immediate thoughts as I lay in the hospital bed after the transplant were: How can I pay him back? What can I do?

I wanted to undertake something memorable and immediately after the transplant, I began to train for the London Marathon. I wanted to earn money for charity and help other patients by raising awareness. During the preparation I fell in love with sport again. I continued to race in different events and suddenly, without any real training, found that I was not far behind the professional athletes who were competing in the British Transplant Games. This became my new aspiration. I gave up my job in the building trade to concentrate on athletics full time and with expert coaching, I learnt how to run properly with economy of movement.

In 1992, I took part in the British Transplant Games and won gold medals in the 400m, the 1500m and the 5000m. I became obsessed with running and was elated to be selected by Great Britain to run in the World Games in Vancouver in 1993. My conscience was finally letting me sleep, as I felt that I was now beginning to repay my brother for the sacrifice he had made for me.

However, my world was shaken to its core once again. I fractured my foot six weeks before we were due to depart for Canada, which meant I couldn't train. Hobbling around the track, the medical team looked on shaking their heads. 'Forget it, Terry,' they said. 'You have no chance.'

But chance and luck were with me for the first time in my life. Browsing through a magazine, I stumbled upon an article about how running in a swimming pool was helping people recover from injury. This was it! My chance. No sooner had I dropped the magazine, I was in the pool.

I trained by tying a foam band around my waist to create resistance in the water. I used this band for two weeks before the Olympic doctor assessed me and confirmed that the fracture had healed. This was incredible, and left many of the medical team speechless.

Inside my hotel room in Canada, I paced up and down. Not because of homesickness, but because I felt ill inside. 'Please God, don't let me come down with anything,' I whispered to myself. I knew all too well how easily opportunities can be lost.

With the curtains closed, I sat in the darkness not mixing with any of the team through fear that I may be withdrawn. All I could do was mobilise my mind to think of the race and nothing else.

These kinds of opportunities are so precious that although I could accept losing to other athletes, I had to make it on to the track.

Shaking with nerves and filled with adrenaline, my preparation had been far from perfect, but with the sound of the gun my legs carried me around the circuit and like a homing device, I locked on to my main opponent, who'd not been beaten in years.

I pushed my body with each punishing lap until the sound of the final bell echoed around the track, the screams from the crowd encouraging me even further. This was my chance, but I still chased the shadow of my rival who crept further ahead until the final 200 metres.

Like a ship's winch, I slowly reigned in the champion until it seemed as though each stride was synchronised between us. Reaching out for the finishing line, I propelled every muscle, vein and limb over the line. It was the closest race in the game's history and was over the most gruelling distance of 5000m. I collapsed on the floor with a mixture of elation, tiredness and joy. Finally, after all these years, I had won. YESSSSSSSS!

NOOOOOOO! On the flight back from Canada my face suddenly began to swell. It became saggy and soft like a water balloon and I had to be moved to a special area at the back of the plane. After we landed, I raced to the hospital where I was told the transplant was failing. We had to find another kidney donor. The breath was just sucked out of me. There was a two-year waiting list and numerous complex factors to juggle – the search to find a match, the need to identify the right time, and ensuring my blood pressure was at the correct level.

I was in utter despair. I had lost my football career, my military career and now it seemed, my running career. During my time in hospital, the only thing that made me feel sane and alive was training in the water, and for the next 12 years it was the only thing I could do.

Dialysis took on the role of my kidneys. For approximately seven hours each day, for six days a week, I lived connected to a machine. When I returned home, I was so weak and drained that I would lie on the carpet in my living room and curl up in the foetal position.

My wife couldn't take any more. The emotional pain of living with this situation was too much for any person to have to bear. I couldn't do anything or go anywhere. I was a walking corpse: toxic yellow in colour and barely able to speak. All I had at that time were my thoughts, and they were killing me. There were times when I did think - *I should just end this*.

My daughter went to live in the south of England with Sue, my wife, and our son, Terry Junior, stayed with me. I felt I could not let him down as he was just a child and he saw me at my worst; depressed and sometimes deranged.

Hospital was like living in a prison because I lost my independence and self-esteem. I was crushed mentally from having to spend 12 years in hospital.

Throughout that time, I was unable to go to the toilet or, as unbelievable as it sounds, have so much as a sip of water. Even a cup of tea could kill me because the fluid would collect on my lungs. The most I could be given to quench my thirst were small pieces of sponge containing a little moisture.

The slightest heat against my skin would send me into a frenzy of scratching to try and relieve the pain. It was so intense and ferocious that I would have gladly used sandpaper against my body, and a cheese grater against the skin on my head. The pain caused me to pull clumps of my hair out. In the end shaving it off became the only solution as the blood would matt my thinning hair.

Even in winter I had to take ice cold baths to get washed because the pain was so debilitating. The average waiting time for a kidney transplant was two years. However, mine took 12. I waited for one from 1993 to 2005.

I was given hope seven times during that period, which meant that seven times my dream of living a normal life again was dashed. This happened at the eleventh hour because of sickness, low blood pressure or infection.

Treated like a piece of meat, carted around from ward to ward, I lost my identity. Throughout this ordeal, I was pleading inside, pleading to God, to anyone who would listen, to let me live again, let me run again, to let me drink instead of eating sponge. Hospital could be a cruel place at times. I was there to recover, but really I felt worse. The huge grey building, with its pebble dash exterior, was an imposing sight and appeared to act as a magnet for the grey clouds which seemed part of its design.

After 12 years of this life sentence chained to the metal frame of a cold hospital bed, hope presented itself again through my brother. His wife was a match and decided to donate one of her kidneys to me – a second amazing and selfless gift.

I was overjoyed to be free from the hell my life had become. My only salvation during that time was exercising in water. Specialists had even attempted to assess the effect exercising in water was having on me.

When I got out of hospital, I was curious myself. I sold my house and traded a mechanically operated hospital bed for the warmth and freedom of the Californian sunshine. There, I learnt everything I could about training in water; many medical professors and scientists were performing studies on how people recover from injury in water. Running in a swimming pool became my new obsession and I absorbed the information like the sponges I used to eat.

I invented a product that I felt would be perfect for the pool. My vision was to produce a full body buoyancy suit, which would help people train if they were recovering from injury, or wanted to improve their health and fitness. I started the project knowing nothing about business. But I was committed and determined to succeed. It's helped that since 2005, I have been fortunate and blessed to live in good health.

I genuinely believe that we are all here in this world for a reason - to do something special with our lives and to make them count for something, no matter what obstacles are thrown in our path. It would have been easy for me to give up, and on many occasions I nearly did. All my hopes and dreams were built and shattered - one after another.

In 2011, I had to have my right leg amputated. Calcium had collected because of a problem with the parathyroid gland in my throat. I could have let this affect me, but no way.

Regardless of my physical disabilities, my mind still functions and I have desires and goals that I want to achieve. New aspirations led me down a different path and my experiences, desperate though they were, have made it possible for me to help many succeed.

I feel gratitude for each breath and have a passion that wants to burst out of my chest like a beam of brightness from a lighthouse illuminating the sea at night. If you are experiencing turbulent times you can get through them by focusing on what you want.

The primitive flotation belt that I began to use all those years ago when I was suffering the most has been developed into the TNAR (Terry Nelson Aqua Running) Suit. I poured all my energy, determination and passion into it, as well as my financial resources.

I wanted to work with the best. However, when I started out, I received a lot of criticism. People told me to start small and try and work with local sports clubs. 'Test it with them first,' they said. Not a chance. I was thinking big. I thought, *if I could just demonstrate my idea to some global sports teams*, then I could really make a difference.

Even though my dreams had been trodden on in that muddy field all those years ago, the result of thinking big is that I now train some of the most successful people in sport. I have worked with Real Madrid and Manchester United, and I have personally trained Cristiano Ronaldo, Kaka and Maradona. My idea has enabled me to meet so many interesting people; the TNAR Suit is used by the England football team, and I am now training professional boxers.

My next step is to create a factory so that I can manufacture my suits in the UK. I will be employing disabled people, with the aim of providing hope and opportunity. In the meantime, I am travelling the world to raise awareness of the suit and its benefits. I am full of passion and living my dream, for which I am extremely grateful. You can do it, too. Whatever dreams you hold inside you, you can pursue them. I have been dogged by 12 years spent in hospital. I've had my leg amputated and seen my dreams dashed as a young man in football. But the will of the mind is the strongest force. It's the most beautiful of assets and you must use it to grow bigger than your fears or adversities, because nothing is more powerful than your dreams. If I can do it, you can too.

Shock is the only way to describe how I felt when Terry and Lisa left. Terry's story had a powerful effect on me. His passion and enthusiasm reminded me of singer Sinead O'Connor's famous music video for her hit song, *Nothing Compares 2 U*. If you haven't seen it, you can do so on YouTube. It's powerful. She looks directly into the camera, expressing nothing but pure emotion. Terry did something similar. He described the rawness, and exposed the truth about how he felt. He looked me directly in the eyes and made me feel what he went through. It's hard not to have empathy when someone shares such a powerful story. That's why I thought of him as a warrior, because he had the spirit and heart to overcome such mental and physical adversity. But what euphoria, what inspiration to say, 'I'm not settling for second best, I'm going to Real Madrid.'

Terry's influence lingered throughout the day. His amazing personality had a profound effect on me, making me feel like I was wearing a Super hero's cape and could achieve anything. But still, he would offer yet more inspiration.

Nicola Rowe and Adam Dugdale - Angel Jude

I hadn't visited my next destination for a decade. Driving to the Huyton area of the city, I was heading to the Derby Lodge. Once a stately home, it now operates as a hotel and bar. The building is made of sandstone, is surrounded by lush landscaped grounds and has an interior which is modern yet homely and rustic. When I arrived, tall Victorian-era windows, eight to 10 feet in length, were open, and the thin white drapes framing them blew gently in the August breeze.

I felt a little apprehensive as I walked in. I knew a small piece of this story, but didn't know what to expect. Luckily my friend Helen, who had helped me contact Nicola, had already arrived.

Helen is always cheerful and positive, and she constantly looks for ways to gently poke fun at me. It didn't take her long, as a wasp invaded my personal space and wouldn't leave me alone, much to her amusement.

Helen and Nicola have dark hair and both look young for their age. Until recently, they taught at the same school together.

We sat down in a semi-circular booth and chatted for a few minutes. I described my encounters with the people I had met on my journey so far. Touching on some of their traumas, and the ways in which they had come back from adversity, led to Nicola to tell me her story, which was so raw and recent that it moved me in a variety of ways.

Nicola Rowe

Nothing can prepare you for the horror of your child being taken away from you at birth. I was exhausted and lying in a bed with nothing to accompany me but the haunting question:

is Jude, our baby son, OK?

My boyfriend Adam and I had dreamt of starting a family together for some time. We had been together for eight years and were so excited when I discovered I was pregnant for the first time. I had just begun my first year teaching primary school children and Adam was fulfilling his sporting ambitions by playing professional football for Crewe Alexandra. Plus we were moving into our new home - life was just as we had planned it.

The pregnancy had been perfect throughout. The timing and the treatment, even the date that was predicted for Jude's birth - 25th March 2013 - was precise.

Born at 4.35pm and weighing in at 7lb 13oz, Jude resembled a floppy doll with loose limbs. I distinctively remember there was no crying as he lay there. My instincts, however, knew the truth. Something was seriously wrong. Doctors were reading numbers to each other and performing blood tests. 'It's just a precaution, don't worry,' one of them said. Suddenly, there was a distinct change in the atmosphere of the room. The usually calm and caring expressions on the faces of the medical staff began to reveal panic and concern.

Like a scene from a hospital drama on TV, Jude was flashed in front of my face, but instead of being placed into my arms, he was whisked away. Immobilised and confused from the drugs, I didn't understand what was happening. Medical staff wheeled me in the opposite direction to Jude and worried faces peered over me as we raced along corridors. Looking up from my bed, I asked a junior member of the medical team, 'am I going to die?'

I lay alone, wrapped in bandages and blankets, with nothing

to occupy me but a cold, lifeless room. Shivering, I stared in shock at the white walls and the hard floors. All I wanted was my family and Adam.

Instead of being a time of celebration, this was a horror story - and we didn't know how severe it would be or how long it would last.

Three long, excruciating hours passed before we had the opportunity to see our son, and approaching the incubator was overwhelming. Perspex plastic encased Jude, and I gazed into his perfect deep blue eyes. The room was silent and in semi-darkness. A gentle light shone down upon him and his tuft of dark hair.

This was a magnetic and amazing experience – a moment of serenity amid the anguish, but it would soon be disturbed. On the other side of the incubator, where Adam was standing, I noticed that his demeanour was completely different. Standing at 6'4", he towered above the incubator, but he was upset and I could see the torment on his face as he repeated, 'Has he got a face? Has he got a face?'

When Adam spoke those words, I knew that this was more serious than just a bruise or birth mark. But at this point, no one could deliver a true diagnosis.

Unimaginable trauma followed; the worst possible experience of our lives. A huge purple mass consumed almost one side of Jude's head. After a few hours he was transferred from Whiston Hospital to the famous Alder Hey Children's Hospital in Liverpool. Still weak and exhausted, doctors wanted to retain me for observation, but I discharged myself. Nothing was going to stop me from being at Jude's side.

In Alder Hey, I lay next to my son who stared out from the incubator. I felt lonely and desperate. All I wanted was my mother there for guidance and support, but visitors couldn't stay overnight at the hospital.

I had so many questions, which stopped me from sleeping. There wasn't a single moment of peace in my mind. My auntie, employed as a phlebotomist at Alder Hey, knew something was not right. She had witnessed many babies being born and instinctively knew this mass was not a bruise.

It was her who identified the potential cause of Jude's condition and presented this to the doctors. Specialists confirmed her suspicions, and diagnosed Kaposiform hemangioendothelioma with Kasabach-Merritt syndrome. Extremely rare, it caused Jude to have almost no platelets in his blood. When a healthy person cuts themselves, the blood clots and forms the scab that protects them, but Jude did not have this function, which is something we all take for granted. The problem was the mass on the side of his face. We initially thought it was a birthmark, but it was a tumour that acted like a leech, absorbing all his blood. He only had nine platelets, while the average person has hundreds of thousands.

When doctors gave him blood transfusions, the tumour continued to absorb and feed on his blood. Blood was being pumped around the tumour as well as his body. This caused his heart a great deal of stress.

During this period of waiting for answers, my shock turned to anger. My pale reflection looked back at me through the glass in one of the waiting areas, and I felt an overwhelming sense of desperation. The same questions span around in my head - Why us? Why Jude? We had planned everything. Jude's room in our new home, even the school he was going to attend.

I raged at the thought of people who are fortunate to have children yet abuse, ill treat or negatively condition them. There were many news reports at the time about the cruel killing of a two-year-old. It was heartbreaking and soul-destroying to think that people could do this to children. I couldn't stop myself from questioning the justice of life.

Our poor little baby. We felt powerless to help him. Once, the tube that was carrying fluids around his body came out and blood started pouring from him. Four test tubes full of it were collected. Life was flowing away from him as the doctors attempted to stabilise him, but the blood was constant. I remember a pinprick of blood being taken from his foot and it ran like a river, soaking his clothes and flowing and seeping through the sheets in my bed. Shock once again took charge. Whilst trying to stay positive, we could sense and see the consultant's body language change as the pandemonium of activity intensified. The panic and pressure dominated the atmosphere in the room. At any one time, some of the best children's consultants in the country were huddled around our tiny baby. But there was hope. The operations Jude had were successful and he began to respond well to treatment.

Over Easter weekend, we sat down with the consultants to ask whether Jude's condition was life threatening.

'Yes, it is,' came the reply.

'Will he pull through?' I asked.

I didn't get the answer I was looking for. I asked the doctor if he had children and he replied 'yes'. I remember saying, 'if you were in our position, would you not want an answer?'

He then revealed the truth. Jude was seriously ill and might not pull through. Tears streamed down my cheeks as I ran to another room. I sat in a plastic chair and placed my fingers in my ears, dreading the echoing sounds of footsteps along the narrow corridors. I knew if I heard those it would be someone coming to tell me the inevitable. Adam continued to speak to the medical team and we made a decision.

With Jude in my arms, safe and at peace, his suffering was over. The humming sound of the life support machine closed down to a complete silence. We looked down at our perfect child feeling proud of the fighting spirit he had displayed through such a rare condition, which only affects one child in millions. He was our angel - 'Angel Jude'. He passed away from heart and multiple organ failure. The overwhelming pressure of supporting his own body as well as the huge tumour caused his body to shut down. He had endured chemotherapy and multiple operations, one that lasted over six hours. The doctors, consultants and even scientists who had been involved with trying to save Jude had given their all.

Stripped of all will and full of confusion and sadness, we approached our new home. We were destroyed. I think every young couple in love looks forward to the day when they can bring their child home.

We took comfort from the support of those around us, and from a game that would have been one of the biggest days in Adam's professional career. Just five days after Jude's passing, The Johnson's Paint Trophy Final was being played at one of the most iconic football grounds in the world: Wembley. It was arguably the most significant day in the history of Adam's club, Crewe, and more than 45,000 football fans attended the game.

The number on the back of Adam's shirt is six, and it was as if Jude was watching over us as applause reverberated around the stadium. Supporters from both teams stood and clapped in honour of our son in the sixth minute. The overwhelming sense of pride and emotion from the fans touched us deeply. Adam and I watched the game at a friend's, and the tears rolled down my face. The most symbolic moment, which felt like a direct message to us from Jude, was when applause turned to celebration as Crewe scored - also in the sixth minute! This gave us great comfort. It felt like our baby was walking with us, his tiny feet leaving footprints in the clouds as he looked down on us.

Adam and I have grown stronger as a result of what we've been through, and we want to help others by sharing our experience. There are so many cases affecting families around the world on a daily basis, and the loss of a young baby or child can devastate lives. Not many people are as fortunate as we have been to have such close-knit support. This is why we are opening the door to our experience in the hope that it may shine light on those who are encountering the awful challenges that we were confronted with.

The loneliness you can feel as a mother or father; the not knowing why and trying to cope with such an ordeal is our main inspiration for sharing our story. In truth, we didn't know how to come to terms with this situation ourselves. In my search for answers, I read the stories of *X Factor* and *Britain's Got Talent* judges Gary Barlow and Amanda Holden – both of whom have lost children close to birth. I was desperate for answers, desperate for people to talk to who could help me through this pain.

Through the darkness we have learned that life is so precious and can't be wasted. Each day needs to be lived. The positives we have taken out of this most horrific experience have come from the faith, love and support shown to us by so many people.

Too much of the world goes unnoticed as we are subjected to waves of negative moaning and whining each day from news and TV programmes. In contrast, however, Adam and I have learned that there is so much good in the world; amazing people who go above and beyond in giving their support to those who need it most.

Our overwhelming desire is for our son's name to continue and never be lost, as he is an inspiration to us. The fighting spirit he showed fills us with enormous pride and we can't let him down. In the six months following his passing, we made it our goal to raise £10,000 to build a room in a new ward at Alder Hey Children's Hospital. This will be in Jude's name.

It is the beauty and strength of many that has helped us through the most difficult of times. One of the most comforting poems that was shared with us, and will always remain in my mind is:

'An angel in the book life wrote down our baby's birth, she whispered as she closed the book:'Too beautiful for earth.'

You can come through your pain, you can experience joy, and you can live again. To overcome such tragedy you need the love of many – it helps you channel your grief and natural negativity into a positive force, which your child can feel proud of. If we can do it, you can too.

When Nicola had finished talking, I was unsure of what to say. It was only August. The tragedy happened in April, and it's every parent's worst nightmare.

I agreed with Nicola's thoughts about the mistreatment of children and how some parents just don't care where their offspring are. Nothing makes the blood boil more ferociously than the thought of vulnerable babies, children and animals being exposed to preying adults.

I sat in the car with my head in my hands. I ran my fingers over my temples, my attention firmly gripped by the story of Jude. How could I help? What could I do? The only way to offer my support would be via fundraising, but how? I even questioned whether I could write this story. Where would I start?

Tapping the steering wheel trying to summon an idea, I eventually came up with one. What if Terry Nelson could help? We were due to meet again the following day, and all I could do was ask.

Arriving at his apartment block in the morning, I stood at his intercom and out of frustration pushed every button. I couldn't gain access. I shielded my eyes from the blazing sun and looked up at the building's endless row of windows, with hope rather than expectation that I might see Terry waving me in.

Luckily for me, a group of builders returning to finish a job were going to the same floor, and they let me in.

'Thanks lads,' I said, relieved I could now navigate through the different levels of security.

Terry opened a white wooden front door and revealed Samson, a gorgeous black dog with bulging eyes and a short fluffy coat. He was as excited to see me, as I was to see Terry.

'How's the book coming along, Antony?' Terry asked.

'Oh, Terry, I need your help, mate,' I replied.

He sat on the edge of his pine office table, leaning his head forward and holding his hearing aid. Reciting Nicola and Adam's story, I explained how they were trying to raise money for Alder Hey Children's Hospital, and wanted to build a room in Jude's name. Clearly moved, Terry paused for a few seconds before standing up and taking three paintings from the exposed brick wall where they hung.

They were original acrylic paintings of Liverpool FC stars, both past and present. One was of Ron Yeats with the League Championship in the 1960s - the then equivalent of today's Premier League. The other paintings were of modern day professionals, including Jamie Carragher and Steven Gerrard, with the Champions League trophy in 2005.

The paintings were huge: three feet wide and four to five feet in length. I don't think I've ever been so astounded or moved by a person's generosity. It was incredible, beautiful and inspiring, but that was Terry - and he wasn't finished.

'I'm seeing Joe Hart's (England and Manchester City goalkeeper) agent on Monday, I will get his shirt signed,' he said.

Terry was true to his word and when I unravelled the shiny green England shirt it revealed Joe's signature and the words 'Just for Jude' - the charity set up in Nicola and Adam's son's honour.

Listening to and writing this story had a profound effect on me. Like the two previous ones, it took my thoughts beyond the sphere of my own concerns. The only difference was that this time I questioned how I could help. I found the feeling to be addictive, and it was like no other.

I felt privileged to assist Nicola and Adam by transporting the paintings and shirt to them. They are the epitome of strength and show just how important the people around you are. I admire them because of the way they have channelled their focus towards doing everything they can to help others.

I would, however, need to muster their resolve and strength as life was about to spring yet another shock...

Richard McMunn – How 2 Become

My dad was referred to Broadgreen Hospital by our GP and this brought a great sense of uncertainty. Tests and biopsies equated to one grim reality - prostate cancer.

Walking out through the automatic doors of the hospital, the sun's rays wrestled with the thick white clouds as they tried to burst through. Ambling through the grounds, there was plenty of time to wonder and think: *what is going on this year*?

Questions immediately sprang to mind following Dad's diagnosis. How bad is it? How long does he have? More biopsies followed and I was more worried for my mum because she was still recovering from the loss of my nan at Christmas. How would she manage the news?

Dad's response to cancer was to meet it with a sense of humour. His immediate treatment required him to have an injection of female hormones. 'Will my hair grow back now?' Dad asked the doctor in his Cockney accent.

The amount of time Dad spent bouncing to and from the hospital for injections, blood tests and monitoring took its toll. He suffered with hot flushes, dizziness and sickness, which resulted in him being unable to work for an initial period of time, something he wasn't used to. A self-employed joiner, Dad is a big man, standing at just over 6' tall and weighing in at 15 stone. My cousin James reckons he has a look of the actor Chevy Chase about him.

Now in his 60s, the tan on his bald head was fading and his duties had changed from knocking in nails to nursery runs. The change brought financial anxieties and extra tension. My parents had always supported me in any decision I made, but as I was living under their roof I now felt that I needed to find a secure job. When Mum was stressed, she would even tell me as much.

I could understand. At 32, I shouldn't still be at home. In the past I would have changed course for something less challenging. Indeed, I probably would have dropped my writing project at the slightest inconvenience or for the chance to earn more money.

And this time I was in real shit. It was still mid-August and it would be October before I was due any kind of payment from the work I was doing with Archbishop Beck High School.

I was now relying on loans from family to bridge the gap. Watching my bank account was like watching an egg timer, all the while knowing the last grains are soon to escape.

Writing meant no earnings while earning meant limited time to write. What fuelled me was passion - passion to be inspired and to inspire others. But how could I find other people to talk as openly as Ben, Tim, Terry and Nicola had done? I was not even 10 per cent of the way through my project, yet I did have my next interview lined up with Richard (Rick) McMunn.

I first met Rick in November 2010 at a seminar about how to market your business on the internet. It was the first seminar I ever attended. This was held at the Renaissance Hotel at Heathrow Airport and I remember sitting with 12 others around a large table with a white tablecloth draped over it.

Rick was one of the speakers on the day. He is of average height with a bald head and a muscular frame. At first glance, he reminded me of Ross Kemp, the actor who played Grant Mitchell in EastEnders. Stood on stage in his black jacket and jeans, his words were profound. He made me believe that I could do something other than work in a job, and it was the first time I'd ever considered this. I would not have written this book had I not attended this event – I have absolutely no doubt about that.

As we spoke on the phone, supportive as ever, Rick let me into his world.

Richard McMunn

My life began in Blackpool in North West England, but my childhood was very unsettled. My father worked in the fire service, which meant my early years were spent moving to different parts of the country. During the 70s and early 80s, I attended two different primary schools and three different secondary schools. Even setting aside the nomadic nature of my education, school just wasn't for me. I found lessons tedious and my attention span was so short that I rarely absorbed any of the information being thrown at me. I could see no value in any of it. I was constantly looking out of the window and thinking and dreaming of something else.

On top of this, I sometimes felt like an outsider, especially when I attended a school that was over 200 miles away from my hometown. I found moving around at such a young age difficult, particularly having to go through the awkwardness of making new friends. Sometimes, simply having a different accent to other kids made me an easy target. I was also overweight and people would sometimes pick on me because of this, which made me self-conscious about my appearance. I was bullied the most at Chipping Campden High School in the Cotswolds. The teachers were absolutely useless at stopping it, despite my complaints. The impact of being bullied and the lack of action by the teachers aroused a range of emotions in me, from frustration to anger and fear. One day, I decided to fight back. I can remember punching my tormentor so hard that I got myself suspended from the school, even though I was the one who had been bullied for months on end. As you can imagine, my faith in the education system was at rock bottom by this point.

When I was younger, I wanted to be in the fire service like my dad, but I got my first taste of entrepreneurship in my early teens when I set up my own car washing business to do at weekends. I was only 15, but I loved it. I was free to make my own decisions and my customers loved the service I provided because I would do it without disturbing them. I would get up really early on Saturdays and Sundays and use the water from my house to wash and clean all the cars on the estate. I'd haul the heavy buckets from my place to all of my customers' houses, just so I didn't have to wake them up. When I finished at around 11.00am, I would go round the estate and collect my money. I remember feeling enormous satisfaction and my customers were pleasantly surprised to wake up to a clean car. The fulfilment I got from this little business was in marked contrast to the feelings I experienced at school. Not surprisingly, when the day finally came for me to leave school, I was overjoyed. For the first time I felt liberated and able to make my own choices - or so I thought.

I left school with just three GCSEs, in English literature, English language and art. I didn't really care about the limited evidence of my education because I always knew that hard work and determination would conquer all. Moreover, at 16, you have no idea of the world that lies in front of you and you listen to the guidance of your parents or copy what others are doing without really thinking: 'What do I want?'

I remember being escorted by my dad to the local careers office.

'My boy wants to be in the Royal Navy,' he told the careers officer.

I remember sitting down confused, thinking: *No I don't, I want to be in the fire service.* Although there had been no prior discussion, joining the Royal Navy in the interim made sense because you had to be 18 to join the fire service. That would have meant two years of doing odd jobs or office work, which didn't really appeal to me. My dad explained that by going into the Navy, I would learn the sort of skills that would be relevant to the fire service, meaning that when I came out, I would be ready - and he was right!

Starting work in the Royal Navy was scary at first, but it proved to be a great experience. I travelled the world, met new people and worked on fighter jets. It was an amazing life and although it was highly regimented, it gave me skills, discipline and values that have stood me in good stead in the time since leaving. I learnt the importance of hard work, organisation, self-motivation and self-discipline – the latter turning out to be one of my biggest strengths. I loved the life but by my early 20s, I realised that it was time to move on. I looked around at many of the older guys I worked with and thought: *Do I really want to be doing this for another 20 years?*

Moving from the services to civilian life is not always an easy transition. Some of the guys who left the Royal Navy struggled to find jobs because the work they had experience in was so specialised. But once I'd made my decision to leave, I immediately thought of the fire service. My dad told me that the construction of the Channel Tunnel crossing meant that Kent

Fire and Rescue Service were recruiting. I saw my chance and for the first time in my life, I sailed through the assessment process. Entering the fire service fulfilled an ambition I had carried since childhood. I had finally realised my long-term goal and my future seemed secure. However, my confidence proved to be illusory.

I worked hard and was one of the youngest station commanders in the Kent Fire and Rescue Service, but, soon after joining, I began to experience financial problems. I was terrible with money and half way through the month I would have to apply for a payday loan because I had run out of cash. Within a few years of entering the fire service, I was massively in debt with credit cards and other loans. Every month I would go overdrawn by at least £1000. This was embarrassing and frustrating because although I was driven to succeed, I had nothing to show for it. It didn't matter whether I had a good day, a bad day or was off on holiday, I was still getting the same salary each month and this did little to help me cover my costs.

Despite my commitment and dedication, the possibility of promotion - and a salary increase - was limited. Progression within Kent Fire and Rescue Service at the time was tough and although I worked very hard, there were limited opportunities because very few people left the fire service.

As the years went on, I became more and more frustrated with the fire service and I began searching for new opportunities. The only problem was that I was in debt and I couldn't afford to take a pay cut in order to leave the job that I had come to dislike.

Around this time, I was part of a Coldplay tribute band called Coolplay. One night, while in Strawberry Moons nightclub in Maidstone, Kent, a chance conversation with a friend, Simon

Coulson, initiated one of the biggest turning points in my life. I will never forget it; Simon told me he was taking redundancy after 14 years with a large telecoms company. The offer of redundancy was opportune because he had started to make money online, and this was really taking off for him. I was amazed at this because my mindset was programmed to being employed, working hard, receiving a salary and moving up the career ladder - what Simon described sounded too good to be true. Whatever my doubts and reservations, though, I had no choice but to try. I was 34, and even though I had achieved the rank of youngest station commander, I was bored and frustrated with my career and my debts were spiralling out of control. Fascinated by the possibility that Simon had opened up to me, I took action and embarked on a new venture.

I may have been starting from nothing, but I was willing to learn and work hard. All I knew was the Royal Navy and the fire service. I found myself wondering, how can I turn this experience into a business? Then I had an idea. There was a lot of competition for employment in the fire service and the recruitment process was tough, but this was something I had 'expertise' in. So I wrote a 300 page guide on how to become a fireman and it started to sell really well. I had no experience but I went ahead, acting on instinct, working hard and following my heart. I continued to think of ideas, all the time learning new skills and identifying certain focused markets. I then wrote two more books: *How2become a Police Officer* and *How2become a Royal Navy Officer*.

It wasn't long before I was coming home from my day job and working on my own business until 1am in the morning.

At this point, I knew nothing about business; I was just learning. I was hopeless at finances and branding, and didn't know how to sell properly. The jobs I'd had in the past had not prepared me for this. Although feeling stretched, this was a very positive period in my life. I loved the feedback I was receiving from customers and hearing how I had helped them to get a job. This gave me real confidence to move forward, with the aim of writing three pages per day.

In the beginning, I made plenty of mistakes, but I soon had most of these ironed out. I was posting out books each day and was struggling with demand. I was spending more time posting individual books than writing them. Then I figured out that I could get Royal Mail to collect huge quantities at the same time. This one change saved hours each day. This type of learning was happening daily. When I began, I was earning £2000 a month as a fire officer, struggling to make ends meet, in serious debt and feeling miserable. Within one year of working online, I had earned over £300,000. It was an incredible transition from where I had started – although I continued to work in the fire service!

Most people, whatever their situation or background, have the potential to change their life for the better. Although I do think that education is important, it does not determine your life; what determines your life is you and your attitude. None of the challenges I have faced in my life have prevented me from working hard to carve out the life I wanted. You can do the same, but change won't just come to you. You have to act and you have to make the change happen yourself. You have to search and go and find what you want; you can't just wait for it to arrive on your doorstep. There is advice and support out there, but you have to seek it out. One of the most important things I have learnt is to find people who are successful and understand what they are doing. When I was in the band with Simon, I constantly picked his brains about the online world and tried to find ways to improve my business.

Many reading my story will be in a similar position to the one I found myself in. The key point I want to make is to give it a go. Make a plan and break it down into the smallest steps. When I started, I thought I was too old to be doing something new. I knew nothing and had incredible self-doubt, but I pushed through all the mental baggage that so many of us carry around, and in doing so I improved my life beyond all imagining.

I have worked really hard to get to where I am now. Nine years after I began, I have earned more than £4,000,000 from selling my books on Amazon and through my website: how2become. com.

Never in a million years would I have thought it possible that this could happen to me, a fat kid from Blackpool who left school with three lousy GCSEs, was bullied, failed the initial Royal Navy test because of lack of fitness and got into debt up to his eyeballs. However, if I believed that was all I could ever amount to, then I would have given up back then. The only way forward is by taking action. My success has brought me freedom. I am able to do what I want, when I want, but this is entirely the result of the hard work I've put in. I get tremendous personal fulfilment from helping others achieve. I deliver seminars on how to create and publish books, and feel enormous satisfaction from knowing that sharing my experiences has encouraged other people to initiate changes in their own lives.

If you take just one thing from my story, then please take this:

Your life is your own – you have choices. Success is all about mindset and choice... choose to be successful! I hope my story inspires you because if I can do it, you can too!

Bullies can act as prey, circling their victims looking for a chink in their armour. An accent, hairstyle, clothing…Although Rick is a matter-of-fact type of person and doesn't use emotive language, I knew that his revelations about bullying would have an impact.

When we are children, name-calling can penetrate deep into the soul and ignite a self-conscious attitude that causes suffering in adulthood.

Reflecting on what Rick told me, what I learned is the importance of taking action. He took action against the bully, and whether you agree with what he did or not, it worked. Whatever the circumstances you face, action is important, and that's the overriding theme within Rick's story.

He's faced a multitude of everyday challenges, particularly financial ones. Most people, including me, have wondered how to avoid walking to the bathroom each morning like a zombie, facing a day's work in a job that is mind numbingly boring. Well, again Rick took action. He decided to commit to writing three pages each day. After 60 days he had nearly completed a book....When he failed the initial Royal Navy fitness test he took action by improving and making sure that he passed the next time.

This is not to simplify in any way the adversity you may be facing. Every challenge requires courage and determination, and most of all time to gather the strength to address it. However, the correlation between the people who feature in this book so far, is that they all took a stand and decided to take action towards a desired destination.

The ultimate aim of this book is to give examples of how people have overcome adversity. Rick is one of those people who have overcome challenges posed by bullying, weight and financial doom.

Financial burden and the worries it conjures can dampen your spirits, so it was also a relief to see that someone else had come through it and thrived.

Distractions and the promise of a quick earner had always won with me in the past, but now facing even tougher tests, my vision and passion were stronger. They would need to be, and what happened to Rick was no accident. He stuck to his plan of writing three pages a day and produced 150 books during a nine-year period.

So, decide to overcome adversity, write out your plan - whatever it may be - and stick to it like glue. It had taken me four years after hearing Rick touch on these points previously to really understand this lesson. Better late than never, I suppose!

Once you have a purpose that is greater than your fears, you're half way there. All that is needed then is self-discipline.

Bubbling with excitement, I knew for the first time that despite the financial pressures, despite being stuck in a room writing and missing out on fun and holidays, my vision to overcome my own adversity and inspire others was much greater than my fears.

Doubts are never far away, that's life, but it was time to move on, and it would be Terry Nelson who would open yet another door for me.

He gave me the details for Emma Hawkins. 'I met her at a conference and she would be ideal for the book,' he said.

Emma Hawkins – I Wheelie Can

After arranging to meet Emma and getting lost along the way, I eventually arrived at a bright rainbow coloured school conversion in Bootle, Merseyside. The classrooms had been converted into space for small businesses to operate from and this modification emanated a real sense of community spirit. Walking into the reception area, my senses were blasted with the unmistakable feel and smell of a primary school.

Dave, Emma's partner, greeted me first. At 6'3", I'm fairly tall and weigh 15 stone. However, I felt small in comparison to Dave who is 6'5" feet and 17 stone plus. Wearing a t-shirt, shorts and sporting a shaven head and glasses, he resembled the security guards you see alongside celebrities. A giant man with a giant heart, he introduced me to Emma.

Emma, who was in her wheelchair, looked up at me and smiled, her beautiful personality shining brightly. Her auburn hair hung below her shoulders and she was wearing a black professional suit. What struck me instantly was her mischievous sense of humour. She told me that she liked going to the pub and Dave nodded approvingly. Such a gentle couple, it was an honour to be sat with them both as Emma discussed her life so far.

Emma Hawkins

Born just four minutes earlier than predicted changed the course of my life, and the life of my parents. The consequence of my premature birth was cerebral palsy, as not enough oxygen had reached my brain. The condition affects the cerebrum, the part of the brain responsible for controlling muscles and speech. For this reason, I spend most of my waking life in a wheelchair.

My mother's determination to push me into mainstream

education shaped my formative years. She wanted me to lead a normal life, have friends and be part of a school community. Indeed, one of my earliest memories was attending classes at a charity named Stick 'n' Step, near to my home in Cheshire, North West England. The charity is dedicated to assisting children with cerebral palsy, helping them to develop speech and movement at no extra cost to their parents. To be part of such a warm and caring community gave me the confidence to progress.

Mum was my inspiration and later in life, I felt for her and my dad. I realised just how much stress and pressure they were under to care for a young family and a child with cerebral palsy. Despite separating, they always showed dedication in supporting my elder sister and me.

During my time in school, I became more aware of the life I was living. When you're a teenager, you naturally seek freedom to explore different places, such as parks and friends' houses. Being confined to the house only magnified my frustration. Looking out of my bedroom window, I watched young people playing outside while I missed out on life again.

I cursed the old electric wheelchair that transported my body at one mile per hour. How could I go out? Even in school I had to leave 15 minutes before everyone else, which may seem advantageous, but I hated the special treatment I received.

In my teenage years, I became more self-conscious about my appearance. I dreamt of high heels, dressing up and dancing at parties. The desire for my own independence only increased as my mother cooked, cleaned and washed me. It was too awkward and I became overwhelmed with the desire to be free. I possessed a mind and the ability to think, but I felt dangled from strings like a wooden puppet; every movement I made directed by someone else.

Just because my limbs needed support, people treated me as if I was helpless. My own self-worth had been crushed like an insect caught in the shadow of a boot as it plunges down on top of it. To escape, I chose to attend a boarding school where the promise of newfound freedom, trips away and nights out beckoned. Nervous but excited, and aged sweet 16, I left for Coventry.

At first I felt empowered and pleased with my decision, but reality soon set in and it was different from what I had expected. Leaving home made my situation worse, and the strings became heavy chains holding me down.

I had no privacy because my every move was monitored for my own safety. I was lonely and confined to a room just 7ft by 6ft in size. It contained dark orange towels, a thin brown carpet and had a door that couldn't be locked. Living in what can only be described as solitary confinement, my confidence wilted like a flower.

The highlight of my day, my special moment of independence, was a trip to a vending machine to buy a chocolate bar. I was in bed by six each evening, left to gaze out of a dirty window, even on a summer's day.

My weight plummeted. And noticing my distress and gaunt face, my mother stepped in. I needed to get home and after completing my GCSE in Art (achieving a B grade), I did just that, returning after one year of hell.

Looking back at my life, my time at boarding school certainly gave me time to reflect. I didn't have a relationship with my nan, my maternal grandmother. For nearly 20 years, I thought she hated me and I would do anything to avoid seeing her. You see, when I was a young child, I watched as she gave my elder sister money and sweets, but I would never receive anything. I thought there was something wrong with me and wondered, *what have I done to deserve this*? Little did I know…

Attending Liverpool John Moores University afforded me my first real taste of freedom and the chance to meet new people. I attended the fresher's fair and drank like everyone else. I celebrated to loud music and laughter, accompanied by new friends who loved me for who I was. I even wore a fab false tan, even if it smelt horrible when it was initially applied.

I loved the experience. I enjoyed the partying. On a couple of occasions I fell out of my wheelchair and just laughed - it was amazing. I was living free from judgement over my physical disabilities. I could be me and through hard work and determination, I achieved a Bachelor of Arts degree.

Following university, I allowed pessimism to affect me again. After being in a relationship for a number of years, the lines became blurred. My boyfriend became more like a carer and the constant negativity and control he displayed made me feel worthless. I mustered my strength and made a decision to move on. The period after my relationship finished was the darkest of my life. It was a struggle doing anything and my thoughts became more and more tinged with depression.

Alone, I cursed my life. I partly regretted my decision to end my relationship. I feared my ex's prediction that I wouldn't find anyone else. Now living alone, my previous single-mindedness about wanting to be independent dissolved. I thought I would never find love.

Parallel to ending my relationship, I started to look for work. I applied for multiple jobs but each application was greeted with a polite no. Compounding the demoralisation I felt during the actual job-hunting process. I spent hours upon hours searching in vain and staring at a computer screen reading job descriptions that didn't describe me.

While the search continued, so did the rejections that savaged my soul. I sent out 50 applications a week sometimes, but there was no return on my hours of labour. After all the education and determination, I felt lost and this led me to a new level of depression. I had worked so hard for my degree, but felt it had all been for nothing. 'Who would employ someone with cerebral palsy?' I'd say in anger.

Aged 24, I sat on the graduate scrapheap. My frustration manifested itself in the form of negative comments to others, including my family - I hated what I had become.

My mother, noticing my sadness, made a flippant comment about purchasing a dog. I was surprised because my mum is not a big animal lover due to the mess they can leave. But I liked the idea and bought a beautiful Jack Russell, naming her Mathilda.

She was and is a beautiful bundle of energy, and I genuinely believe that she saved me from myself. Blessed with responsibility, I became alive. For the first time in my life, I was supporting and contributing to the survival of another living being. The beauty of animals is that they don't discriminate or care about your disability; they just want to be loved. She followed me everywhere, jumping up, licking my face and wagging her little tail. For once, health and safety protocols worked in my favour, as my carers were not allowed to touch or feed her. She was my responsibility.

Fate took another important twist not long after that. One evening, sat propped up in bed and eating a packet of crisps, I randomly tuned into a television programme. It was a documentary about how people were carrying out despicable acts of cruelty against those with disabilities and mental illnesses.

All I could do was cry. Horrific and repeated displays of violence had been inflicted on vulnerable adults placed in care at Winterbourne View hospital in South Gloucestershire. They needed to receive specialist support but were slaves to sickening torture. A big burly man - a so-called support worker - slapped the people in his care viciously around the head. It was like watching a gazelle with a broken limb. These 'carers' had taken on the role of hyenas and laughed as they smelt blood. They continued to administer physical abuse, and the loud clapping sound that was made as the abuse took place is something that will stay with me forever.

Horrified, I watched as the 'carers' repeatedly poured cold water over one particular young girl. They took turns as she sat there, helpless and soaking wet. Ferocious staff continued to snigger and laugh as she lay on the dirty carpet, her hands shaking violently from fear and cold - such cruelty administered on such an unimaginable scale.

The undercover reporter who filmed the event described on camera how he witnessed the same girl howling in distress as she was doused with mouthwash that seeped into her eyes. Imagining the green stinging liquid splashing over her face made tears of anger roll down mine. The time had come to make a difference. That night something changed inside me. All the doubt I felt about myself seemed to melt away and I knew I had to help others.

I started making calls and began the process of completing paperwork to set up my own business. I named it 'I Wheelie Can' and it specialises in training carers and medical professionals in disability awareness.

I realised I was not a failure or worthless and had the capability to use my mind. Knowing others needed my help, I realised I could make a difference. I stopped worrying about my own challenges and embarked upon a new path, and what I believe to be the secret of living - giving.

With a smile on my face, I crumpled up my CV and threw it in the bin. I looked down at my old life, the rejections and the comments, and decided I did not want to be that person anymore. My goal became focused on serving others who had experienced the same difficulties as me.

Feeling empowered, I realised I was not a wooden puppet controlled by someone else. I have cerebral palsy, but so what! I have feelings too, and while I had experienced turbulent times, don't we all? We all feel pain but we can choose to feel good and pursue work that inspires. With this new attitude, I sought to build bridges rather than destroying them. During this period of awakening, I learnt that the limits I had placed upon myself in the past could be removed. I had believed all the bad things that people said about me. I believed that because I sat in a wheelchair and couldn't write as fast, or use my legs like other people can, I was stupid. How wrong was I? You can achieve anything you want to.

Through my business endeavours, I have been able to support professionals in the National Health Service. My training has helped doctors and nurses to manage disabled people more effectively. It has been amazing to read the feedback that nurses (some with many years of experience) have given. Amongst many things, they have learnt different techniques to feed people with disabilities.

The joy of knowing that I can help to save lives and teach those who may not be able to communicate clearly is brilliant. Fortunately, I have been able to convey the message at conferences and persuade people in power that just because some people have physical or mental disabilities, doesn't mean they don't have feelings and rights - rights to be free.

My work is taking me into schools and recently, I was invited to give a motivational speech to help inspire young adults. I used my own story to show them that they too can achieve. It's important to remember that you can too.

My search for answers led to unexpected discoveries. Remember my nan? Well, she had given the money directly to my mother when I was a child. Of course, this made total sense as my reflexes were not well developed. I couldn't hold the money. The sweets she gave to my sister were boiled sweets, which were far too hard for me, being seven years younger. My nan wanted to give them to me but Mum wouldn't allow it. My regret is that I didn't know about this until many years later.

After holding on to such disappointment and blaming my disabilities for the way I perceived Nan was treating me, I had created thoughts in my mind that had no truth. I felt guilty and embarrassed that for twenty years I had avoided someone who loved me. Since my discovery, I've built a wonderful relationship with my nan and she has the same cheekiness and humour as me. She loves to poke fun at my mother and winks at me every time she successfully achieves it.

With one discovery complete, soon after, another illusion evaporated from my mind. The fears about not finding love were false. I am recently engaged to Dave and so very grateful that I have found someone who loves and understands me.

With the date set for our marriage, I am going to walk down the aisle, accompanied by my dad, and without the aid of a wheelchair. I will do whatever it takes to make this happen. And for my hen night, well the plan is for us to race along the streets of Benidorm in wheelchairs.

And so upon reflection, I know that goodness comes with adversity and while we can become confused, scared and angry, in the darkness there is hope and there is also happiness in knowing that if I can do it, you can too.

How we make excuses. How we say 'I can't do this' or 'I can't do that'. Emma's story laughed in the face of every negative belief I've ever heard.

With a puff of my cheeks I realised that this was it. This was inspiration; a piece of evidence to make you believe. We all host a number of beliefs, which are based on the way we think. What I had learned on my journey so far is that despite physical limitations, the mind is king. Here was the evidence that it could be done; a 25 year old woman with cerebral palsy who has achieved a university degree, started a business and now wants to study part time for a law degree.

Leaving the old school was ironic because my next destination, a few weeks later, would be another converted school, this time in the village of Bromborough, on the Wirral, Merseyside.

My assignment was to train a group of 18 year olds living in foster care. The objective was to help them gain employment skills and experience, which would hopefully provide some hope in a world of chaos.

Who knows what goes on behind the eyes of many young people? Listening to some of their stories, though, produced waves of emotion within me. I heard tales of abuse, loneliness and zero hope. They saw no future for themselves as they sat in a circle feeding off each other's depression. They had abandoned the idea of getting an education, blind to the vision of what life could be like as they hung the invisible noose of negativity around their young necks. They needed to see someone positive, and this meant an introduction to Emma.

At the end of the session, I took the students along the narrow corridors to a traditional classroom filled with tables and chairs. Emma had agreed to speak and as she wheeled in, the boisterous fun and games turned to silent curiosity. I sat behind Emma in order to gain a view of the students' faces and to see the beautiful realisation in their eyes. This was the realisation that someone they perceived as worse off than them had achieved remarkable things.

Emma spoke quietly and with passion about her life and the challenges she faced, but she did so in a way that resonated with the students. At the end of the presentation, one of the mentors, Jenna, excitedly said to me, 'Antony, some of the students now believe they can do something with their lives.'

Emma's inspiration was another piece of evidence that despite my own challenges, I was on the right track. A meeting with Alan, my own mentor, just a few weeks later confirmed this. As I told him about my progress, he could see the difference in me from earlier in the year.

'This book is healing you,' he commented. He was right.

Eileen O'Connor – Eileen versus Goliath

August was proving to be a good month for meeting people, but with just six stories collected so far, I'd run out of options. Panic began to set in as I still had the elusive task of finding a further 35.

My next strategy was to go public, which meant speaking to audiences. Immediately my attention turned to Number 1 Maryland Street, the home of the International Coaching Academy, which was founded by John Haynes. I first met John in March 2012, at an event to promote entrepreneurship in schools. He is a motivational coach and hosts a number of training events and seminars. If anyone could help, it would be John.

His business is located in a Victorian building in a trendy part of the city. It's just walking distance from Liverpool's two famous cathedrals and numerous tourist attractions.

Inside I was greeted by a beautiful blend of authentic posters and inspirational quotes, which competed for attention on the walls.

A nice aroma of coffee engulfed my senses and also reminded me of painful conversations I'd had with my ex. John was one of the first people I'd spoken to after the events at Christmas 2012, and naturally I turned to him again.

Back then, I was full of anger and frustration, and I was in torsion as I started to relive that dreadful time. Luckily, I was also preoccupied with the task of sharing my request for stories in front of an audience, and turned my attention to that.

I stood up in the green room, which was aptly named as three green fabric sofas, positioned in a horseshoe shape, dominated the room. Light beamed through the thin green curtains forming a natural spotlight for me to stand in. Twenty people were seated before me, obviously wondering what I was going to say. I was nervous as I outlined the purpose of the book. I'm always anxious when I have a public speaking engagement. I speak fast and have always been more comfortable talking to young people. But the one advantage of speaking to adults is that generally their concentration span holds out for a lot longer.

Sat to my left was a man who introduced himself as John Byrne. John is an entrepreneur but more golden hearted than hardnosed. As result of my talk he became a friend, and it wasn't long before he got in touch about an exciting new venture he'd been introduced to by a woman named Eileen O'Connor. He thought I'd be interested to hear more about it for my book.

'Let me speak to her and see what I can arrange,' he told me. Within a couple of days, I received Eileen's contact details and we spoke on the phone to discuss my book.

Soon I was on my way to Formby, a coastal town about 40 minutes from Liverpool. Conscious of not being late, I always arrive at meetings stupidly early, especially when I don't know where I'm going.

Approaching a crossroads, I spotted what can only be described as stables, but it was the height of summer and hard to see through the canopies of huge trees. Turning left towards the stables, I could see two beautiful black horses grazing in a large enclosed field. I immediately felt that I was entering somewhere special.

Driving slowly in my sister's car, with my hair brushing the roof, I was like a shark trapped in a tin can designed for sardines, and

I laughed when I hit potholes the size of craters. There was just no avoiding them!

My off-road adventure continued around another bend as I recalled my first conversation on the phone with Eileen and some of the features she'd told me to look out for. I was excited about meeting Eileen and intrigued about her. She mentioned that she lived on a beach and that had always been my dream; I wanted to live somewhere sunny like San Diego or the South of France. I had not visited either locations, but it's where I visualised myself.

I continued to slope past the huge houses that were situated sporadically on either side of the winding dirt track. They were a fantastic and unusual mix of bungalows and other unique properties, which all had different coloured brickwork and beautiful long windows. Creeping around the corner, the car rocked gently from side to side as I navigated the craters. The sun shone down through the clouds and I knew I was getting closer. The sand dunes Eileen described were now in front of me and the roar of the Irish Sea was breathtaking. Rabbits danced around the car before disappearing back into the sand dunes of National Trust land. I looked up and saw an amazing building - it was the type of house you'd see on a postcard in Scotland or Wales. Huge, long and white, it sat like a diamond encrusted by golden sands.

Locking the car door, I walked up the path to the sounds of nature, which had a magnetic quality that made me feel calm. Eileen opened the door and welcomed me in with a broad smile. She had short, almost bobbed platinum blonde hair and bright blue eyes. I could tell instantly that I had met a gentle soul.

I sat down and stared through the kitchen window in awe as the rolling waves attacked the beach. I proceeded to tell Eileen of my San Diego sunshine dream.

'Oh, that's where my best friend Susan lives,' she replied. 'I'm going there in November.'

No way, I thought. Transfixed and relaxed, I listened to Eileen's story.

Eileen O'Connor

The squawks of seagulls dominated the sky as I opened the door of the pub where I lived. The cold air would blast in from the Irish Sea and had the power to bleach my skin red.

The pub was named The Stadium and I lived there with my mum, dad and younger siblings. It was housed in a tough docker's area and it was the swinging 60s. I shared my hometown with The Beatles, but the new life they breathed into the city contrasted sharply with its unwavering economic decline.

The huge shadows cast by the tankers and cargo ships which had governed the docks had been replaced with the shadows of unemployment. But darker shadows were about to be cast over the pub.

I felt safe growing up until I heard my father say:

'I will be back soon.'

I watched his pale yellow face, as he said those words and walked gingerly down the stairs of the pub. I didn't realise that I would never see him again. He died of liver failure, causing heartbreak for all, especially my mother. My parents adored each other and at the age of only 31, my mother was left alone to raise four children on a widow's pension.

Having to grow up fast, my role as big sister involved helping with the household chores, preparing breakfast and collecting my siblings from school. My mother gave us the best life she could and I would witness her grief from the doorway; seeing the many tears she shed splash against the kitchen table.

Walking to school was horrible, as my thoughts always turned to the past. Following the death of my father, I moved schools three times and missed four months of learning due to tonsillitis. I enjoyed being at home. After all, school was the least of our problems. We needed to survive and I wanted to be there for my mum – she was still longing for the comfort of my dad.

As time progressed, our wounds began to heal slowly. It was only in high school that I tried to regain some of the time I had lost.

Growing into my teenage years, I longed for independence and to further my education. By 18, a decade since Dad's passing, Mum had remarried and I worked part time in a hotel to fund my studies.

While at college I met my husband, Paul, who worked as a photographer in the Royal Navy, based in Portsmouth. We were together throughout my years in further education, snatching weekend visits whenever we could.

At the age of 42, Mum gave birth to twins and I enjoyed helping to support her on my days off from work and college. She and my siblings were now settled, so I made a decision to leave home. It was painful and emotional because of the bond between us all, and tears once again streamed down our cheeks as I traded one industrial dockland for another.

With a fresh new life and feeling proud of my qualifications, I found employment as a cashier working in a local supermarket. My responsibilities included checking money, counting pennies and ensuring the floats balanced. I loved the people but longed for something more challenging to do. Once I'd understood the job, it became a monotonous routine. The predictability of the work and seeing my career mapped out for me made me feel deflated. However, when I made the decision to leave and take a new role in a bank, the job was just as similar and predictable. Each year that passed, it felt like someone was burying me alive. Every task and meeting dampened my desires. I'd look at the black plastic float inside the till where the coins sat each night and think how it would soon be as empty as I was.

After five years of working in such roles, my emptiness was filled with complete joy when we had our first child, George. By then we'd moved to the Midlands as Paul had got a job with Land Rover as their in-house photographer. Life was good. He managed an extensive library of photographs, which contained a treasure trove of images, including one of Winston Churchill with the first ever Land Rover.

Paul's career flourished. Travelling extensively to photograph new vehicles, he even got to take pictures of Princess Diana when she visited the Land Rover plant at Solihull. He loved the job and was shattered when he was made redundant. By then I was pregnant with our second child, Grace, and I worried terribly about how we were we going to live.

Land Rover had decided to cease the operation of managing such an extensive library because of the costs and labour required in dealing with multiple agencies around the world. I could understand this – Land Rover's business was manufacturing cars, but it didn't make the news any easier to swallow. However, the decision to disband and dispose of the photos would be a blessing in disguise. Paul had been the only person managing this operation, and calls continued to flood in after he had left. We could see an opportunity and agreed to purchase the library from Land Rover, setting up our own business and rescuing the photographs from a skip. I used my skills as a cashier to manage the finances and we ran the business from the garage attached to our house. I was able to work from home while spending time with my children. Life was finally looking brighter.

We worked hard to provide the best life for our children. Our business flourished, growing until it consisted of a workforce of 12. In fact, it was expanding so rapidly that we needed to move, so we invested in a beautiful new home.

We purchased a barn conversion and outbuildings, and began to craft a home and business premises on the same plot of land. Our new property was surrounded by fields, trees and outbuildings. We felt like we'd come a long way since facing up to the redundancy a few years earlier.

Outside, the long garden was separated by a stone footpath which led to the boundary of an adjacent field. There sat a beautiful stone and wooden alcove with a cone shaped roof. We'd light a fire and sit inside it with family and friends, listening to the crackling of the wood and watching the flames glow against the darkness of the warm summer evenings.

Wishaw, England, may have been a quintessential chocolate box hamlet, but it was also cursed.

An alarming series of accidents occurred on the country lanes around us, which had become a rat run for motorists accessing the M42. We were woken up many times by the sound of screeching, as drivers slammed on their brakes in an attempt to slow down fast. The acrid smells of burnt rubber and the sounds of people crying in despair became all too familiar.

The last straw came when a Volkswagen Golf collided with an 84 year old lady in a wheelchair. The pensioner sustained serious head injuries and later died in hospital. In the same week, other motorists were involved in serious incidents. One driver was lucky to escape with his life when his vehicle skidded and flipped over, trapping his head in the open window. Another couple miraculously escaped after their car plunged down a steep, grassy embankment.

Neighbours had witnessed similar accidents over the years and continually helped to drag crashed cars from the ditches using their four-wheel drive vehicles.

Just a couple of months after the pensioner's death, it was our turn to taste tragedy; our beloved cat was hit by a car. Seeing our pet lying in the road, her distinctive white fur making her immediately identifiable, was horrendous. We picked her up but there was no life left in her body. The overwhelming sense of anger I felt made me shake like the rattle of a snake, and I was ready to inject my own venom into the policy makers that were allowing this to happen.

This is when my life began to change. Igniting a campaign, I got together with people from other villages to demand an end to the carnage. Fuelled by rage, I spoke to newspapers and designed leaflets, posting them through letterboxes with the aim of shepherding together representatives from the council, police and community.

I hoped that I'd be able to get around 20 or 30 people to attend a meeting in the main hall of the local golf club. You can only imagine my shock when I opened the doors to the hall and discovered 200 people waiting. I panicked. I had never spoken in public before. I coughed, spluttered and my face burned. What had I done?

An elevated seat sat on the stage in between representatives from the police and council. It was signposted for the chairperson - me!

As discussions evolved, the local community formed the Wishaw Action Group. And with the support of our MP, Andrew Mitchell, the media and the police, we eventually led the road campaign to success. Within 12 months we had succeeded in securing new road signs and lower speed limits. Cars could no longer race along the winding roads of Wishaw, threatening themselves and all who lived in the hamlet.

The curse, we thought, had ended. But it hadn't even started. No sooner had we begun to sit in our gardens free from the horrors of motor vehicle accidents, we were fearing for our lives again.

Each day I walked the short distance across our driveway to the office, and each day I would find our employees suffering terribly from nausea, rashes and eye infections.

Worried by the decline in everyone's health, it was not long before I was woken up in the night by screams of pain coming from George's bedroom. Bounding into his room, I switched on the light to reveal the horror. He was sat on the bed with blood pouring from his nose. As a mother I was shocked as all I wanted to do was protect him. But taking him to the doctors terrified me, as they suggested an operation to cauterise his nose.

Grace, our daughter, was also suffering. She was experiencing horrendous night terrors and hallucinations, but it was me who was next to wrap my knuckles on the doctor's door.

I had a lump in my breast. I was sick with worry, but to my relief I was told it was cyst and therefore nothing to worry about. Relieved by the news and free from the pressure of my own health concerns, I could focus on my family and the business.

The pace continued to accelerate and we became partners with three other directors. Our workforce swelled from 12 to 20, and then to nearly 50, between two locations.

But as the business grew, so did the cyst in my breast, and it just didn't feel right. My instincts were telling me to investigate it further, but the doctors were adamant that it was fine. To put my mind at rest, I had a biopsy. I left the kids with my mum while Paul drove me to the hospital to get the results. We had a joint of beef in the oven and a bottle of champagne in the fridge; I wanted a divorce from the cyst once and for all.

As I sat in the hospital waiting room, my appointment kept being delayed. My intuition told me that this was more than a routine hold-up. Minute after minute I watched as patients scurried in before me, and slowly my head sunk into my hands.

Finally, my name was called. Entering the doctor's room, I noticed that his eyes were bloodshot and his face was wrinkled with worry. Their assumptions had been proved wrong. In November 2001, I discovered that the illness which had being festering inside my breast for the last nine months was cancer.

I was so angry and upset because all along I had known that something was wrong. Sadness slowly turned to rage, and as the blood in my body boiled, my tears could have burned metal. I was 38, with two young children.

I feared death, and not only that, I feared standing in our home and saying those words that had always haunted me: 'I'll be back soon'. I also wanted to know the cause of the cancer. After all, there was no history of it in my family.

The worst moment of my life happened back home in our living room, as my children looked up at me in anticipation of my words. They were 11 and nine, understandably naïve to the world of cancer.

Grace was so upset that she started screaming. George dealt with it in his own way. His reaction was to look after me by becoming the new cook of the house. He made soups with stainless steel pans so big and heavy they weighed more than him.

I worried for my family, as anyone would, but I was only able to escape putting a brave face on when I was alone. My tears in the shower could have filled the bath. I had cancer, but I had to fight.

I started regular treatment at the hospital and recognised that many of the faces around me were constricted with worry. A number of women from the village were diagnosed with breast cancer, or with precancerous cells on the cervix, which meant that they could not conceive.

Sitting at the kitchen table, I looked out the window, cradled my cup of coffee and wondered why? Why was everyone sick? The rattling of the mailbox and the delivery of a letter, however, would ignite a new quest.

I received an application from a mobile phone company to put more antennas on the mast. *The mast*! I thought. The monstrous 22 metre metal structure with massive antenna panels had scarred the landscape since the day we had moved into our dream property. I had always thought it ugly, but never before had I considered the possibility that it might be dangerous.

The potential cause of the cancer that was thwarting my life, and the lives of many others, was now resting in my hands. The mast was situated only a hundred metres away in an open field.

I found it hard to switch off as I tried to continue 'normal' life. Blasts of chemotherapy led to the thinning of my hair and a weaker reflection greeted me in the mirror.

We used the latest technology to test the levels of radiation in the atmosphere. They were high. Furthermore, the metal beds my children had slept in acted as conductors, increasing the flow of radiation into their bodies. I was furious and determined to tell our story to anyone who would listen.

This relentless determination consumed my whole being. I couldn't sleep and pursued everyone I could think of who might be able to provide insight into the case.

I rang university professors who had investigated the effects of radiation. The cancer/illness cluster correlated with published research and we discovered that we were not alone. It was confirmed that cancer could be caused through this form of radiation.

My immune system and white blood cells had been decimated from being exposed to radiation from the mast. My scalp was now visible, my skin was grey and my body was battered by the regular visits to the hospital for increased doses of chemotherapy.

Scared and shaking, I watched on as injections were pumped through a plastic tube in my wrist. Likewise, Neupogen was injected into my stomach to increase the level of white blood cells in my body. Doctors kept a microscopic eye on my progress and were amazed to see the rebirth of many white blood cells after a five-day break from my home. It was clear from my own perspective that microwave radiation from the mast was cooking the blood, organs and every cell inside me.

Just as I regained hope that I might be right about the cause of my cancer, an independent scientist's report was published stating that it was not the mast. Results confirmed that the levels of radiation were satisfactory and within the guidelines. Maybe I had been wrong. As a community, we accepted the results until a further twist of fate took place a few days later.

Looking through my kitchen window as I washed plates and cups, I saw a man half way up the mobile phone mast. I was shocked and immediately (and with purpose) went to speak to him. Before I could vent my frustration he said, 'you may have been having trouble with the reception in the area but you won't now!'

What? I thought. He must have mistaken me for a customer.

Rushing into the house, I rang the mobile phone operator to ask why we hadn't been notified of the repairs. They responded by saying they knew nothing about them and stated that I hadn't spoken to one of their people.

With lessons learned from my cancer misdiagnosis, I trusted my instincts and rang the police to inform them that a white van had been seen in the area and we were a little concerned. It was not long before they returned my call. They had investigated the men in the white van and concluded that they were industry technicians employed to work on the mast.

That was all the confirmation I needed. I suddenly saw a shadowy explanation for the presumed safety of the mast in full technicolour. The levels of radiation were hardly safe. The power to it, and thus the radiation coming from it, had been reduced before the independent testing had been completed. Now that we had been given the all clear, technicians were climbing the mast, adding even more power, and thus more danger. We had been duped into thinking all was safe.

Infuriated, I couldn't accept this. The mobile operator had lied to us about the so-called 'safety' of their mast's emissions, and with that, my response to the operator was:

'You are going to have one hell of a battle on your hands now. We are about to start a campaign that you will never forget and I want you to remember our faces and the damage you have caused until your dying days.'

Repeating the blueprint from the road campaign, leaflets were distributed and I informed the local media what was happening. I had my photo taken in George's room, next to his bed draped with a military radiation net - which we'd installed to protect him - and this made the front pages of newspapers. Headlines such as: 'Mast War: Resistance is Useless' regularly appeared in newspapers in Sutton Coldfield, Birmingham and national newspapers throughout the UK.

As a community, we came together once again for a David versus Goliath battle. Cancers, sleep problems, headaches, skin rashes, depression and electrosensitive sickness had destroyed people's lives. Not only that, Wishaw was an affluent area and the reports jeopardised the value of people's homes - homes we had worked so hard for.

The mast appeared unannounced one day, with its danger undeclared. When we asked for the truth, it was covered up. This deceit and the destruction of our right to feel safe in our own homes unified the village in a common cause. We fought that tower and the mobile phone industry with everything we had. Alerting the public to the health dangers of these structures was more important than the value of our homes; we had a duty of conscience to alert the world.

When the mast collapsed in the field behind my garden some two years later, our campaign became magnified. The landscape looked like a medieval battleground as we staged round the clock vigils. The mobile phone operator wanted to repair the mast and gain access to the land. They were as furious and as determined as were we. They still kept coming, threatening to bring the police and take legal action against us. Thankfully, part of the right of way to gain access to the mast was on one resident's land, and of course, permission to access the site was declined.

We wanted to rid ourselves of the metal giant that was now positioned horizontally on the field. As a community, we took turns to guard it on a rotational basis, sleeping four hours on, four hours off in the freezing cold of winter. We sat in deckchairs, roasting marshmallows around a fire that burned in a metal drum. Passers-by tooted their support as they drove past and the campaign gathered momentum. We felt that we had no option but to go public and this was the moment when the national newspapers and TV stations really grabbed hold of the story.

I travelled to London by train one dark, cold morning, I was nervous but excited. I was about to appear on *This Morning*, the national daytime TV programme, to talk about our campaign in Wishaw.

I looked down at the full English breakfast in front of me and persuaded myself that I must eat something. As I cut into the egg, it exploded, the yolk rising like lava from a volcano and landing all over me. I was horrified. How was I going to get a new outfit before I was due at the studio?

The shops weren't open yet and whatever I tried to do to clean myself up only made it worse. I was mortified at the thought of appearing on national TV, egg stains and all!

Sloping into the *This Morning* studios, I begged the staff to help me. They initially wanted to replace my top with a black lace one, but there was no way they could persuade me to wear it. Luckily for me, the amazing team managed to salvage my own top and I was ready to face millions of viewers live on TV.

The interview went well, but when it ended, I walked off set in front of the cameras while they were still live. 'Oh, and off she goes,' said Philip Schofield, the presenter. I'd thought you just got up when you were finished. I was embarrassed but then I thought about the exposure I'd got for the campaign. I focused on my passion rather the shame of making a mistake.

With each new challenge, I had to grow. We were embroiled in a battle with one of the fastest growing industries, and we were exposing the health risks relating to it. In the early 2000s, the industry had invested billions of pounds in 3G licenses, but the lives of people were more important. First it was smoking, then alcohol, then sun beds - with all warning signs ignored until it was too late.

Back in the village, the fall of the mast meant we were safe from radiation. The community could now continue life as normal. The objective for Wishaw was complete. We had won the battle. The mast would never return. All the campaigning and hard work had paid dividends, but my feelings were so strong that I wanted to help others realise the dangers across the world.

From the start of the new millennium, I dedicated my life to the investigating, researching, speaking and educating about the dangers of 'RF radiation' in all things wireless (or mobile). I travelled to different conventions and continued to unravel shocking information.

There was so much corruption and lies - evidence that scientists had been employed by the industry to turn the other cheek. Equally, I also discovered amazing scientists who know that radiation from mobile phone masts can have biological consequences. I wanted to bring this debate from both sides together, to see if a common ground could be found. Was it possible for people to work together for the good of all?

Determined for history not to repeat itself, we wanted to make everybody aware of the health risks. In 2003, my colleague Mike Bell, an environmental lawyer, and I formed the Radiation Research Trust (charity). We made tremendous progress and warnings circulated that I was on a 'hit-list'. By raising and exposing information on cancer clusters, I was threatening the profits of one of the largest industries in the world, but I didn't think I was really in danger until I received evidence of it.

I was working flat out while delicately negotiating with and encouraging scientists from both sides of the debate to attend and present at the 2008 Radiation Research Trust conference. This was the first time that such a conference was organised to include experts from both sides of the health debate (those who believe electromagnetic fields have negative effects on health and those who believe the opposite is true). Just weeks before the event, on August 27 2008, I telephoned Mike Bell only to hear a 'click click' sound. I tried again and couldn't believe it. I was through to the Police Monitoring Station, the POLICE! Yet I had phoned my colleague...What in the world? There could only be one explanation. The phone wires weren't crossed. Our phones were tapped, but by the police. Exactly what 'hit-list' was I on – an industry or government one?

Stunned, I suddenly believed all the hype about me being in danger. Instead of making me fearful, this incident provoked greater anger. I tried the number three more times before finally pressing redial and getting through to Mike. My suspicions were confirmed. We were being watched.

The intimidating setting of the Royal Society in London is the birthplace of science. It is home to huge Roman pillars and decorated in history from the 1600s. As I walked in the footsteps of time and absorbed the beautiful portraits of the great and good, including Sir Isaac Newton, I hoped that it would be a suitable environment to bring 150 of the world's leading minds from both sides of the debate together.

A year in the making, I'd organised a dinner at the Palace of Westminster for all the delegates, as well as their hotels, flights and transport.

With the event fast approaching, the government decided not to send its people. This had a domino style effect, providing an excuse for other agencies and scientists, that were under pressure not to attend, to pull out. The event was crumbling just weeks before it was due to happen. It was the school holidays and I took a short break to take my daughter shopping. Yet as I sat having a bite to eat in Selfridges, Birmingham, tears streamed down my face. I was embarrassed about crying in such a public place, but I was hurt and felt destroyed. A year's worth of organisation was slipping away as fast as the tears hit the food on my plate.

In a bid to rescue the situation, I sent a plea for help to Sir

William Stewart and spoke about my breast cancer with every bit of passion I had. I was not giving up. Sir William was the chairman of the Health Protection Agency and he had served the government as chief scientific advisor for decades, advising Margaret Thatcher and Tony Blair. He listened and agreed to represent the Health Protection Agency. A couple of days later, and with just one week to go, the event was back on the agenda.

With relief and euphoria, I rushed to tell everyone I knew about this latest development. It was not over, though. There was yet another hurdle to cross. An American journalist wanted to film the event, which was not part of the plan. Once again, people became scared for their jobs or worried that they would be exposed. We had to plead with the journalist not to come and refund the money for her flights. With days left, the clock was counting down until I heard from the Royal Society. Rumours had spread that there was going to be mass demonstrations outside the building, and they feared riots, unrest and unwanted attention. Once again, I had to speak to all the groups and literally beg the various speakers from industry and government agencies to keep the event alive. It did happen in the end. I opened it at the Royal Society with a speech. I closed it by saying:

'When you are told that you have a life threatening illness you realise what is really important in life. What is important is our partners, our sons, our daughters, our mothers, our fathers, our brothers, our sisters and our friends, and we need to think about every one of them. No one wants to see their loved ones suffer and I'm sure you will all agree that this is the reason why we need to put health first. I have come to realise that differences of opinion in science can be good, as they help each side to strive for perfection and answers. I have also come to realise that the debate is not just about science, but about how such knowledge is taken forward into developing appropriate public policy. I hope we can all open our ears, open our minds, open our hearts and accept the truth and find a safer way forward together for everyone.'

I had practised my speech and I was determined to deliver it with passion as I looked into the eyes of those in the room with a plea for help.

The event led to the formation of the first EMF (Electromagnetic Fields) Dialogue Group at the European Commission (a court in Brussels where decisions that affect millions of people around the world are made), which involved both sides of the scientific debate. I helped the commission to bring the team together and I am an active member to this day.

For me, it has been a journey of incredible pain and sacrifice. I was left heartbroken after my marriage ended in divorce after 25 years. But I continued to fight to protect children everywhere, including my own. I am an ordinary working class woman from Liverpool. I am a daughter and a mother and I have fought all the way to present at the European Commission. And after 10 years of campaigning, on May 31 2011, the cancer committee of the World Health Organization finally voted to recognise RF radiation as a 2b or 'possible human carcinogen'.

But throughout everything, it is the beauty of people that makes life worth living - especially those individuals who genuinely want to make life better. So many people helped to lift me out of the emotional pain of divorce and failure. Indeed, while I was languishing in the worst of my adversities, I met my best friend at a conference in America. It was a speaking event that I very nearly didn't attend. The divorce and emotional hurt was a battle I could not recover from. I fell into despair and didn't feel able to function. The heartbreak was too much to bear and after fighting with councils, the mobile phone industry and cancer, the divorce had left me in a mess. I didn't want to speak to people or take part in any activities; I just wanted to hide away. Yet sometimes in life, we find the people we need the most and I found my support in the individuals whose paths I believe were meant to cross with mine.

Encouraged and cajoled, I was scraped off the floor, which was incredibly timely as this was one of my greatest opportunities to continue my message. The talk took place at The Commonwealth Club in San Francisco, which is America's oldest and largest public affairs forum, and has been host to a distinctive array of speakers such as Martin Luther King, Jr. and former president, Bill Clinton. And here was me - a woman with no university education and no public speaking training. All I possessed was a raw passion to protect.

The case is still open and the research and facts continue to pour in. It is incredible to think that I have been involved in such a project. I am amazed when I look back on the coughing and spluttering of my first presentation during the campaign to protect Wishaw's roads, and how I've overcome cancer. For six years I endured radiotherapy and chemotherapy and five years of taking tamoxifen tablets. In 2007, I had all my reproductive organs removed. Since then, I have been fortunate enough to be in good health.

It has been lonely and arduous at times, with no promise of success and every guarantee of uncertainty. Yet somehow I felt that each time I took one more step along my path, I was stepping into a footprint that had been ever so discretely mapped out for me. Perhaps this is what destiny feels like when one is working on behalf of a greater good. If I can do it, you can too.

Inspired, I sat glowing with admiration. Eileen, fast approaching a birthday milestone of 50 years of age (I know, I am breaking a cardinal rule by revealing a woman's age, but it's to demonstrate something important), had been fighting various challenges since the age of eight, from death and disillusionment with work, to divorce and the disaster of breast cancer.

What I learned from Eileen is the importance of overcoming fear. You have to have passion for what you do. It was a story that reminded me of the significant time I'd lost in the past by thinking, *nah, that won't work.* Every doubt contributed to my reluctance to start or try anything new. I'd simply focused on what could go wrong rather than what could go right. Here was a woman with no real education, who had gone from working as a cashier to speaking on the same stage as Martin Luther King, Jr. Wow!

Eileen told me about an unfortunate spelling mistake she'd made when delivering leaflets to raise awareness of the campaign. Instead of saying 'condemning' the mast it said 'condomed.' I couldn't help thinking of a condom over a mast. Maybe it could have become a marketing campaign - 'safe text'. Jokes aside, a simple human error such as this would have probably made me think, *I'm not good enough.* I'd made mistakes in the past. In fact, I was in one of the poorest sets in English at school. I did well in other subjects, but can't help wondering where I was when the lessons on full stops and sentence structure were delivered. As I began my professional career, many of my colleagues used to laugh at how poor my English was. I used to read emails back and think, *did I really send that to a customer?*

Eileen demonstrated that fear and doubts accompany us each day. However, we can overcome them. And the solution to achieving this was becoming clear. Start discovering your passion. Craft and mould it until it grows greater than your fears. The evidence had appeared in Emma's story of helping disabled people, in Rick's of overcoming financial difficulties and in Eileen's cancer cluster campaign. In fact, passion appeared in all the stories.

Pain is part of the process. I was experiencing it, but Eileen had shown me what was possible. I walked away and drove back towards the craters, watching the grass in the sand dunes sway in the breeze. As I did this, I knew I had made a friend for life.

Sai Prasad - Indian Superman

In the week that followed I played catch up. Furiously trying to write up the stories, I bobbed backwards and forwards between meetings and asking the people I'd interviewed so far, follow up questions. On some days I could sit quietly with two fingers resting on my skull and literally feel the pulse of intensity as I spun many stories at the same time. August had been jammed packed full of learning, and now September was here.

The fresh month presented some new but exciting challenges. I wondered about submitting the stories I'd gathered to a publisher. Would they see the possibility? In addition to this thought, and given my concerns about the standard of my English, I decided I needed a person to correct my mistakes. Searching on the Internet, I found what I had been looking for - a writer's workshop. This concerned how to write and submit a book proposal. Delivered by Hay House and located in London, I had a strong urge to attend, but I cringed over having to fork out for an expensive weekend away. With no money, I decided to apply online for a credit card. I squinted at the screen in nervous anticipation of the decision and let out a gasp of relief when the application was accepted. All that remained was to book the train tickets to London.

Throughout the weekend event, I closed my mouth and opened my ears in order to listen and learn. There were some good speakers, including author Robert Holden and CEO of Hay House, Reid Tracy.

Hosted in a modern building near Blackfriars tube station, it was your typical seminar setup - almost like a church congregation. An aisle that led towards the stage dissected a path between 40 rows of chairs.

From the stage the message came through loud and clear to an audience of at least 200. Platform! What was that? A platform means your audience. How many people do you have on a database? How many people follow you on Twitter and Facebook? Simply put, how many people are going to buy your book? You could almost feel the energy drain from the room – it was as if someone had just popped a balloon. Bang! There goes that dream. It didn't happen to me, though. I have no doubt that without having the evidence of people who had overcome adversity I may have reverted back to my Catherine wheel approach and looked elsewhere for something easier. I reminded myself that we all need to start somewhere. Every tree starts life as a seed. Remember Tim Reddish's pastime of skiing when blind? Remember Terry Nelson who practically lived in hospital for 12 years and now teaches Cristiano Ronaldo?

I thought of this on the way home. I knew the platform was the overwhelming piece of evidence that I'd need to submit as part of my book proposal. The proposal is the business plan for the book. It was required so that the publisher could understand how the book would be sold, who would buy it, and how many pages it would have, etc. Plus, there was a whole raft of other questions that needed to be addressed, all of which had the power to diffuse the desire of anyone who had their heart set on writing a book.

The proposal would be a book in itself, and this is where I felt some pressure. Even though my faith was stronger, I still had to revisit many of the stories to ask more questions, as well as search for new people to interview.

I'd started to prepare many more lessons in school after a new project had presented itself. In addition to this, the proposal now loomed. *Oh no*, I thought - writing this book is going to take a lot longer than I expected.

The intensity of writing and the thought it required meant that I needed time away from the bat cave of my room. My usual spot was in an enclosed paved area in the back garden. Here I'd stand and throw a tennis ball against the wall. It had reaped rewards just before I left for London. I was throwing and catching when I thought of Somi, a friend whom I'd worked with when I'd moved to Guildford to take on a role with Ericsson.

Somi is a great guy, and throwing the ball reminded me of him because he loves cricket. I knew he had moved back to India and I sent him a message on Facebook seeing if he knew of anyone inspirational. He didn't disappoint. Within a couple of days, I was introduced to Sai Prasad.

After trying to align our diaries, a Friday evening in September 2013 finally presented us with an opportunity to connect. I spoke to Sai through Skype, with no knowledge of his story. At first, I was simply excited to be able to speak to someone from a different country.

Sai Prasad

The tentacles of karma touched my spine as I was born into my new life. The doctors, noticing an abnormal growth, spoke to my parents about operating. But the situation got worse, much worse, as the operation to remove the growth changed my life's path.

Karma, that's what it was. Karma means that if you have carried out a wrongful act in a previous life, then the justice for that act can be administered in this life. Whether people believe in karma or not, it is a huge part of the culture within my country.

Being born in India with a disability leaves many at the mercy of negativity. Families hang their heads in shame, particularly in rural areas, and many are subjected to solitude in their own homes. Without support, opportunity and education, disabled people are often forced to hold out a bowl and beg passers-by for money in order to stay alive.

My mother and father were deeply distressed. If you have a child or member of your family with a disability and expose them to the outside world, the blast of negativity is so violent that it can singe all hope - and it did so in my life. The intensity from people staring at me made me feel overwhelmingly worthless. The operation to correct the growth on my spine resulted in limited use of my legs and bladder, and it also affected my kidneys. It introduced me to a world of emotional struggle and the confines of a wheelchair.

The infrastructure in India - the roads, buildings and public transport - is not built for people like me. The speed at which life moves on the arid, dusty and chaotic streets of Hyderabad, where I live, is intense. Throughout the day, noise booms from eight lanes of traffic. The bustling of people fighting their way on to public transport and the arguments as market traders battle for space provides a taste of everyday life in India.

If I was waiting for a bus, I would feel even more degraded. The drivers would look down at me from their lofty seats, their tired faces casting judgement as they drove past, leaving me stranded. Was it any wonder that so many people in similar situations to me gave up hope?

The fact that there are so many old buildings in India magnifies the complexity of growing up with a disability. Cast aside with no respect, it often felt like I was being tossed into an oubliette with bricks chained around my ankles. The emotional torment destroyed my confidence. I attended eight schools in six years, and the loneliness of having no one to confide in was difficult. I dreamed of a life where I could be free and respected, but to achieve this I needed to learn - it was the only way.

The long trips to school often ended in humiliation. The class I was supposed to be in was on the first floor but there were no facilities to transport me there; no ramps and therefore no accessibility. I was told to go home, as they would not move the class for me. I became an irritation, like a stone in a shoe.

I kept persisting. The constant change of schools and wheeling myself along blistered my hands. Salty tears regularly rolled down my face. Just as I had built a relationship with a teacher or classmates, my newfound contentment would be snatched away. The fees that parents were required to pay, coupled with the competitiveness of schools and the pressure to deliver results, meant that many students with disabilities became circus acts. I didn't want this for myself, but I had no rights and there were no laws to enforce change.

Classes often consisted of 70 students with just one teacher, and lessons were delivered as seminars. Like crocodiles peering above water, the other students would lock their gaze on me. It wasn't long before the teacher would turn and discover this, deciding that I was to blame. I was a disruption, and without mercy, I was sent home.

Too many students who wanted to learn were falling behind. The survival of the school was jeopardised by me being there.

The pain played like a song on a repetitive loop in the depths of my mind. Too many disabled young people stayed at home, weighed down by the mental boulders of embarrassment and fear. My decision was to keep persisting or suffer a life even worse than the misery and rejection I faced at school. Many parents kept their children at home because of cost and the stigma. They would rather protect themselves and their children from the ridicule and bullying, and who could blame them?

Looking out of the window as the other students played and built relationships, my only company was my loneliness, which is the worst of all human emotions. In my adolescence, I made a decision to learn and make a difference. Disability had reduced the options available to me. I knew I would never play cricket for India. I could, however, use my mind for the country.

In order to reach that goal, I knew life would be a continual battle. My determination to prove people wrong became a crusade of will, and with my parents' support, I continued to study, read, and devour all the information I could. Gradually, teachers started to take notice and they saw the benefit I could bring by boosting the school's performance in the league tables. Invigorated by their faith in me, I decided I wanted to progress to university and competed with more than 200,000 other students to win a place at one. Finally, and after 17 years of adversity and suffering, I proved to the teachers and myself that my determination and tenacity to achieve were my strongest assets.

The dawning of new economic opportunities at the start of the 21st Century resulted in India benefiting from investments brought by the West. There were companies like Deloitte, which valued my mental capabilities over my physical appearance. Its equal opportunity policies became part of business culture and gave hope to many, particularly me. Given an opportunity to study for a master's degree in the US, my life really began.

Landing in America, the door of the aircraft opened, exposing my skin to the fierce cold air and the chance of new opportunities. I was amazed at the smoothness of the transfer between the airport and the halls of residence, but there was a lot to get used to. Studying at the University of Wisconsin, I'd traded the 32 degree heat of Hyderabad to minus 12 temperatures of Madison.

I'd arrived during one of the coldest winters on record. For eight of the 16 months I lived in Wisconsin, the land was covered in snow. The beauty was unbelievable. The tranquillity was spellbinding. My eyes became magnetised at this new world, and I was filled with new ideas. Despite such significant snowfalls, the accessibility meant I was able to move around without any real concern. The automatic doors, the washing machine in my room, the ability to go shopping without any inconvenience, this was freedom to me, and it was a life that I wanted all disabled Indian people to experience.

Wheeling along a corridor in my student accommodation building, my attention was caught by a poster. It must have subconsciously attracted me because it was in the same colours as the kit of India's one-day cricket team: blue and saffron. The poster was advertising skydiving. Immediately, I saw this as a sign. I could become a voice for the people who sat in their homes gripped by the law of karma. I could show them that despite their beliefs, they could take control and do amazing work with their lives. I could demonstrate that they had the opportunity to create; that what has happened in the past does not determine the future.

Sensing an opportunity, and excited and full of trepidation, I made the call to book the skydive. The night before it was due to take place, my stomach churned. I worried about landing as my wheelchair was to be replaced with a rope that would

111

perform the role of a lever. I would need to pull the rope so that my legs would rise, thus allowing me to land on my back.

Naturally nervous, the significance of the event meant much more than a plunge from the sky. It was a metaphor for opportunity, and with that thought held in my mind, I grew greater and taller than my fears.

As I moved closer to the edge of the plane, the reverberation from the winds circled and roared around my body. Then I jumped and my anticipation was replaced with total liberation. Bathed in sunlight, the up rush of air pinned back my face and I was free. I flew with the birds, sat on clouds and became more confident with each passing second. I filmed the event as evidence. I wanted people to see that if I could do it, they could too.

By trusting my instincts and booking the event, I became the first Indian with a disability to skydive. After uploading the film to YouTube, the broadcast was watched by people around the world. It wasn't long before the footage caught the attention of national media back home in India.

Nothing was going to stop me from raising awareness for people with disabilities, and providing opportunities for them. I had to inspire others to show the one billion people in India, and around the world, that great things can be achieved using the power of the mind. I didn't want another person to experience the pain I had suffered growing up. The feeling of freedom gave me so much hope, but immediately those thoughts turned to others. If I was the first disabled Indian to do such a thing in the 21st century, then surely others would be grateful for the opportunity to do the same.

Two years later, another life changing opportunity presented itself. In 2013, I was selected as one of 30 young ambassadors to visit Antarctica. To be exposed to such an incredible landscape was truly breathtaking. Navigating icebergs, the summer sun kissed the ice and it melted gently into the ocean. As I sat on the rocks overlooking the expansive water, I reflected while watching thousands of penguins going backwards and forwards. There were no arguments, no fighting and no hierarchy amongst them, just cooperation. And this was in one of the harshest environments on earth to survive in. If only the same attitude to survival was adopted in India. That was my dream, and as I sat draped in the Indian flag, I realised I had reached a new milestone; I was the first Indian with a disability to experience this amazing landscape.

Arriving home in Hyderabad, the momentum gathered pace. The news of my trip was spreading fast and I had the opportunity to appear on national television to raise awareness and talk about my experiences. The significance of my expeditions ignited discussion and debate. My exposure was so great that opportunities and projects emerged from different places.

One of the challenges for the traffic police in India is noise pollution. Many of them suffer terribly with headaches and illness resulting in them being unable to do the job. Part of my role was to create a solution to this problem. Working with local government agencies, my purpose was to create opportunities. After much thinking and analysis, I asked myself, what could be better than employing those who are hard of hearing? The result of a trial has proved a blessing. 15,000 Indian people with hearing impairments have now gained employment. They now manage the traffic using sign language, and this has proved very successful. Many people who were cast aside are now able to contribute to society.

Subsequently, I have been involved in the creation of Dine in the Dark - a restaurant operated by blind people. When customers enter the restaurant, they are greeted and taken to their seats to eat in complete darkness. This allows them to really experience what it is like to be blind. It also provides an opportunity for blind people to establish their own businesses and thrive as able-bodied people do.

What is beautiful is that I sit in India now and see how the heavy fog of disdain for people with disabilities is beginning to lift. Although there is a long journey ahead, I am witnessing shopping centres being constructed where the accessibility requirements of disabled people have been taken into account. It's progress and it's wonderful to witness.

Using my passion, I have co-founded a company called Sahasra. The idea behind it is to help young people gain access to higher education. It provides workshops as well as lifelong mentors to aid and guide people to success. Students participating in the Sahasra Programme pay a $5 admission fee for the workshops. They are given practical information together with inspirational stories and leadership examples. More than 20,000 students have attended the programme at college and university campuses, generating $100,000. We use that money to provide $80,000 worth of scholarships to fund university places. Sahasra was named as one of the top-10 business plans, among those that were submitted to the Global Social Venture Competition at the University of California, Berkeley. This made me feel incredibly proud.

My life and my disability have become my asset. Why should millions of disabled people in India suffer?

The pain of my youth is so prominent in my mind that I never want anybody else to have to experience anything like it. I want people to taste the air in different countries, to experience the different climates, rivers and oceans, and to respect different cultures and see that we are all equal. Each of us has so much to offer the world. In my own beautiful country, I am just one person in a population of over a billion. I believe that if I can do it - if I can come through the pain of adversity to move forward and create a new and full life - then you can, too.

After I'd finished speaking with Sai, I immediately ran downstairs to tell my mum and dad about the interview – it was the first time I'd shared one of my stories with them.

'You're not going to believe this,' I told them, 'it's unbelievable'.

They'd been chattering away, as they did most nights, with a glass of wine and a beer, and they were making spaghetti bolognese. Supportive and appreciative, their silence said it all as they digested the story. They were moved.

There was such a gentle strength within Sai's voice. His calmness reminded me of Ghandi or Nelson Mandela. He possessed a soft, non-violent way of addressing challenges. I watched his videos on YouTube, impressed by one of him sailing on a small boat designed for two to three people, his hands skimming the ice-cold water of the Antarctic. It was thought provoking stuff.

Unaware of the gravity and culture of karma, admittedly I was shocked by it. Karma is a word that's used in the West, but perhaps it's used in the wrong manner. Whenever I read articles or comments on it, it's referred to as a tool for revenge. 'What goes around comes around,' is a phrase that springs to mind. I regarded it as a flippant comment, more of a figure of speech, but I was naïve to the significance it has within India's culture, or how binding its hold is. I spoke to Sai about this and he said:

'The essence of karma will always be there, but regardless of belief, any bad act that has been performed in a previous life does not affect your response in the present.'

In others words, many parents of disabled people, and even those with a disability, accept that there is a debt to pay, and they accept this without thinking that they can contribute. Therefore they live in the shadows, hanging their heads in shame.

Sai's work provided India with a different observation. Many disabled people don't leave India, but he pushed the barriers to enable 15,000 people a chance of employment. He did all this while still in his mid-20s. He'd seen more of this world and made more of an impact than the vast majority of so-called 'able' people do in a lifetime.

I couldn't hide my excitement and wonder, but I also reflected on the stigma surrounding people with disabilities. This shapes the minds of many, particularly children. I had seen the effects of it, shyness and fear, but how Sai had come through it and achieved something amazing should be a story told to all children. I wanted my students to believe that they could do what they wished – just like Sai had.

Within a couple of days I was teaching a group of 14 and 15 year olds. Sai had agreed to sprinkle some of his inspiration around the classroom and appeared to them via Skype.

Later that day, I received a tap on my shoulder. Turning around, I was confronted by a tall young man with brown hair and pale skin. He looked smart in his maroon coloured school uniform, white shirt and maroon tie.

'Sir, could I really go to India?' He said. 'Could I go to a different country to work?'

'Yes, of course,' I replied. 'You can go wherever your thinking takes you.'

What Sai had demonstrated is what's possible when you live without restriction. His story inspired me to think big. Think big so you are consumed with excitement, whatever that dream may be.

Debra Lindsey-Santoro - Walking with Angels

After speaking to Sai, I had to press the pause button on the progress of my book. The proposal took priority.

The word 'platform' continued to dominate my thoughts, so I rang and emailed people who I knew might be able to help. Frank McKenna said I could speak on the radio; others contributed until eventually I had access to almost 250,00 email addresses. Surely that was a good start?

Without question, it was a tough and tiresome process. To reread pages time and again was a painstaking process. The sheer administration of thinking about and writing nearly 100 pages in just over 30 days left me sliding down my chair with mental exhaustion. But it was worth it to be able to talk about such amazing people, be inspired and ponder what others may think.

By mid October I wanted to submit my proposal to Hay House, but there was always something that could be improved, reworded or changed. Luckily I'd met Georgie Moore on my search for stories. I discovered that she was an editor and she agreed to help me. I'd found the person I'd been looking for to help correct my mistakes at the most critical of times.

I'd been living off adrenaline in the lead up to submission, but as soon as I clicked the send button I went to sleep. My mind and body had been like a flower leaning over and kissing the soil in the baking sun. Now I needed the shade. There were no more ideas left in me; just a writing 'hangover'.

After my short recuperation, I was back on the trail for stories.

Remember earlier when I mentioned Rick McMunn and his

influence? Well, on the day I met him back in 2010, I encountered another person. He was sat at the same table as me; a giant of a man by the name of Ben Brophy.

Ben's tall: 6'5", maybe taller. In his mid-30s he, like many of the men I've mentioned so far in this book, has a completely bald head.

Back when I first met him, he stood out like a skyscraper in a village. He was dressed smartly, in a grey suit jacket, black shirt and jeans, and he was the coach on our table, employed as part of the team to teach us.

What was/is cool about Ben is that he shares so much information and his passion is infectious. But one of his greatest assets is using YouTube.

One of the reasons I attended the course in the first place was to learn how to promote and sell products online. Alan McCarthy paid the fee for the three-day event, and what an investment it was. I always point back to those days as being the turning point in my life.

In January 2011, I went to Manchester so Ben could teach me how to use YouTube. The video we worked on featured Alan talking about negotiation tips. I had already filmed the video, so Ben did the editing. Within six months, it was the most watched video on YouTube on the subject of negotiation. At the time of writing (October 2013), it remains top of the listings - proof that the training worked.

In order to receive additional guidance on negotiation, the viewer was directed to a website where they could leave their name and email address. *This gave me an idea. I'm going to chance my arm and put a request out for stories*, I thought. In over two years, I had collected 1000 email addresses and done nothing with them. That was about to change.

Even though it was a completely unrelated subject and a few people might get pissed off about receiving such a request, I sent an email out anyway appealing for inspirational stories.

Waking up bleary eyed a week later, I opened my mailbox and saw a name I didn't recognise. Debra Santoro was one of the thousand people I'd randomly emailed. Wow! That little video had led me to my next story.

I trusted my instincts and contacted her later that evening. It was as if it was meant to be, as if I had known Debra all my life...

Debra Lindsey-Santoro

It's every parent's nightmare to receive a call from the emergency services and hear a stranger's voice say that their child has been involved in a serious accident. For my parents, it was worse. Aged just 21, I was sprawled in a hospital bed in the emergency room. A sheet had been pulled over my face; I'd already been pronounced dead.

Growing up in Bangor, Maine, in the US, I was very close to my family. I have five brothers, and each of us was born approximately one year apart. I lived on a farm and played amid the beautiful trees, grasslands and vast open fields. Being part of a family with five boys, I became involved in everything they were interested in. Dirt bikes, farm machinery, motorcycles and trucks. I loved the action and excitement just as much as they did.

It was a landscape that experienced the wonder of all four seasons. One pastime I loved was exploring the woods and countryside on my horse. Huge oak trees would shed orange, red and yellow leaves, which danced in the sunlight as they floated to the floor.

My dad came from a large family, and the roots of our family tree grew all around us. My aunts and uncles lived next door and were within shouting distance to us. Afternoons consisted of my five brothers and me arriving home from school and racing each other to our grandparents' home. We would all sit in their kitchen, munching on homemade cookies and drinking fresh cold milk, all the while mesmerised by their storytelling.

This routine continued for many years, until the passing of my grandmother. I was only fifteen and the loss of such a beautiful mentor left a huge void in my life, and the lives of my family. But although I didn't know it then, my grandmother would continue to play an important part in my life.

For the following five years, I focused my attention on education. I developed an interest in accounting and finance, hoping to become successful and to make my family proud. And constant study was my routine until the age of 21, when a trip home from college started in atrocious conditions. It was March 1985, and the ferocious weather breathed a lethal concoction of snow and ice into the New England countryside. Driving along the long and winding country roads, the calm and serenity of my surroundings was disturbed as my car struggled to find traction. I extended my arms so that they locked, gripping the steering wheel so tight that my fingernails dug into the rubber. I clamped my foot down on the brakes, but the car screeched out of control. I became a passenger, gliding along the ice towards an old stone bridge. The force and momentum of the car exploded through the barriers and I trembled with fear thinking, *this can't be happening to me*.

Plunging 90 feet to my death, I felt like I was trapped in a giant tumble drier as the car rotated. I can remember seeing a vehicle on the road below, but that's all. I died in a flash as the emergency services tried to revive me. The dreaded call was made to my mother and father, who were both grief-stricken.

Dad was told he couldn't see me but he wouldn't let anyone stop him as he bounded through the hospital and into the room where I was lying. Dad naturally wanted to say goodbye to his only daughter, but as he leant over me, he saw two of my fingers move ever so slightly below the bloodied sheet I was under.

Unconscious and unaware of my father's presence in the room, I floated upwards, like the steam off a hot cup of coffee on a cold day, comforted by a brilliant white light somewhere between this world and the next. I was at peace until the calm was interrupted. Suddenly, I heard my grandmother's very distinctive voice and knew I must be close to heaven. She had always been a protector, a mentor and a friend, but this day she took on another role – she became my guardian angel.

'It's not your time to die,' she soothed. 'You must return to your body. You have too much left on this earth to do.'

'I don't want to go back,' I replied. 'It hurts and it's too painful.'

I begged my grandmother to let me stay in peace and remain free of pain. But no sooner had I uttered those words, my spirit was enclosed back in my broken body.

I was badly burned from the waist down. My legs were charcoaled and resembled meat that had been left on a searing hot barbecue for hours. Twisted and mangled, my bones extended out of my legs in different directions. The left side of my face was also destroyed as my cheekbone had been crushed. My lower lip was split down to my chin and many of my teeth were fractured. My right arm was mangled and my left leg was so severely burned on the inside that my femur had broken. Both bones in my lower leg were sticking out, and like a sword they had severed my tendons and damaged many nerves and veins. I had broken almost every bone in my body, all apart from my neck, back and two fingers on my left hand.

The driver of the car that I had briefly seen on the road below me had pulled me from the wreckage. He had saved my life while sustaining second-degree burns on his hands and arms. To this day, this incredible person has remained anonymous.

Air lifted to Massachusetts General Hospital in Boston, I spent seven months in the burns unit and three further months in the orthopedic unit. I was in a coma for almost six weeks, and while unconscious the doctors worked on reassembling my broken body.

Third degree burns covered a third of my body. Doctors used 'cadaver' skin, harvesting any viable flesh from my body. A rod was placed in my broken femur, and likewise in the fibula of my left leg.

I can still remember the excruciating pain. My screams could have shattered glass. Unfortunately, I developed an infestation of gangrene in my right leg and after seven months of undergoing futile operations, it was finally amputated.

Worse was to follow. Doctors and my family feared that my reflection could kill my esteem and they would not allow me to look in a mirror. The left side of my face had been crushed so severely that I was unrecognisable.

A few months later, I did see my reflection. Horrified at my alien and shredded appearance, the words of my grandmother were lost on me. I saw no hope and wanted to die. My body had been crushed and burned, and so to had my spirit.

Fortunately, the doctors sedated me throughout my early days in hospital, but there was nothing they could do once I started moving again. I was put into physical therapy to try and regain some of the movement in my left leg as it began to heal. Every twist and turn of my remaining charcoaled limb felt like being mutilated alive. The pain stamped out any flicker of courage I possessed. And the final damnation finished me off. I would never walk on my left leg again, without the aid of a brace. This hit harder than the physical disfigurement and I remember thinking, *how could this have happened to me? How can I ever hope to live a normal life again?*

The worst point of my ordeal came when I looked at the bottom of the bed only to see one foot sticking out of the sheet. I felt unimaginable psychological pain and sunk into the darkness of depression. All I did was feel sorry for myself, and I wished that death would arrive at my door many times.

Then my older brother came to visit.

'What is wrong with you?' he said. 'Look at what you are doing to Mum and Dad, to all of us. You need to snap out of it and start fighting. We all love you and we don't want to lose you.'

The words penetrated deep and allowed me to think and reflect during the endless days in hospital. Indeed, my thoughts had pointed inwardly on my own misery and not on how I was affecting others – particularly those who cared for me the most.

My parents were constantly at my bedside. What happened had left them devastated and although they still had five other children to think about, I was always in the forefront of their minds. I owe my entire life to my parents and my brothers. They have been there to support me every step of the way.

Following my brother's visit, I made the decision to fight. His words of passion and encouragement made me determined to think of others and not just myself, especially when the doctors told me that I would never walk again as a result of the injuries to my left leg. I became fixed on proving them wrong - and I did. Numerous operations were performed on my 'residual limb' in order for me to comfortably wear a prosthesis and learn to walk again. I now walk just as well as people with two legs.

I'd snatched some hope back on the day my brother spoke, and I was not allowing it to leave. I was not going to let the opinion of a doctor confine me to a fruitless existence, and with my brother's words humming in my ears, I began the journey to take back my life.

I started on the road to recovery by working with a fantastic physical therapist. She taught me a number of techniques and although painful, they worked. While I was lying in bed or sat in my wheelchair, I would take a towel and wrap it around my foot, pulling it up towards my chest by bending my knee.

'This may encourage the growth of your tendons and nerves,' the therapist explained.

Trusting her guidance, I diligently stuck to the routine and regained 70 per cent of the motion in my ankle, which meant that I did not have to wear a brace. This amazed my doctors. It was an extremely painful process, but to be able to move around unaided made everything worthwhile.

The simple action of moving my foot and bending my knee invigorated my soul and stimulated the belief that I could recover. As a consequence, I completely removed the word 'can't' from my vocabulary. If someone told me that I couldn't do something, it was all the motivation I needed to prove them wrong!

After spending so much time in comas, hospital beds and confined to the four walls of a hospital ward, it was time to let myself be free and close the loop on the healing process.

After leaving the hospital and feeling settled within my skin again, I decided it was time to see some sights and make up for lost time. I'd been influenced by the outdoor adventures of my childhood and already owned a motorcycle. Now it was time to get out and see my own country.

In the late 1980s, many advances in technology were still in their infancy, particularly mobile phones. My dad and brothers, all naturally protective, feared for my safety, but they also accepted how determined I was to experience how amazing life could be.

So I set off on my own adventure, the wind ruffling my black leather jacket as I rode my Honda Shadow 600CC through 36 US States. The roar of my bike echoed through the open spaces, and long mirrors, resembling periscopes, stuck out right and left. *No looking back now*, I thought.

Seeing wild elk, buffalo and coyotes roam across miles of open space was breathtaking. The journey represented the purification from pain and the freedom of choice.

In Yellow Stone National Park, I witnessed Old Faithful erupting powerfully - shooting boiling water from the earth's crust. As the water travelled 150 feet into the sky, I reflected on my own ascent towards the heavens. Had I not faced the pain and listened to the words of my grandmother, I would have gone towards the light. Consequently, I would not have had the opportunity to live.

Spending six weeks riding cross-country, I visited many amazing places and shared my story with a host of wonderful people. In the Midwest, I watched wild mustangs roaming the open lands as I roared into the glow of the orange sunset. The open road and the horizon provided a new perspective as all areas of my life began to improve. Not long after my soul-searching trip, I got married and my career in accounting and finance began. In parallel to this, my desire to serve grew.

The stark reality of my experience provoked my attitude to give back to those who needed help, encouragement and hope. I subsequently used those legs of mine to ride a bicycle 100 miles in just one day, which I did to raise money for our heroes in the forces, as well as various cancer organisations.

My work has enabled me to experience new lands, new people and support soldiers who risk everything daily to preserve our liberty. I support those who diffuse roadside bombs. I also encourage those who become victims of conflict and end up in a hospital bed like I did. I do this because I empathise with them. I've experienced those feelings of hopelessness and pain – losing a limb is also losing a vital part of yourself. I know, however, that you can overcome your adversity and lead a life of your choosing. I'd realised this by the end of my time in hospital. During my long recuperation, I set goals for myself. I have since met each goal, and I have also accomplished some things that I never dreamed of doing before my accident.

More than 20 years have passed since the accident, but the challenges continue. Shortly after my sponsored bicycle event, my left knee started giving me trouble. In 2009, I had to have a total knee replacement. I told my doctor that I was very, very nervous about the operation, but he assured me that my body wouldn't reject the materials, as it had previously (every piece of metal in my body had had to be removed following the initial accident). But if I had not had the replacement, then I may not be walking now. Well okay, I probably would, but maybe not as well. If you haven't guessed it yet, I am very determined and stubborn (the New Englander in me). I would need this trait in abundance for my next challenge…

Early in summer of 2012, I found out that I had breast cancer. I was horrified! I thought: *Why me? Haven't I gone through enough?*

After wallowing in misery for a month, I said, 'Wait! Why am I feeling sorry for myself? This is not me – I am a fighter.' Because of my attitude, I was able to encourage two ladies to seek treatment, and had I not shared my experience with one of them, she may not be with us now. Once again, having a positive attitude saved not only myself, but others as well.

Breast cancer is very personal and many women keep it to themselves. I want to share my story and encourage people to be proactive about performing self-examinations. I found a lump in my right breast in December 2011. I didn't do anything about it immediately, and after a few months I noticed that it had grown substantially larger. My doctor ordered a mammogram, which came back negative. I was then sent to a breast surgeon who ordered an MRI scan. This was also negative so I agreed to a lumpectomy. Less than a week later, I received an urgent call from a nurse who told me to come into the breast surgeon's office. I refused as I was very busy at work and went in the following week instead. I kind of knew what the result was going to be by the urgency in the nurse's voice. After the breast surgeon had told me the dreaded news, she talked for about 40 minutes, but I can't tell you what she said because I just tuned out. I'm sure that many of you can empathise with this.

Subsequently, I decided to go to Moffitt Cancer Center in Tampa, Florida for treatment and that was the best decision I could have made. After five surgeries to remove the cancerous tissues from my breast, I then began radiation treatment daily for three months. Now I am in excellent health.

The fighting, hard work and the desire to make a difference have given me a second chance to live. With a lot of determination and perseverance, I have carried the fight into my work. I am proud to have reached a management position in my current job and I have had many opportunities to lead and inspire others throughout the organisation.

Senior leaders reach out to me to lead events because they know I will give 100 per cent of myself. There is no greater satisfaction than the one that comes from successfully implementing and leading a team of people, and seeing warm, smiling faces on each person you have helped.

Today, you would never know that any of this has happened to me. People could walk past my desk and would never know the true story. My trouser suit conceals my prosthetic leg. At one point in time, I used to constantly hide it, but now I embrace it because it is part of who I have become. My once mangled face has healed through the help of surgery. I hope this shows that despite the most graphic of physical adversities, life can be fulfilling and amazing - once you decide it can be.

My decision to live has helped raise thousands of dollars to support others who need it the most. My mission now is to help others achieve confidence and strength, so that they too can become empowered and inspired. But what I want you to know is this: If I can do it, you can too.

I don't think I said a word during my Skype interview with Debra. I was totally absorbed as I listened to her describe her out-of-body experience. It's only as I write this now, after our initial conversation, that I realise I have no idea what she looks like. I was so fascinated by her story that I didn't even ask.

What happens when we pass on, or come close to death, is something that almost everyone has an opinion about. For me, the overwhelming message within this story is one of faith. Regardless of religious beliefs or what happens after death, ultimately within life we have to be able to trust ourselves.

The brutality of Debra's physical experience is without question the most horrific I've ever heard. At just 21, she was battered, broken and burned, had a leg amputated and wanted to die because of the pain she was in. She didn't even know if she would recover, never mind how. But after the natural darkness and uncertainty, she made a decision to recover and keep the faith. It was a key message. Especially when doctors told her that she would never walk again. She did, and much, much more.

Riding a bicycle 100 miles for charity and exploring North America on a motorcycle is amazing. It made me realise that as long as you have faith, it doesn't matter what tripe the naysayers come out with; you can overcome adversity.

Through Debra, I really started to understand the concept of faith. Faith for me was an overused word. I'd so often hear, 'you have to have faith'. The problem I had in the past was that I didn't have a purpose to put faith in. Well I did now.

Andy Bounds – Weakness into strength

It was ironic, as faith is what I would need to discover more stories, and to trust in myself. I wish I'd had faith back in 2008, but like I said, with no purpose, it's hard to have it.

Back then, I was sat in an audience at Celtic Manor resort in South Wales. Just a couple of years later it would host the Ryder Cup. At this point, however, it was the venue of a sales conference. It was my first day working for a new company and I didn't want to be there. There must have been 1000 people there, and they had descended from all over the British Isles to listen, learn and indulge in the financial year-end celebrations.

Forced to meet new people and act enthusiastically, I just wanted to jump into my new shiny black BMW and bolt home. My aura exuded the essence of a miserable man. I knew I had made a mistake. I had moved for a larger salary, I had moved because of a car, I had moved for all the wrong reasons. I thought this was success; I had made this mistake before.

I didn't want to speak to anyone. Instead, during the two-day conference, I sat listening to the guest speakers and their pearls of wisdom. One guy spoke of his trip to the North Pole. Amazing, but how do people even begin to think about doing such a thing? Why couldn't I do something like that? How the hell did I end up here?

The lifts were crammed with people bustling backwards and forwards. There was a buzz of chatter as swarms of salespeople gathered to drink coffee while I looked for my table. The next act was a guy delivering an interactive training session. That guy was Andy Bounds. *Brilliant*, I thought. I'd love to do that.

At the end of the event I drove north, battling with the traffic.

With the country roads clogged, I opted for a different route as I reflected upon the past couple of days. Inspired by what I had witnessed, my positive feelings had disappeared by the time I got to Birmingham. My desires were diluted by fear. How could I end the pretence? I would be unemployed if I left my job, surely that was worse? Would anybody else employ me? And what about the car? If I didn't have it, how would I get around? Later that year I did make a decision, but more about that a little later…

Five years on, in March 2013, I heard Andy's name mentioned three times in the same week. I'd made the assumption that because of his soft Lancastrian accent he lived elsewhere, yet here he was on my doorstep. At this point I was in the midst of adversity, but I had a bone to hang on to. A project - the opportunity to restart my quest to help young people into employment. I wondered if Andy would speak to the students.

My first thoughts were, he's not going to speak to me. But to my surprise, and after speaking to Emma Platt, his assistant, the date was set for a meeting at Prêt A Manger in Castle Street, Liverpool.

Prêt A Manger would become the hub for this and many more meetings. As I sat and waited, I looked out of a huge glass window, which was over two metres high and probably ten metres in width. It was like sitting in a goldfish bowl as I could study the people shopping or heading to work. Then I saw Andy walking past. He was dressed in jeans and a baggy shirt with the sleeves rolled up. His most prominent feature is his bald head and, of course, his ability to communicate. As small talk ensued, he explained that he could help with contacts and help me build my network.

Eight months later, as you know, the business had finished and I'd started on my writing project. In fact, Andy became the nucleus helping me meet people like Frank McKenna and Terry Nelson.

Talking to Andy was easy. He made everything simple, but what struck me was his willingness to help others without looking for anything in return. As we sat and talked, never in a million years could I have guessed the story he was about to tell.

Andy Bounds

Sometimes our greatest weakness can become our greatest strength.

This is a great saying, although as an 11-year-old boy with a bandage wrapped around my head (which was helping me recover from an operation on my right eye), it was difficult to comprehend...

Born with a genetic eye condition, I'd just lost the sight in my left eye. And with a prescription of -14.5 in the right, that one wasn't much better.

I did find some things hard, such as feeling lonely during games lessons when - for the few months after the operation - I wasn't allowed to join in. I remember leaning my forehead against the

glass of the gym window and watching my classmates messing about on trampolines. I was so jealous of them. It felt like everyone but me was having fun. I know that everyone feels like this at school sometimes, but it just felt so isolating. And with me, it was so visible. I felt it was my label:

'Andy Bounds? Oh, he's the one who can't play games. Weirdo.'

During these games lessons, the only place that teachers could send me was the library. Libraries are pretty cool now, but that one wasn't. It was silent and dirty, to the point where I'd often write my name in the dust on the books. It had an old fashioned, eerie atmosphere; like Hogwarts, but without the magic.

It was weird, school. You know how schoolkids hang around in packs, a bit like wolves? Well, I often felt like I was the runt. Many relationships and bonds are forged on fields and playgrounds. And I couldn't be part of that. To me, it wasn't just evidence that I was different, it was evidence that I was worse.

As I got older, games lessons became less of an issue. But, in sixth form, it kicked off again, because that's when people learn to drive. As a result of my poor sight, I couldn't do that either. As you know, for any young person, driving is a symbol of freedom. It's a significant achievement to share. But people passing their driving test was bittersweet for me. I was happy for them (well, sometimes), but each success reminded me that I wasn't like them. I also wondered what impact my non-driving might have on my love life (which is pretty much the most important thing in the world to a teenage boy).

Then came university. That was much better. I loved it. A new lifestyle came with new habits and new friends.

The uneven sports field was replaced with a level playing field - the students' bar. And, like most students, I lived the vampire lifestyle of sleeping away many a day while nursing a hangover.

But whereas my first 'isolator' – my eyesight – wasn't my fault, I was about to get another one. And this one was…

You see I discovered that the best cure for hangovers wasn't paracetamol, but pizza. And kebabs. And McDonalds. I had many battles with my weight, and pretty much lost them all. I loved having a Pizza Sunday. But when this turned into a Pizza Monday, Tuesday and Wednesday, it wasn't good.

And, because my eyesight meant I could never be the designated driver, I always had the opportunity (obligation?) to drink. So I did. A lot. And then had a kebab on the way home.

As the pizzas got bigger, so did I. I went from 200 to 280 pounds. I had a 44 inch waist, with trousers more fitting for a clown. I wasn't an unhappy eater – far from it. I was really happy. I loved food; there was no need for an off button. But it also left me tied to an umbilical cord of frustration and I just could not free myself from it. Every time I stretched out to improve my situation, I snapped back to my starting position. I needed to cut this cord and become reborn.

And I saw evidence of my 'weakness' every day. My wheezing showed me that I was out of breath. I used to be too blind to play sports, now I was too fat to! I was just into my early 20s, but had the health of someone two or three times that age.

Summer would be difficult because of the heat. My 'Fat Suit' made me sweaty and self-conscious. Everywhere I went, I knew I'd be the heaviest person there. It's funny, but I still remember that feeling really well - the experience of being about to go into a room and knowing - absolutely knowing - that I was about to be the fattest person in it. These aren't the feelings of someone at ease with himself! So I'd make jokes to diffuse other people's (OK, my) negative perceptions.

With clogged arteries and a gut hanging over my trousers, it was time for action. So I dieted a bit. And I'd make progress. But it never lasted. In fact, my approach to losing weight was similar to that of being overdrawn. My thought process was this: Since I'm overdrawn by £900, it doesn't matter whether I spend another £20 or not, I'll still be skint either way. So, I might as well spend it. And, since I'm so fat, it won't make me thin if I don't eat this enormous pizza. So I'll eat it.

When university finished, I remember thinking: *Well Andy, if your school years were your 'blind years' and your university years were your 'fat years', what will your work years bring?* I was excited about making a new start.

My job interviews were illuminating. They showed me I had something that people liked. I received amazing feedback. There was one interview in particular where I remember absolutely smashing it. It just couldn't have gone better. They told me they'd ring me on Tuesday morning to confirm whether or not I'd got the job. I got up early and waited by the phone. And then, as I paced around the lounge, it rang. I snatched it up, and heard the call I'd been waiting for…well…for what seemed like all my life.

'Andy, you were the best person we saw.'

I'd never heard anyone say that before.

'We're offering you the job.'

At last! I was up and running. This was going to be the new start I'd been waiting for. I instantly started thinking about what this meant for my life and my self-esteem. Then I realised I'd stopped listening to what the company boss was saying. So I tuned back in…

'We'd like to discuss your company car – you'll need one to do the job.'

I stopped. My shoulders slumped. I couldn't believe it. Just as I'd got the start I wanted, my non-driving had stopped it. I couldn't do the job.

Now, I'm a pretty resilient kind of bloke, but this was a hard one to take. I'd just impressed someone. I'd stood out ahead of my peers. I'd found something I could do. But at the same time, I couldn't do it. Impressing people wasn't enough. And, as anyone who has been through young adulthood will know, it sure is easy to find things that are unfair in the world. And I felt that this was.

So I had a huge sulk. I mentally kicked the cat around the room. But eventually I settled down and realised, once again, that I had to do something about it. So I changed my outlook again. I recognised that I needed a career where I could sit in an office, one that I didn't have to move far from. I decided to become an accountant.

Now, I have to admit, I'd never thought of myself as 'accountant material' (whatever that means). But it proved to be a good choice. I got a great job with a wonderful firm. My role combined working full time and attending college to study for professional exams. The pressure to pass them proved tough for many, but I thrived on it. Also, I didn't realise it at the time, but this college was about to change things for me...

One day, as I was sitting in class, a thought crossed my mind: I'd love to teach this stuff. And, as I studied, it became clearer to me how I'd teach 'my' students. So, while everyone else seemed to be focusing solely on learning the material (and rightly so – we had exams to do!), I was listening to the tutors, thinking, how would I have explained that differently?' I wrote my own training notes, making them as simple as possible. It wasn't long before other students asked to borrow them. My notes were making our complex, boring subjects easier to understand, and fun too.

It was becoming obvious to me that I'd be good at teaching, so I plucked up the courage to ask the college to tell me if a position ever came up. It was one of those conversations where you come away thinking, 'yeah, like that'll ever happen'.

But, to my surprise, it did. Shortly afterwards, I received a call asking me to come for an interview. It went well and they offered me the job.

Now I had a decision to make. And it wasn't easy – head or heart? I was working for a great accountancy practice and had good career prospects. I enjoyed working with my talented colleagues, many of whom had become good friends. I liked it.

Should I risk all this for a training job? Something I'd never done in my life? The risks were clear, particularly the lack of job prospects. I mean, where do you go if you get better at training people? Do you teach bigger classes? Harder subjects? Cleverer people? And, although I had this feeling I'd be good at it, I'd never actually taught anything before. I hadn't even made a stand-up presentation. And that was obviously a fairly fundamental flaw in the plan.

So, I asked my dad for his advice. His answer changed my life.

He asked me: 'I know you like your current job, but do you go to bed happy and fulfilled?'

'No, not really,' I replied.

'Do you think that if you took this new job, you'd be more

likely to go to bed happy and fulfilled?'

The answer was obvious.

'Yes, I would,' I replied.

Dad's advice?

'Go for it. Throw yourself into it. Enjoy it. If you want to stay in it, do. If not, it will stand you in good stead whatever else you do.'

So here I was, about to take a job where the job prospects seemed worse. This was something that I had never done before. My eyesight was still bad, my belly size even worse, but I had this very strong feeling. It was like I knew I was about to go to bed happy and fulfilled. I was excited and felt alive. So I accepted the job. And I took to it like a duck to water. My mission was to be the best I could possibly be. So my first task was to learn. I watched as many other tutors as I could. I practised harder than anyone I'd ever met. I attended every skills-building course I could go on. I learned from every type of presenter I could think of: teachers, leaders, politicians, TV presenters...everyone. Whenever possible, I asked them what they thought made a good presentation and what they did to engage audiences. I read as much as I could about the behavioural and psychological aspects of learning. In short, I became a total geek.

But, most importantly, with each new class I delivered, I improved. I used people's feedback to continue my evolution as a presenter. And the student feedback was brilliant to hear:

'Andy's great because he communicates difficult topics clearly... Andy takes the boring subjects and brings them to life...Andy's great at communicating in simple language...Andy makes it easy to pass.'

And my favourite feedback at the time was: 'Andy's lucky, he only teaches the interesting subjects.'

Interesting subjects? Have you ever studied Information Analysis? It is, without doubt, the most tedious thing that anybody has ever seen. Yet people were saying that I was lucky because I taught it and it was interesting. If I was making that stuff interesting, I must have been better than I thought!

I loved everything about the job. And the best thing was that the better I got, the better the pass rates were. My skills were transforming people's careers and prospects. At that time, in some accountancy firms, passing your exams meant a pay rise and promotion and failing meant you were out. What a responsibility to help people pass!

I was beginning to realise that my ability to communicate was my biggest strength. For so long, I'd felt tied to that stupid umbilical cord of frustration. But, at last, things were clicking. My mum is blind and all those years spent reading stories to her, describing characters, scenes, landscapes, shops, restaurants and houses in order to help her visualise them...it had all helped me to get to this point of being brilliant at explaining things. Then came the big realisation:

My poor sight was actually my greatest strength, not my greatest weakness.

Over the following years, I achieved unprecedented results. Three of my students became national prize winners (at a time when 12,000 people took the exams). Believe me, that was a significant slice through the frustration cord.

And Dad was right. I went to bed happy. And with that fulfillment, other areas of my life blossomed and I met my wife Emma (you'll be hearing more about her further on). It seemed that being unable to drive or being fat didn't matter. It was all in my mind. Who'd have thought it!

So, aged 34, I'd grown in resolve and confidence, so much so that I wanted to start my own business. This is very different to someone who thinks: I'm not different, I'm worse.

But I knew it would be difficult. I'd 'only' trained accountants. Just what was I going to do? I knew I needed to know more than I did, but I didn't even know what I needed to learn. I decided I should meet other business people, so I got up early for weekly breakfast meetings at an organisation called BNI.

BNI is brilliant (if you haven't been, go!). It's an organisation that helps its members grow their businesses by introducing them to new contacts. Every week my wife Emma (I told you she'd appear again) would get up at 5.30am to drive me to the meetings. Now that is love! And, as we drove, I'd rehearse with her what I would say. She coached me, and I got better.

It was a combination of the impact I had at BNI and Emma's support that gave me the confidence to set up on my own. And so I did - training businesses how to sell and communicate better.

Emma's confidence in me was such that she gave up her job just a few weeks later. You can look at this either positively or negatively. Positively - she must have had a lot of trust in me, and in us. Negatively - we had absolutely no money coming in. And as they say, if you want motivation, get desperate.

I realised that for our business to be a success, I needed to make some changes. And if we wanted it to get bigger, we needed me to get smaller. So I searched for more permanent answers to my weight problem (apparently, having one less slice of pizza isn't enough). After speaking with a number of people about this, I had a pivotal conversation with a nutritionist. He asked me who I wanted to be in 10 years' time. So I told him what I wanted my future to hold, what I wanted people to think of me, where I wanted to work and what I wanted to do, and so on.

'He sounds cool, doesn't he?' The nutritionist said.

'Yes, he does,' I replied.

'And would this guy eat pizza every week?'

Silence.

'No, of course he wouldn't.'

Almost instantly, I began to cut down my food intake.

Shortly afterwards, I presented at a BNI conference in Bradford. I was nervous about it. It was going to be the biggest audience I'd spoken to – 150 people. I had a feeling that it would go well, but I could only be really sure of this once it was actually over. Emma performed her usual trick of giving me confidence and reassurance, and then telling me to practise again and again.

The talk went brilliantly. It's probably the best presentation I've ever delivered. It was certainly the most life-changing one.

The audience actually interrupted my ending to give me a standing ovation. I don't know if you've ever had the privilege of watching 150 people stand up to cheer and clap what you've just done? It is brilliant.

And, if the immediate response was wonderful, it was nothing compared to what came afterwards. The UK BNI bosses came over and asked if I'd speak at their world conference in America (I'd be the first UK BNI member to do this in their 20 plus year history). Three different people came up to me in tears to tell me that I'd shown them how they could enjoy their jobs more. I smile as I recall this now. Talk about a transformational 40 minutes! I guess this feeling is what a contestant on the *X Factor* experiences – the rush of excitement and amazement when you realise you can do something that makes others cheer.

Immediately afterwards, as Emma and I enjoyed the moment, I told her: 'I'll never weigh 280 pounds again.'

She looked at me, realised something was different this time, and replied, 'I know'.

And the weight went.

Six months on, I'd shed 80 pounds. A decade on, it's still off. In fact, it's weird how similar my life is now to the guy I described to my nutritionist all those years ago.

Shortly after delivering my presentation, someone suggested I write a book. This had never even crossed my mind before. But, whereas the old me might have wondered whether I could do it, the new me knew I could.

My friend Paul McGee introduced me to his publishers and we got on well. Six months later, *The Jelly Effect: How to Make Your Communication Stick* came out. It became a best seller overnight.

I still remember the launch day. My publishers had set up radio interviews for me and after each one I called the office to see how sales were going. Each time, the book had shot up the

Amazon chart. I remember being amazed when it hit the top 25. What an achievement for a new author, I thought. But, 30 minutes later, it was number 18. Then it was in the top 10. Finally, it reached number three. The only two books above it were the two versions of the final Harry Potter book. I thought that was pretty cool. Weirdly, I'd rather have been third behind those two than at number one. The answer to your next question is, 'I don't know why. I can't explain it.'

But it wasn't just the sales that meant so much. There were other, more personal things that came with it. The book was such a team effort. Two of my customers helped to edit it and my friends, family and other clients aided the promotion. BNI - remember them? – well, they were brilliant. Their leaders endorsed it, not just by writing testimonials, but by telling their members to read it in order to help grow their businesses.

And the good news about Jelly didn't end there. I'd written it by scrawling notes on paper, dictating them, and then editing the typed pages that came back. And who was my typist? My mum. She's been able to touch type for years, and she'd given her blessing for me to tell our story in the book. And, as she typed up my dictation, she heard me describe the impact she'd had on my life. She called me to say that this had helped her feel there was a purpose to her being blind.

I find it hard to find the words to describe what this meant to me. So here's what she said: 'I'd never wanted to be blind, but I've got used to it, even if I'd rather not be. But, as I heard you on the Dictaphone, I began to realise there was a point to it. It's had a huge impact on our relationship, and your ability and passion to help people communicate better. It's taken 50 years, but it's wonderful for me to have this closure about it.'

It was one of the most memorable, emotional conversations I've ever had.

It's funny looking back at Jelly now. A lot of people, quite understandably, don't care that I once wrote this book. But if I hadn't written it, my life wouldn't be what it is now.

Since then, I've been blessed by what's happened in my professional and personal life. I've worked with some of the world's largest companies in over 30 different countries. I've helped them to win billions of pounds of new business. I've won awards recognising the quality of my work. My second book *The Snowball Effect* sold its entire first print run on launch day. I have four wonderful children, and Emma is still the perfect mixture of soulmate, confidence giver and taskmaster. As I say, I'm very blessed.

I still can't see very well. I used to believe that this made me useless, different, worse. But obviously I'm not. I was just a victim of my own thoughts, fears and – the most powerful driver of all - habits. I wasn't really unhappy, but I wasn't happy either. And I certainly wasn't fulfilling my purpose.

To progress, I had to make big decisions. I spoke to Emma, my parents, others I respected…and I took action to pursue my dreams.

And as for that umbilical cord of frustration, that's long gone. I barely even remember it now. I'm nothing like the person I was. There's no more wondering if I'm good enough. In fact, now it has to be the opposite. I have to be able to go into any room, with any of my customers, and know they're thinking: It's ok. Andy's here now. Things will be alright.

I'm fulfilled and happy now; the way I wanted to be when I

answered my dad's questions all those years ago. Since that conversation, this question – and my answer to it – has been my measuring stick for whether I'm succeeding.

I'd like to finish with a question for you: How would you answer Dad's question?

I hope you are happy and fulfilled. If you aren't, remember that you too have the power to cut your umbilical cord of frustration. It might take some time. But there are always people out there to support and guide you. Sometimes it isn't easy to find them, and it definitely isn't easy if you aren't looking for them, but they're there. And, if you can't find someone, feel free to contact me. I'd be pleased to have a chat with you.

One of the messages I share with my customers is this: 'it's not what you do, it's what you cause'. So, I don't go to an accountant because they do tax returns, I go because they cause me to pay less tax. I didn't see the nutritionist because I wanted him to do some sessions with me, I went because he was going to help cause me to lose weight.

And in your life, it's not what you do, it's what you cause.

And it's not just what you cause for others, it's the life you cause for yourself. The wonderful news is that you have the power to make it brilliant. And if I can do it, you can too.

To learn more from Andy, sign up for his free weekly tips at:

www.andybounds.com/tips

The invisible cord of frustration pulls on many, and it did on me. Severing it takes courage and decisive action. Sometimes in life, the adversities we face can be ones of confusion, lack of direction and living an unfulfilled life. Like with any adversity, active steps are required to overcome these challenges and move forward in order to grow from the experience. Andy proved this in his story.

Returning to 2008 and my own dilemma about whether to quit my job, it's no exaggeration to say that I lost a lot of sleep over it. I wondered: Should I leave and feel a failure or do I grit my teeth, ignore my feelings and hope it will get better? I'd been the same over my previous job and the one before that. In total, I had wasted three years deceiving myself that life would improve.

But, just six months after hearing Andy speak at Celtic Manor, a combination of factors forced me to make my most fearful decision. I quit. I gave back the car, the salary and the bonus. I had no job, but I felt amazing, not like the failure I had feared.

Andy's path resonated with mine because of his profession, his writing and his decision-making. But it also reminded me of the importance of direction and the beliefs we collect through our lives.

Beliefs remind me of the papier mache projects I used to do as a child. You blow up a balloon and it's free to float anywhere. But then you start applying strips of paper drenched in paste to it until it hardens. You apply another layer, and so on, until a boulder of thick paper is created. The balloon bursts and you're left with a hollow shape. Static, it sits in the same place. The same happens in life and in this analogy the balloon is your mind. At first it's free, then sticky beliefs cover up possibilities, which then harden over time. This is what I learned from Andy. In school he believed he was worthless. The same belief applied when he couldn't drive. If you are to bring down the guillotine and sever the cord, it helps to know who you are.

After quitting my job I had some time on my hands. This is when I began looking within to find out what I really wanted. In the past I'd researched a lot of concepts on personal development and noted down my own opinions. But now I wanted to get deeper and really comprehend what I wanted and understand who I was.

I drew the chart below to help me:

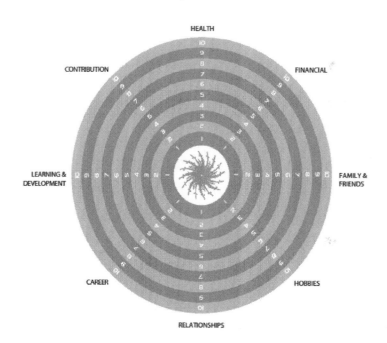

Step 1 – Self-Assessment

Starting clockwise at health, I rated myself on a scale of 1-10 for all segments of the wheel. Try doing the same.

- A score of one would mean your life is in despair and turmoil - you are feeling very upset and depressed.

- A score of 10 is bliss. You love what you are doing, you feel amazing and have never felt better about this area of your life.

- My career was by far the worst for me as I rated it a score of one. But more importantly, I wanted to do something about it. I didn't want to live tied down to a job because I thought it would impress other people. At the same time, I was scared of leaving because I didn't know what else I would do.

Step 2 – Soul Searching

Once I'd identified my career as the area I wanted to improve, I searched for lists of words to describe work. I found hundreds, and I filled several A4 sheets of paper with them. But as I started searching through them, I looked out for words that stood out, that I resonated with. I wanted to find words that described what I wanted work to be like.

I spent an hour a day on this for a few days until I had my final list of words. These were:

- Goals – I wanted to work towards goals that were exciting.

- Fun – I wanted to love my job. I wanted it to be fun and for time to fly by.

- Wealth – I wanted to earn well from my profession.

- Contribution – I wanted to be able to make a difference to people.

- Freedom – I wanted to be able to choose the hours I worked.

Step 3 – Seeking

I began to seek out a new career. Fortunately, after leaving my job, I had enough funds to live for a couple of months. I'd reached a point where my happiness was more important than just existing in a job that was not suited to my values. A month later, I landed a position within the education sector and ultimately started my own business, which has fulfilled the values I identified on my list. Even though I have encountered some rocky times since then, this has been one of my most rewarding jobs. I hope that reassessing your own life will help you find greater happiness, too.

Susan Foster – Fighter

I could barely sit still on the train. My legs were twitching nervously underneath my table as I approached London. Each stop heightened the concoction of excitement and trepidation I felt inside, and I could neither eat nor drink.

Waiting in anticipation of my final stop at Euston station, memories of my days working in the south of England resurfaced. I hated selling products that I had no passion for, and I had made this journey so many times before. Now I just wanted the doors to open. The stuffy Virgin train always smelt the same. A mixture of food odours wafted through the carriages, combining with the stench from the toilets. When the doors finally opened, I accelerated out like a wound up toy, joining the hoards of people descending down the escalators and into the Underground.

What was ironic was the date - November 19 2013. It was exactly three years from when I first met Ben Brophy and Rick McMunn - the day when I was inspired to change.

On this particular day, Ben and Rick were speaking to a number of my students while I travelled to London. Ben even knew one of the people I was meeting. I couldn't help romanticising about all these little facts and coincidences. Surely they were signs. Surely this was it!

Dizzy from weaving my way through people on the bitterly cold streets of Notting Hill, I waited for 2pm to arrive. The sky was clear but the breeze was cold and I couldn't wait to get inside the Hay House offices. In the lift I psyched myself up, summoning the courage to say my piece. This was my big moment, my opportunity to persuade a publisher to buy my book.

I waited in the small reception area scanning through a vast array of books, but not really concentrating. The place was as I had expected: small, relaxed and trendy, with a nice vibe. Led into a meeting area, I sat down to discuss my idea with a team of four. They listened and asked questions, but as each minute passed I felt my will and confidence plunge from a great height. It was like driving over an unexpected bump in the road, and I was left breathless. My stomach was also churning. Were my expectation levels too high? Had I over prepared and crammed too much information into my mind?

The meeting was constructive and the friendly team gave me some great advice, but I felt defeated. Deep down, there had been a part of me that expected the book to be whisked to the top of the pile and that I would be driving towards a completion date. After all, the meeting was set up quickly - there must have been a reason why? Surely they would want me to sign something? But no, that had been my excitement running wild and the reality that it wasn't going to happen the way I had imagined led to a miserable afternoon.

With around five hours to kill before my three-hour train journey home, the dream was over. All the effort I'd put in... the scrimping and staying disciplined, the cutting myself off from society. Had it all been for nothing? As the minutes ticked by, I became more and more dispirited. Trying to remember the team's advice, I wandered through the streets with my shoulders hunched and my hands buried deep inside my suit trouser pockets. I looked for the nearest pub. Drowning my disappointment seemed the logical option.

So I sat and watched the clear chill of the November sun being replaced with bright Christmas lights that flashed around the shop windows outside. After a couple more drinks, my disappointment deepened simply because I was stumped.

Working furiously, I had collated nearly a quarter of a million emails, agreed radio station slots and provided ideas on how I could involve the audience. I'd gathered a mountain of evidence to show how I would make this book a success.

Despite this setback, I knew I was stronger now. In the past I may have looked for alternatives - a new job or a new project. I would have fretted over not having a huge following, or the fact that this was a massive gamble. The little money I had was flitting like sand through my fingers.

However, emotions are emotions. We can't switch them off but we can decide how long we linger on them. By the time I arrived at Euston station to head north, I knew I needed to regroup. I would get a good night's sleep and go again. Nothing had changed. I was still just as focused on my pursuit of making my book the best it could be.

Reflecting the next morning, I wrote down the feedback from the meeting:

1. There is potential for a film.

2. What's my story?

3. My idea of 40 stories would not stand up alone. I didn't really get that. Surely people would want to read 40 inspirational stories, right? Well, apparently the Dalai Lama had written a book on the same theme and it didn't do that well.

Steadfast in my approach, I would stick to my own plan. There was a lot to write and a lot of catching up to do as I had interviewed many people, so I needed to lock myself away.

I made a promise to myself to concentrate on writing my book without speaking to publishers until I believed it was finished. My thoughts after my Hay House experience were that it had been like trying to sell a cake while it was still in the oven. Potential cake customers are not going to consider buying one until it is baked and has the decorations along with the icing on top. I was presenting something that was not fully baked.

Just a week on from the meeting with Hay House, I already had another appointment with an interviewee set up. It was time to move on.

It was Monday November 25 2013 and I loved Monday nights because I played indoor football at Calderstones High School in Liverpool. It provided the opportunity for exercise and freedom, and I was able to think about something other than the book. However, at 9pm after football on this particular day, I would be speaking to Susan Foster.

Susan is Eileen O'Connor's best friend and she lived in San Diego. I was jealous. I visualised the warm sunshine and sitting in wet sand and letting the water roll over my legs as my hands touched the white froth from the waves. It was hard to imagine as the days in the UK seemed to get shorter and shorter and my hands were constantly covered with gloves.

Making the long distance call to San Diego using Skype, I was online from 9pm to 1am, and those four hours just flew by. Susan is very in tune with British culture, and even understood some slang words. She is also the mother of three children who are a similar age to myself. I looked at pictures of her on Facebook. Long waves of blonde hair cascaded past her shoulders and she had a perfect all American smile, as well as a natural elegance in the way she dressed.

Susan is a writer and like Eileen, she is campaigning hard to raise awareness of radiation emitted from mobile phone masts. It was during our call that a transformation in my thinking occurred as Susan shone her experience as a writer on my own project.

'I want to hear what happened to you,' she said. 'Your emotions, your feelings and your meetings. You're much more than a storyteller.'

Bingo! Wow. The murky confusion in my mind evaporated. I needed to become the glue that linked the stories together. I now understood what Hay House were saying.

I've only written this book the way I have - interweaving the interviews with my own story - because of Susan's ideas and foresight. Her advice made so much sense and I have a lot to thank her for.

After chatting about my book, I sat with my elbows resting on my mum's mahogany dining room table and my head cradled in my hands while I listened to Susan speak.

Susan Foster

It all started on a very unsuspecting, beautiful San Diego morning, which was unusually warm for late September. The year was 1993. I was driving into La Jolla for an appointment, singing along to the radio. I still remember feeling extremely happy, almost joyful. My youngest son Jason was six years old, and I had just dropped him off at school. He was so happy with his new teacher and school. When my children were happy, I was happy. My career was going well and life was good. No, life was great. I felt, for the first time in a very long time, that I didn't have a care in the world.

The road ahead of me was clear apart from a large pickup truck that was travelling in the opposite direction. When it was within passing distance of my car, the driver suddenly swung wide to the right, then even more rapidly jerked to the left so that the truck was heading straight for me – as if a bull's-eye had been painted on my driver's side door. I glanced quickly to the right. The street was lined with parked cars. There was no escape. I could not stop short of the truck's trajectory, nor could I speed up quickly enough to escape a collision altogether. My fate, whatever it was to be, was nanoseconds away.

As the grill of the truck speeded towards my face, I screamed a never ending 'NOOOO!' - a plaintive wail to the heavens. I was the mother of three children, aged 14, 11 and six. I was not about to leave them. I refused to die. A series of thoughts went through my head with lightning speed, though I processed them logically, as if time was my friend. I couldn't imagine not raising my children. I knew they needed me and there were things about each of them that only I understood. I was not going to let this bullet of a truck speeding towards my car take me away from them.

Suddenly, everything slowed down. Four distinct images flashed through my mind. They didn't come from me, but were shown to me. I saw an image of my daughter, Dana, then my son, Michael, and finally Jason, my youngest. My heart leapt at seeing Jason. He had been sick as a little boy and we were 'attached at the hip'. I truly felt he wouldn't make it without me. Then I saw a book. My first thought was that it was the Bible. But as I looked, I could see that it was a fairly thick book open to…completely empty pages. They were pure, white and unmarked. I knew I was supposed to fill them. I didn't know what the book was going to be about, I simply knew that

157

writing it was part of my destiny. In this sliver of time before an explosion of trauma and chaos, I also knew that I needed to be there for my children.

My children…my last thought was of them before the out-of-control truck hit my car with a force that picked it up and smashed it into the concrete curb. I was reasonably confined within the seat belt, yet my thin body went through extreme trauma with the severity of the impact. I would later learn that some of the roots of my teeth broke and moved sideways in my jawbone. I eventually required 10 spinal surgeries, seven to my back and three to my neck.

With a crack that reverberated through the car, I heard my neck snap. It sounded like a large, dry tree limb being cracked in two. With that sound, two distinctive yet concurrent things happened. The people gathering around the car saw a woman unconscious. She was trapped and motionless, her head dangling to the right.

While this was happening, I was suddenly in the back seat of my car. I was conscious, fully aware and completely free of pain. With a sense of serene acceptance, three male visitors came to me, appearing in vivid colour. I felt completely immersed in love. My beloved 'Gump', my grandfather, who was more like a father to me, was on the left. He had died 19 years earlier, ravaged by an eight-year battle with cancer. Yet Gump looked vital. I noticed the colour in his cheeks and the adoring look in his eyes. John, the medical student I had dated in graduate school, and who was one of the finest men I've ever known, was on my right. His brilliant life as a surgeon had been cut short by the senseless violence of a deranged patient. His look was one of gentle, confident concern. Both Gump and John were slightly back from the man in the centre. It was clear to me that their positions reflected their respect and deference for him, and they remained silent throughout our time together. My eyes then came to rest on the man. He had an exquisitely beautiful face, framed by brown hair that fell almost to his shoulders. I recognised my visitor immediately. I was looking into a face of wisdom and compassion. Before me was Jesus Christ.

Prior to this transcendent moment, I had believed Christ to be a great prophet, but I am an empiricist, so if someone had asked, 'Do you think Christ has extraordinary powers possessed only by a deity?' I would have answered no.

Yet on September 27 1993, at 10:30am, Christ was real, he was omniscient, and he was supremely powerful. I was bathed in peace, freedom from pain, immense love, and, finally, wisdom. To go with these men rather than return to face such extreme trauma would have been almost expected. Yet my destiny was my three children, the book with the blank pages and my desire to fulfill that fate. I met the gaze of the three men who had come to be with me in this encapsulating moment where I had one foot in life and one foot in death; there was no question that I would only accept life.

There were no words exchanged, but thoughts acted as speech. Though I felt immense love from Gump and John, my only communication was with Christ. He told me that I could return to my body, but he cautioned me that it was going to be an incredibly difficult journey, and I would only make it if I surrounded myself with healing and compassionate, brilliant people. This advice has become my inner mantra and I live by it, and because I have clung to Christ's guidance, I have come back from the brink more than once.

I now know, without a doubt, that I have given my children the courage and understanding to get through their own travails, and my children helped me find laughter and purpose as I fought my way through years of pain. I cannot take any narcotics due to a severe allergy, so to go through major spinal surgeries without the benefit of any pain medication has been gruelling. Without my children by my side, the thought of giving up might have been irresistible.

Family vacations to a cottage in northern Michigan were a summer tradition, but following the accident I had to stay home - travel was out of the question and for many years I was confined to my home, working, writing and overseeing the education and upbringing of my children.

On one hot August afternoon in 1999, the phone rang, breaking the lonely silence of the day. I would later come to recognize that my destiny to fill those empty pages was about to begin...

A firefighter named John had called after seeing me on the news. I'd being interviewed because I'd helped to defeat the building of a large cell tower (or mobile phone mast as they are called in the UK) in my neighbourhood.

As a medical writer, I'd got involved in the campaign after doing some research and discovering that the radiation these towers emit, which is powerful enough to reach mobile phones many miles away, penetrate every living cell with the potential to cause adverse neurological effects and not only promote the growth of cancer, but possibly cause it.

John told me that there were plans to build 24 mobile antennas on the fire station roof so that mobile phone signals could be transmitted and received. The local union had no money to hire an attorney, plus they had less than 48 hours before the deadline to appeal the proposal. John asked if I could write an appeal. I explained I would help if I could, but it was against the law to complain about towers based on health concerns. John was speechless – just as I had been when I first learned about something called Section 704 of The Telecommunications Act of 1996. Passed by the US Congress, it prohibited health concerns as a legitimate reason for denying a cell tower. If a citizen expressed any concern about health risks before the local planning committee, and the tower permit was rejected, the telecommunications company would automatically be granted permission to build the tower. I explained to John that it was passed without most members of Congress knowing the implications of this provision, and that the adverse health effects, though known by the industry and the US military, were kept deeply buried.

Even though our hands seemed tied, I promised John I would give it some serious thought and he suggested I drop by the station to meet the captain and offer my help. But under no circumstances was I to show any recognition when I met him, or it could cost him his job. The fire chief had made a deal with a telecom company, so for a firefighter to try and upset the deal was against fire department policy. I wanted to help John, and I wanted to help the firefighters. The more I learned, the more I realised that these dangers were being hidden from the public. The industry had spent billions of dollars buying the airwaves claimed by the US government. This went a long way towards balancing the budget under the Clinton administration, but even more lucrative were the annual profits realised by the industry. By purchasing the airwaves (licenses), the industry had greater potential to deliver vast profits and expand around the country.

Careful planning by both government and industry had gone into establishing the laws that gave the wireless industry immense freedom to build the cell tower infrastructure across the US. Promising John I would try to find an angle was much easier to say than do. I hung up the phone and reached for the two-inch thick copy of the Telecommunications Act in my files.

I am the daughter and granddaughter of attorneys, who taught me that if you can't solve a problem one way, you have to think outside conventional boundaries and find an alternative solution. I had written about the dangers of neurotoxic chemicals on the brain, and suddenly a particular safety angle, which was separate from the 'untouchable' health concerns, started forming in my head. I pulled my books on toxic chemicals and their biological effects off the bookshelf. I then ended up writing an appeal based on the toxic chemicals in the rechargeable batteries that power the back-up generators for cell towers. The appeal worked in that we got a delay of 18 months while the batteries were sealed properly, and that delay eventually caused 20 of the 24 towers to go elsewhere.

When I went to the fire station to meet the captain as suggested by John, Captain Currier introduced me to each of the firefighters. When I was introduced to John, it was an almost impossible task to contain my recognition and my shock. Looking into his face stole my breath. John, a man I presumed I had never met before, was the face I had seen over and over again in my memory since the events of September 27 1993. Had John recognised me when he had seen me interviewed on TV? It was unlikely, as I could not possibly have resembled the woman who was screaming and crying while trapped in her car on a La Jolla street. These are the times when I firmly believe that destiny takes over, though we may only recognise how our paths are meant to cross, and for what reason, years later.

John had played a key role at the scene of the accident. The so-called Jaws of Life truck had been brought in because the firefighters who initially responded were having difficulty getting me out of the car. The Jaws of Life truck can literally bite down on metal and pull it with great force, freeing trapped accident victims. Over a dozen firefighters had been at the scene of my accident, but John was my true hero once I was finally extricated from the car. I later learned it is the job of one firefighter at every serious accident to lock eyes with the victim. It has a calming effect and helps to keep the accident victim from going into shock. I had never forgotten the immensely kind man who gently locked eyes with mine, telling me, 'It's going to be okay. You're going to be fine. Just stay focused on me.'

On September 27 1993 that man was my lifeline. As I stood before John at Station 24 in San Diego some six years later, I could barely hold back my joy, which was mingled with disbelief. When John volunteered to take me on a tour of the station, I finally had a moment alone with him and I asked the question I already knew the answer to: 'Were you working the Jaws of Life in 1993?' His answer, of course, was yes. I felt the unmistakable brushstroke of destiny.

After the victory at Station 24, other firefighters in California were starting to hear about the successful appeal. And I was now beginning to hear about the plight of some very courageous men in the Santa Barbara area. They had towers within nine feet of their fire station dormitory room, and had all suffered from neurological problems including severe headaches, disorientation, anesthesia-like sleep, depression, severe mood swings and cognitive impairment. Some had got lost on emergency calls in the very town they had grown up in. One 20-year-old medic forgot where he was in the midst of basic CPR on a heart attack victim. Thankfully, his captain had been counting the chest compressions and was able to take over, but the larger implications for society were daunting.

When the strongest of the strong – our firefighters – are impaired by technology, we are all at risk. Our firefighters are the guardians of the gates of society; if their health is jeopardized we are all in peril.

I decided to take what savings I had and collaborate with Gunnar Heuser, MD, PhD - a renowned neurotoxicologist from Los Angeles, California - to devise a study to measure the status of those firefighters' brains. Due to financial limitations we could only do SPECT brain scans on six firefighters, but all showed brain damage, which was far more significant than anything we expected to find.

With this disturbing knowledge, and with a forthcoming meeting of the International Association of Firefighters, my son Jason - then 17 - worked with me to write a resolution. Jason sat at the computer and typed as I dictated – I still couldn't use my hands without nerve pain.

I then formed a coalition of five US and Canadian science experts and firefighters. We met in Boston in August 2004 at the aforementioned IAFF Convention (International Association of Firefighters). I spoke before the Canadian Health Committee and showed the brain scans to the audience. Word spread quickly amongst the 3,000 US and Canadian union delegates. When Resolution 15 came to the floor, it was passed by an overwhelming 80 per cent margin - with a standing ovation. The resolution called for a moratorium on placing cell towers on fire stations throughout the US and Canada until further studies could be conducted.

The reality is, money speaks more loudly than almost anything else these days, and the moratorium was never honoured. But we created awareness, and the effort to protect firefighters continues. The men who were there for me 20 years ago became part of my destiny. The erosion of the health and performance of the bravest and best among us is a story that deserves to be told. If our strongest are being damaged by cell towers, what will happen to the rest of the population who are living with these as well as mobile phones and WiFi?

In what I can only describe as a blessed twist of fate, I have joined forces with Eileen O'Connor, director and founder of the UK's Radiation Research Trust, to fill the once empty pages of the book I was shown during the accident 20 years ago. Eileen is a survivor of breast cancer, which she and many experts are convinced was acquired from a large cell tower that stood outside her home in Wishaw. We met at the famed Commonwealth Club in November of 2010 when I flew to San Francisco to hear her speak, and from there a bond of friendship formed. This grew over the years as we shared information about hidden science on both our continents, and 'safety standards' that are written with industry help and provide anything but a measure of safety.

Together we fear for humanity, together we work to create awareness around the globe and together we are filling the pages of a book that has become, with a sense of urgency and brilliant force, a shared destiny. If we can do it, you can too.

Susan's story instilled in me the knowledge that guidance from those you trust is priceless, and a belief that throughout any challenge, special people are waiting around the corner to bless you with a new perspective.

What encapsulated me more was her out-of-body experience. It was the second I'd heard, and was very similar to the one Debra had described. In my mind, I have no doubt that there is a God and no doubt that we are given the freedom of choice to do what we wish while living in our physical bodies.

It's ironic because Susan's scientific background goes against the grain of believing in such an experience. Science is based on evidence, proof. But what her story highlighted to me as I reflected in the days and weeks after our conversation is that at the very heart of creativity and life lies something which cannot be seen. For instance, a vision in the mind must be created before it can be turned into reality.

I'd watched biographies on TV about historical figures such as Nelson, Lincoln and Alexander the Great. Imagine you'd said the following to Nelson in the late 1700s: 'Forget wooden boats and cannons, huge metal ships the size of an island will be home to flying metal objects which will be able to screech through the air faster than the speed of sound. This is the future.' You would have been locked up in an asylum!

The dream of flight and the dream of creating aircraft carriers was once someone's fantasy. And no doubt in the beginning, that person, like many others who have dared to dream, was ridiculed. Whatever you dream, whatever the circumstances or adversities you face, you can control your thoughts. This is what I learned from my experience with Susan.

We all have blank pages; it's just a case of writing down what we want and believing it can happen. Along the way there will be waves of emotion that will threaten to bully us into a corner, but having people to protect you from the brute force of them can only inspire.

Susan's ability to listen and mentor, her compassion to help others and to give her own money to save the lives of firefighters, reveals her special character. I'd craved this type of guidance, and from the shores of San Diego, I would find someone to steer this book gently and more beautifully in a slightly different direction.

Clarence Sarkodee-Adoo
What is there to be angry about?

The pendulum of emotion swings back and forth for me, as it does for many people. A mixture of feelings accompanied me on my travels around the north-west for various meetings. Trapped in a world of doom and gloom, my emotions rose from the pit of my stomach. I recalled many of the things that happened in the past, the relationship, business and trying to complete this book. I'd thought I was OK, but obviously I wasn't today.

The lid had been taken off the pressure cooker, and walking along the Albert Dock, the sound of a horn from a large boat made me jump out of my skin - my anger then focused on scowling at the idiot who had done it. Needless to say, my nerves were frayed.

On top of the anger and frustration, I felt guilty for feeling this way because of the people I had met and the stories I had heard. I knew I should be grateful, and deep down I was, but sometimes negative emotions can temporarily take the shine off the feeling of gratitude.

Luckily for me, when I arrived home there was an email waiting for me. Tim Reddish had helped me yet again by giving me the number of Charles Hazlewood, an orchestra conductor who was one of the founding members of The British Paraorchestra, a team of musicians who performed during the closing ceremony of the London 2012 Paralympic games.

After connecting with Charles, he introduced me, via email, to a man named Clarence Adoo. Charles told me a little of Clarence's story and after receiving an email from him we agreed to speak on the telephone.

By now it was the end of November. Autumn seemed to continue to linger as if the seasons were confused. Leaves were still falling outside. In fact, they were six inches deep. Orange and brown flooded the garden so there was not a blade of grass to be seen. I looked out of the dining room window to see flashes of lightning scarring the sky. I love thunder and lightning. There's always a bit of excitement when such a freak flash of weather performs an almost natural firework display.

Nervously I rang Clarence and I listened intently as he spoke with clarity in a beautifully calm English accent. He resonated serenity and sophistication that was almost James Bond-esque. I actually saw a photo of him standing in a black tuxedo and bow tie looking debonair; he could indeed be the first black James Bond.

Clarence Sarkodee-Adoo

My parents travelled from Ghana to England in the late 1950s and I was born in 1960 in rural Shoeburyness, Essex. My father had come to England with a desire to further his education. He owned farming land in Ghana and wanted to learn new agricultural techniques that would help him grow his business prospects back home in Africa.

The loud African voices of my mother and father projected through the walls of our home. There was always a hive of activity taking place. As well as my parents, I lived with four of my siblings: Harry, Patience, Helena and Richard. My elder two siblings, Julius and Esther, lived in Ghana.

My mother loved family life and stood tall with her back straight and perfectly upright, and her chin slightly raised.

She resembled an African queen and wore traditional brightly coloured garments that flowed all the way to the floor. She had loved music and singing from a very young age, and I too became immersed in music.

Every waking moment was spent listening and learning and I became a member of the choir. Aged six, I was given a cornet to play in the young people's brass band of the Salvation Army. I would sit for hours with my legs crossed watching and listening to the senior band practising live before me. One of the members of this band, who was also a milkman, gave me a couple of music lessons, and this started me off on my musical journey.

I taught myself how to play the cornet by generally listening to music. The sounds and waves that poured out from the radio and from live performances encapsulated and inspired me.

Meanwhile, my brother Harry, who is 18 months older than me, loved sport - particularly football. We used to play together and I chose to support Leeds United while Harry supported Chelsea. I don't even remember how we came to support the teams we did, but Harry would often remind me that my team was not very good. Come the FA Cup final in 1970, we were very excited as Chelsea was playing Leeds. Disappointingly for me, Leeds lost. Around the same time, when I was 10, my father decided to return to Ghana. However, a military coup, violence and unrest made for an uncertain future. When my mother decided to return to Ghana, we as children questioned whether we should follow suit. We now had a foster family, whom we'd met through the Salvation Army, and many friends. We loved our parents, but we wanted to stay in England, and although my mother, father and youngest brother, Richard returned to Ghana, the rest of us were allowed to stay, giving us a chance to fulfil our dreams.

I enjoyed school and my passion remained with music, but not everyone saw this as a rewarding career path. A teacher in my school asked me what I wanted to do with my life. When I told him that I wanted to be a musician, he responded by growling, 'be realistic, Clarence'.

He looked down at me, a child of 12, with a dismissive glance and grunted as if trying to intimidate me out of my ambition. But someone saying that I couldn't realise my dream stirred a passion inside my heart. I became determined to prove him wrong.

When I left school, I applied for a place to study at the prestigious Royal College of Music in London. It was extremely competitive and young people from around the world attended auditions to try and earn a place there.

Having specialised in the cornet since I was six, you can only imagine my trepidation when I discovered it was not the instrument of choice within the college. The trumpet was favoured.

Following this troubling revelation, I rushed home, panicking and spluttering my words to my foster mum. I needed to buy a trumpet for my audition, which was due to take place in five days' time. This was set to be the biggest day of my life so far. My dream hung in the balance, and it was all I could think about. But in a matter of seconds, music slammed into the background as tragedy struck.

A more debilitating piece of news made me forget my audition. My father had died in Ghana and the funeral was taking place on the day of my audition. With my head in my hands, the tears flowed through my fingers as the devastating truth sank in - my father had gone.

My attention was focused on travelling to Ghana, but my mother told me to stay.

'It's what your father would have wanted,' she said. 'Make him proud.'

Those words ignited the focus within my heart and I respected my mother's guidance. She knew that my father wanted me to pursue my dreams. If they had not journeyed to England all those years ago, I may have never have had the opportunity to discover my passion. I therefore decided that the best way to honour my father was to earn that place.

Aged just 19, the pressure of the big moment was upon me. My journey there was full of apprehension and nerves. The home of The Royal College of Music is an imposing red brick Victorian building, which is framed by two huge towers. Inside, the sound of footsteps echoed and music dominated the corridors, from which old-fashioned classrooms led off. Thick wooden doors and a grand sweeping staircase added to the building's magnificence.

Hearing the sounds of trumpets playing faster and higher than I could play, made me feel even more nervous. Although the cornet and trumpet are similar, there are considerable differences and I'd had just days to learn.

Then the moment I had been waiting for - my big chance - arrived. I played in front of a stern looking panel who then proceed to ask me questions:

'How long have you been playing the trumpet Clarence?'

'Since Tuesday,' I replied nervously.

But once I had expelled the nerves, my heart opened like a flower and I began to talk of my passion for music. My enthusiasm and knowledge relaxed the panel and the stern looks on their faces dissolved. It was not long before I heard...I had secured my place. I was overjoyed and danced around my house like an excited child on Christmas Day. I punched the air, declaring: 'I did it, Dad!'

The fulfilment I found from music inspired me to accomplish more, and for the next 18 years I travelled the world as a trumpet player. I played in West End musicals and in the Salvation Army's band; it was an organisation that had been close to my heart for many years. However, now I had progressed within the band to become a bandmaster, directing and leading productions.

Music carried me along a path of adventure. I travelled to Brazil with the Royal Northern Sinfonia Orchestra and my trumpet playing featured in a BBC television series called *The Paradise Club*, which starred Leslie Grantham, a former *EastEnders* actor. I even participated in a world record attempt for the most people playing one instrument at the same time - the huge double bass. This was televised on the TV show *Record Breakers* with Roy Castle, and we did indeed break the record!

More amazing opportunities flowed, and in 1993 I experienced the beauty of Ghana for the first time. Here, my acute hearing tuned into the songs of exotic birds while the warmth of sun's rays beamed down on my skin and I breathed in the clean air.

Sitting on the steps of my mother's porch in Ghana, I reflected upon music, home and my father. I took my trumpet out of its hard black case and began to play. It was a special moment because my mother had not heard me play live. As she leaned against the doorframe and listened, I played the theme tunes of her favourite TV dramas. It was a great feeling to see her smiling with appreciation.

Back in England, more happiness was on the way. In 1995, my brother Harry and his girlfriend decided to tie the knot. On the day of his stag party in Shoeburyness, I finished work unexpectedly early and decided to head there from my home in Newcastle. I'd previously told Harry that I couldn't attend his party due to work commitments, but now I could surprise him.

It was August 19 1995 and the sun was shining. I'd just bought a new pair of shorts and was filled with excitement about heading south. Driving south along the A1, my friend Emma, who was accompanying me, soon fell asleep. This gave me time to reflect on the special moments I'd shared with Harry. I was so delighted that he had found happiness and that my mother was travelling from Ghana for the wedding. Most of our family was going to be reunited.

I was listening to a song called *Fragile* by Sting when I reached Retford, East Midlands. Suddenly, I began to lose control of my car. I gripped the steering wheel of the red Honda Prelude tightly. The steering column began to shudder and vibrate violently. Sensing danger, I moved towards the hard shoulder, travelling at around 60mph. By this point, the moving mass of metal was proving uncontrollable and in this most fearful of moments my brain brought back an experience from when I was a child - bumper cars!

The last time I'd turned a steering wheel and it didn't respond was at the funfair. Only on this occasion it was a real car that was out of control and wouldn't respond to my commands. Instead, it careered into a grassy embankment that ran parallel with the motorway.

Shock gripped me as in a flash the car rolled on two wheels at an acute angle. This caused it to somersault twice and face oncoming traffic. Groggy and dazed, it took a few seconds to realise where I was. I couldn't move, and then I thought of Emma.

I shouted her name and became concerned because there was no response. I shouted again and again, louder each time, until I was roaring 'Emmmmaaaaa!' It was then that I saw her begin to stir as she drifted back into consciousness.

Trapped inside the car, I heard the cries of people from the emergency services communicating with each other. Flashing blue lights reflected against the windows of the cars that were stationery nearby. I could hear screeching sounds as sharp industrial tools sliced through twisted metal to help me escape from the crushed tin can that I was lodged in.

Emma and I were placed in separate ambulances that rode in unison to the hospital at a slow speed. I overheard the paramedics saying that they didn't want the rush of other cars and lorries to rock the ambulances back and forth in case there had been damage to our spines.

In hospital, I was given strong painkillers.

'A couple of cups of tea and you will be home in no time,' said one of the nurses, jovially.

My biological mother was at my side every day. I would hear her authoritative voice from a distance asking the doctors about my progress. Since I was a child; her presence was always strong, as was her faith in God. Wearing her beautifully coloured African gowns, she would sit next to my bed, grasping my hand which I couldn't feel. Looking me deep in the eyes, she would repeat every morning despite whatever happened during the previous night:

'You know, God is good.'

But weeks passed and I was still in hospital. In intensive care, I drifted in and out of consciousness. Nurses' faces dominated my vision and I could hear the high-pitched noises of hospital machinery beeping like a submarine's sonar.

Life was like a film reel. I could remember a clear frame of what was happening around me, but suddenly the next three frames would be deleted as I drifted back into unconsciousness.

However, a male voice constantly sounded in my head.'If you think you were fulfilled before, it's nothing compared to the fulfilment you will experience in the future,' it said.

I instantly recognised this calm, clear and precise voice – it was God. With those few words came the flickering of my eyes as a haze of peace descended. How could I be more fulfilled than I already was? Did God not know what had happened and the true extent of my injuries? After being in hospital for weeks, I still couldn't move a muscle. How could that compare to travelling the world and pursuing my dream?

A little while later, when I'd regained full consciousness, one of the nurses said nervously, 'We thought we had lost you that time'.

It was clear to me that words transmitted into my thoughts by God had come to me somewhere between this world and the next.

Then doctors told me the full extent of my injuries. I was paralysed from the neck down and was unable to move my arms and legs. I would require 24-hour care for the rest of my life. I had to be fed and couldn't even write my own name, let alone play my beloved trumpet.

The communication from my brain to the rest of my body had been severed. As I sat in hospital in a wheelchair, I looked down at my hands; they were my creators, my tools, but now they were lifeless. I would never play again.

The only part of my body that moved was my head. I was able to speak, and the medical teams who deal with people suffering this kind of devastation every day tried to comfort me. One doctor said: 'Clarence, it's OK to be angry.' 'What is there is to be angry about?' I asked.

Dumbfounded, he was not used to this type of reaction, but then he didn't know who I'd spoken to. I thanked God for Emma. She was OK and would go on to make a full recovery and continue with her life.

I trusted the words of God, but I really didn't know how it would work out. My mother was at my hospital bedside and her faith was strong for me.

While I was calm, the only feeling of injustice that lingered was with the insurance company. Although I was paralysed, I wasn't due any compensation because I hadn't lost a limb. Aged 35, I was worried how I would survive financially. What would I do? The cost of any care was expensive, and I required it 24 hours a day.

Not only did I require expert medical attention, I needed a van and lots of special equipment such as beds and wheelchairs. Any meetings required significant planning. I required three full-time carers who rotated on different shifts to support me each day. I found it shocking that there was only minuscule financial support available to help me with this.

I had to learn how to write with a pen lodged in my mouth. To read a book or music, I got to grips with using a mouth-operated instrument to turn the pages. At first it took 20 frustrating minutes just to turn one page. Imagine that.

But this is not to moan. I speak of my challenges only to portray my new life. My friends were not surprised when they came to the hospital and found that that my mood was as positive as it was before the accident. My mind was aroused by God's words. I possessed no resentment, just curiosity. What would the future hold? How could I become more fulfilled?

Spending more than six months in hospital provided me with a lot of time to ponder those questions. But during that period my enthusiasm for music never waned. Then the Royal Northern Sinfonia orchestra, which had been so prevalent in my life so far, offered me a new role as an animateur.

The job aims to inspire an interest in music in young people.

Travelling through the spine of the UK and Ireland, I visit schools, orchestras, churches and universities to help young people grow and develop their capabilities.

I am grateful that I am able to teach, mentor and pour out my knowledge and encouragement. Being able to share in the children's excitement, to see their reaction when they play a difficult piece of music, or witness their reaction when they progress in an orchestra, gives me such pleasure. It was the same encouragement that I received when I first started, and it helped me to overcome the negativity from those who told me to be realistic.

Dream big, that's my message to the children. Do not let adversities ruin your hopes. I had to apply the same sentiment to my hopes following the accident. Perhaps it's a human response to feel pity for those who lose the freedom of physical movement. Of course, there are many adjustments to make and life can be scary, but I was fortunate to have a job, and for the decade following the accident, I used my spirit to propel my ambition; practising gratitude for the use of my mind helped.

Many children who were initially shocked by my appearance in a wheelchair soon forget about it when we discussed music and how we could improve. I suppose that is part of the value of my story; appearances aren't that relevant, the mind and how you use it to benefit others is more important.

Not only did I use my mind for music, but I also used it to help raise awareness for people with disabilities. I consulted on many building and accessibility projects before they went ahead, which was a very rewarding experience. It enabled me to meet new people, in particular one amazing man by the name of Rolf Gehlhaar. Rolf has developed many unique musical instruments for disabled people, and he set to work on one for me. Luckily, he enjoys a challenge. After time spent thinking and planning, he developed a headset much like the ones used in call centres. A white blow tube snakes down the left hand side of my face, and a mouthpiece touches my lips. In addition, the instrument has three small black sensors. One located on both my left and right temples, and the third on top of my head. To play, I blow through a mouthpiece and by moving my head I control the sensors that connect with the mouse of a computer. This has given me so much freedom and it is the only instrument of its kind in the world – made just for me! After the excitement of learning to play a new instrument, I can now perform and be part of a band. Was this the beginning of the road to fulfilment?

Maybe it was, as the end of 2011 brought an unexpected surprise in the form of a letter from Buckingham Palace. It was the New Year honours list and I was being awarded an MBE for my services to music. For the past 15 years, I took part in many music projects and inspired people, it would seem. As I read the letter, I felt humbled; included in it were the words 'role model'. People travelled from around the UK to celebrate with me, and my older sister Esther even came from Ghana.

But the momentum didn't stop there. With the London 2012 Olympic and Paralympic Games fast approaching, I became a founding member of the British Paraorchestra. Led by the aforementioned conductor Charles Hazelwood, the orchestra is currently made up of 28 musicians, who have a range of disabilities. It includes an amazing woman with cerebral palsy, who uses her nose to play a keyboard. We have a very celebrated one armed pianist, as well as blind saxophone and guitar musicians. And we are joined together because of our love of music.

From the moment I was paralysed back in 1995, it would have been so easy to miss out on amazing opportunities just because I'm confined to a wheelchair. However, the magic of life can be breathtaking. The hard work and togetherness of my orchestra mirrors all others and we had the great honour of playing in front of 80,000 people live on national TV at the closing ceremony of the London 2012 Paralympic Games.

Wheeling out across the running track and towards the stage, I realised what I was about to achieve. Sprinkling flashes of light lit up the night sky from thousands of cameras, and a sea of colour and celebration danced around the stage. To be entwined with that energy and to be able to perform with Coldplay was the ultimate experience.

The games were a symbol of achievement, desire, hard work and determination from people around the world, all of whom had faced adversity. It was special as we played the music that expressed the emotion - something words cannot describe.

That experience was just the beginning, and despite my initial curiosity in trying to decipher the message from God, I understand that I am fulfilled. I now conduct some orchestras by simply nodding my head to control the flow, direction and harmony of the instruments. I have contributed to the music that has played during the Queen's Speech on Christmas Day, as well as being part of the Royal Albert Hall carol concert, where I spoke about my faith to an audience of 4,000 people.

We can find hope in the hearts and minds of beautiful people. Through the greatest of challenges, so many people have inspired me and many have supported the Clarence Adoo Trust to help me live. The cost of my care is very expensive but it has helped me to survive and offer my services to music.

People have cycled thousands of miles to raise money for me. Others have run marathons and gone to great lengths to prepare and train, giving up their precious spare time. It is incredibly moving and shows the spirit of people. Without them, I would not have had the opportunity to inspire and give hope to others. Surround yourself with positive people. Be who you want to be. Let those who snigger at your dreams drive you forward.

I believe that I have fulfilled the words spoken softly to me by God. Miracles do happen when you believe in yourself. If I can do it, you can too.

Just amazing. So here was a man with no resentment, anger or bitterness. I almost cringed when I thought of my moaning just a day or so earlier.

Paralysed from the neck down, nearly every physical movement had been taken away from Clarence, yet he is always positive. Whenever I spoke to him, his upbeat personality shined and he was always keen to hear how I was progressing. What stands out in my mind are the following seven words which Clarence repeated to me - they will stay will me forever, and they gave me goose pimples.

'What is there to be angry about?'

It is a truly breathtaking sentiment, especially when the physical body is unable to respond to the brain's commands. I couldn't stop looking down at my own hands and imagining that they didn't work. But Clarence had relied on his hands to do the work he loved. They had allowed him to play the trumpet, travel the world and be successful in his career. But ultimately, despite such extreme physical adversity, Clarence has become fulfilled. Maybe you believe that a direct blessing from God helped Clarence, or maybe you think this is nonsense. Maybe you know someone in a similar position to Clarence who is bitter and angry and you can't accept that Clarence isn't. The point I am making here is that whatever you believe is your choice.

However, when I spoke Clarence, I decided that I wanted to adopt his mentality - his positive approach to tackling challenges. In my case, what was there to be angry about? I was now doing something I loved. If things had continued the way they were, would I have had this opportunity? I wouldn't be speaking to Clarence now – or any of the amazing people I'd met before him.

Who wants to be angry? Who wants to be miserable? Not me. But no doubt you're smiling now because you know a few people who seem to be constantly cross.

Anyway, regardless of anger, here is what I did after ending my call with Clarence. I decided that the next time I had a problem, I would look for a positive solution. I wrote out the table (on the following page) on a scrappy piece of paper. Here are the instructions:

1. Write out your **challenge** in the first column. (Be' honest with yourself.)

2. Write out some **positive solutions** in the second column. (This will help focus your thoughts.)

3. Under **who** you should list the person responsible for the action. It could be you, or you might need to speak to someone.

4. Under **when** write down the date when you are going to take this action.

Here's an example of a list I wrote for myself.

Challenge	Positive Solutions	Who	When
Angry about my past challenges including business and relationship.	Write out 5 amazing things that have happened since the challenges of last year.	Me	Today
	Write out 5 statements that show how you have improved your life since writing your book.	Me	Every morning for 30 days
	Speak to people in more detail how about how they overcame their own challenges.	Eileen/ Susan	Next Tuesday's meeting

So many times, when a challenge presents itself, swirls of thoughts, mainly unhelpful ones, can swim in and stop you in your tracks. They did with me and I designed my positive solutions to stop them. It's easy to fall under the spell of doom and gloom; to argue, fight, criticise, or look for someone else to blame. If you're doing the same, keep asking yourself the question: What are my positive solutions? It's amazing how much better I felt just a few minutes after performing this task – my brain was far more focused on the positive.

Do you want to feel rubbish? Or do you want to handle challenges quickly and professionally? You choose. Try it and see if it works for you. It has certainly been powerful for me. It's a blessing from a man who could have quite easily blamed someone else.

Calvin Jodisi – Kenya Compassion

My next stop was The Athenaeum in Liverpool where I was due to meet Ken Pye - whom I'd been introduced to by Andy Bounds. I'd never heard of this city landmark before and walking through its doors was like going back in time. The Athenaeum was founded in the late 18th Century as a men-only club, a more professional setting for workers to read the newspapers and engage in business conversation. It still operates as a club today, and boasts a huge library, but in line with the changing of the times, women are also allowed to join.

Entering the newsroom was breathtaking. It is the size of most modern day offices and could have easily seated 100 people. True to its name, I saw men and women relaxing on dark maroon leather sofas reading the broadsheets. I absorbed the atmosphere from years of history. It had a very regal feel, like a room in a country manor. I would not have looked out of place sporting a tweed jacket, smoking a cigar and carrying a pheasant under my arm. Well, this is how I felt anyway as I helped myself to a coffee and waited for Ken to finish his meeting on the other side of this grand room.

Ken is a big advocate of the city of Liverpool, he is always immaculately dressed and has impeccable manners. When I approached him, he sat up straight and smiled broadly. His grey hair was combed into a side parting and his friendly eyes welcomed me through Harry Potter style spectacles.

Ken listened to my request for inspirational stories, while simultaneously flicking through his extensive address book. As he did this, I wondered about the name Athenaeum. There was an obvious reference to Athena, the Greek goddess, and only a couple of months earlier I'd seen a programme about

Odysseus, the Greek hero famed for his role in the Trojan War. In Homer's epic poem The Iliad, it takes years for Odysseus to return home from the war, but luckily he had a 'mentor', Athena. I learned that this is where the word mentor originates (you learn something new every day). Athena guided Odysseus through his troubles and adversities, and now Ken was going to guide me to Kenya, where my next interviewee, Calvin Jodisi, lives.

I watched some footage of Calvin before I logged on to Skype and prepared for my call to Nairobi. If I'd been listening to just his voice, I would have said it was Brian Lara, the famous West Indian cricketer. His tone was so calm and soothing. It would be Calvin who would help me fulfil my truest value of contribution – which to me means contributing to the success of others.

Calvin Jodisi

The soles of my feet could have sliced through rocks. The two-mile walk to and from school each day had hardened my bare young feet. At the end of the day, I was always desperate to return home and help my mother. She was so ill.

I lived in a thatched house made of grass; it could barely withstand raindrops or the strength of the scorching sun. The house stood within five hectares of my grandparents' farm. My job at home was to lead the goats and cows on a pilgrimage for fresh grazing before I left for school. Without brothers or sisters for company, I'd wander through the wilderness holding a brown jerry can on top of my head to help collect any water I was lucky enough to find.

Sometimes water sources were very far apart, especially when local ones were plundered dry. Often there would be a long line of villagers desperate to collect some water. As a small boy standing in line, I was regularly humiliated and bullied. On many occasions I would return home with barely any water at all. When I was fortunate enough to get a substantial amount, I dragged and wrestled the jerry can all the way home, kicking up dust into my eyes and struggling to stand the hot soil. Sweating and tired, I'd arrive home happy that my two-mile mission was complete. I'd then pull together three large stones to balance a rotten old pan on. Placing wood underneath it, I would start a fire. The smoke caused me to cough and splutter and tears streamed from my eyes.

My mother lay on a mat made from reed, her eyes like those of a cat as they reflected in the crackling fire. She experienced so much pain. I'd hear her wailing and notice her ribs, which were so exposed that it was easy to count them. The mat would stick to her, and when we peeled it away, we'd see that it had left indentation marks on her skin. So deep was the pattern the mat left, with its circles and diamonds, that her skin resembled the skin of a snake.

Sitting by the fire, my mother would give me advice about business and following my heart. I would listen to her slow husky voice, giving her my complete attention. She also taught me about farming, cooking and pricing, and as I listened I would perform the role of a doctor, cleaning away her diarrhoea and doing anything I could to avoid losing her.

Returning home one day in 1999, after the daily search for wood and water, I heard crying in the wind. My stomach turned and I knew something bad had happened. Crying was customary when someone had died. I knew this from the death of my grandfather.

When I arrived back at the farm, I realised that my mother had gone. Even though I knew she was ill, it couldn't change the emotion. I cried and cried; I'd lost my mother and my best friend. Her death proved a catalyst for greed. My grandfather's brothers circled the farm like vultures, aware of the potential spoils it could offer. I had no say because I was a male child from the daughter of the family. It was as if I was a stranger, with no rights to the family farm at all.

There were many arguments over the cattle and goats. With the clattering of pitchforks, the battle turned violent as the brothers fought amongst each other. They didn't show any remorse or try to comfort my grandmother and me – they just displayed blind greed. At 11 years old, I was now alone and remained unsure about how my mother had died. Doctors said that it was tuberculosis, but this was never confirmed.

The grief I experienced over losing my mother took everything out of me. Like a soda can after being run over by a car, I was crushed. Taken in by guardians, I was grateful for a home. I couldn't go back to the farm; my intuition told me that if I did I would be killed, such was the desperation of my great uncles to get their hands on the farm. It was a decision I made for my own safety, but it meant that I would never see my grandmother again. Not long after I left, she died of tuberculosis. She, like my mother, died too young.

The people in the village who had known my mother prayed for me and taught me to be strong. Their kind words of encouragement helped me when I was at my most vulnerable.

I'd only just started to feel settled again when life handed me yet another challenge. My guardians, with fat tears in their eyes and their heads bowed, delivered more bad news. They could no longer afford to keep me. The only place for me now was a children's home. I was forced to leave the natural magnificence of the countryside, where I had roamed with the animals, and move into a densely populated house. It was a violent place, devoid of love and engulfed by drugs and destitution.

While there, it was hard for me to sleep and relax in the evenings. The screams I heard from children consumed by drugs were not of this world, and the stench of excrement would filter through the corridors and into my room. I was naïve, but I aged quickly and my skin thickened in order to shield me from the criticism and harsh reality of life.

My mother's warm words were replaced with cold putdowns. The home was for kids from the streets. The only fun they experienced was taking out their pain on others. I'd been allocated a bunk bed in a room with eight other children. The banging and shouting was constant and I was bullied both physically and mentally. I endured horrors that I do not want to share.

My only escape was to amble into a nearby forest. I'd walk along the banks of the river searching for a spot to sit and read. Reading stories always helped, as they were a source of inspiration and proved to be a kind of companion.

It was a lonely life and I longed for my mother. But I found a little hope in prayer. Kneeling on the grass, I trusted in God that I would pull through. This routine continued until I was 15. As I grew older, I thought more and more about the future. I didn't have a home or the means to live, but I wanted to learn.

Three things occupied my thoughts: education, food and shelter. The home had helped me with my studies but I knew I needed further support. One afternoon, I was searching through a rotten newspaper with water splashed all over it, when I found an article about a woman in America who was helping students with their education. This made me think about calling her to ask for help.

Sitting in a dark, narrow hallway, scraping a few coins together in my hand, the beating of my heart was the only sound I could hear - it seemed to echo from the walls. With my nerves jangling, I called Darleen Johnson, the woman who gave me the chance of an education, and a chance in life.

Darleen offered to support me for two years. Following that time, another lady, Aileen Fitzgerald, stepped in to help. Both Aileen and Darleen kept in contact and encouraged me via email as I continued my development. To have strangers so generously offer their support was a new experience for me.

I regularly updated Aileen on my progress and wanted her to come to Africa, but she had her own challenges. She had been diagnosed with Parkinson's disease, which affected her movements and forced her to leave her job as a librarian, a role which she had enjoyed for many years. I was upset to hear this news, but Aileen proved to me that she had a heart bigger than any of my challenges, and this made me determined to repay her faith in me.

Meanwhile, the impact my early life had on me was profound. It made me realise how short life actually is. After seeing so many young people in my village poison themselves with drugs, I knew how close I'd come to living that life. But thanks to the compassion of others, I got to apply myself and studied actuarial science, which incorporated a combination of subjects, including statistics, maths and economics.

Inspired by my mother's words and teachings, I wanted to explore business. But I was left feeling devalued when the time came to look for a job. The reality was clear; my feelings and opinions were of no interest to the employers I spoke to.

Wandering through the fields, which I always did when I felt like escaping, I pondered over ways in which I could help improve life for people. I was determined to make a difference. Later, I walked past market stalls, absorbing the smell of fruit, vegetables and various spices. These brought back memories of the crackling fire and the advice my mother had given me while I learned to cook.

Then I had an idea! What if I could teach school children how to create their own businesses? I wanted to offer stability, to give them the same kind of chance that I had been given. So what about a social enterprise within a children's home?

Reviewing the past through my mental photo album, I saw the pieces that had been missing – opportunity and sustainability. I came up with an idea to utilise some land by turning it into a rabbit farm. This could help feed the children, but the rabbit meat could also be sold to the local markets, which would help sustain the home.

I teamed up with some local rotary clubs to turn my vision into a reality. The more I spoke at various events, the more people came forward with ideas and support. Subsequently, I set up a campaign called 36 meals, which I established to raise awareness of food wastage and to seek donations. It was named 36 meals because our aim was to provide 3 meals per day for 6 days.

I worked with other volunteers, collecting rice and other dried foods from people and delivered it to schools and orphanages. Travelling in cars, we operated a free taxi service, picking up and delivering the food. It was this work that began gaining recognition in Kenya because it was simple and it was making a difference.

I began receiving calls for advice, and radio and television opportunities soon followed. But although the scheme worked, we did face challenges. Corruption, theft and violence tainted many of our missions, preventing aid from reaching those who needed it. It was frustrating how some organisations would keep most of the food or money intended for our projects. However, I continued to search for the right people to help me, and many of our missions were a success. Then I was invited to Switzerland to attend a conference called 'One Young World'. I didn't have a passport or possess any knowledge of Switzerland; I wasn't even sure where it was in the world, and I'd never been on a plane before.

I was 22 and bursting with excitement as I set off on my big journey. After all, I was an orphan with no family. Could this really be happening? Taking my seat on the plane, my stomach churned, especially during take-off, but I couldn't conceal the smile on my face. When a foil container was placed in front of me, I didn't dare touch it. I didn't know what to do and thought I had to pay. I sat and watched other people eat and it was some time before I received a whisper in my ear from an air steward, telling me it was OK to tuck in.

People were attending the conference from Nigeria, Uganda, Ethiopia and Asia, and I made many new friends before it had even started. When it did, I sat in an audience of 1000 young and eager leaders from more than 180 countries. I could not believe that this was real. I wondered if I was watching a movie as I listened to Archbishop Desmond Tutu, Kofi Annan and many other inspirational speakers.

I particularly recall the archbishop saying, 'The future lies in your hands.'

Sir Bob Geldof echoed the same sentiment and told us that it was our time for action and our responsibility to save people and change the world - because we are the future.

That evening I found it hard to sleep. I sat on a bed so big that I couldn't touch the floor when I dangled my feet over the edge. My room had amazing views over a beautiful river, upon which swans and ducks glided effortlessly. As I watched them, my own head swam.

In order to help, I needed to contribute to the youth of Kenya. It would be hard because so many lived in fear, distracted by survival in a world that offered only the potential of AIDS, drug abuse and malnutrition. In awe of my surroundings in Zurich, I was privileged to be sitting in such an opulent setting, and it was important that other children from Kenya (and other parts of the world) could do the same.

As I gazed into space, an idea was conceived: 'Change Mind, Change Future'. This would be the name of my business! I would establish a non-profit making organisation to inspire young people, teaching them positive thinking and entrepreneurship. I wanted them to see a life beyond drugs, destitution and disease. I wanted to eradicate the hopelessness that still rots the minds of many young people, and to teach them how to dream instead.

In order to encourage children to change, I had to use my own experiences to show them that they could take another path. Back in Kenya, I began to deliver workshops and enter global competitions, making use of my mentoring and leadership skills. The pain of any defeat did not matter to me. Growing up in fear, with no one to support me, was much worse. And so, I entered a competition for entrepreneurs called Your Big Year. This was open to 60,000 people from 221 countries.

In order to progress, I saw the importance of marketing and gaining business exposure. I needed to draw attention to my ideas. Living in a rural community, I used every contact I had. It was often difficult to get a signal for the Internet, so it was a constant battle to blog and leave my social footprint on Facebook and Twitter. But I managed it. As a result, I was invited on TV shows, where I talked about my ideas of social entrepreneurship and giving back. It's amazing how my idea had flourished from a seed that was planted by my mother.

It was one of the most surprising things to ever happen in my life when Chris Arnold, the founder of the Your Big Year competition, called me via Skype to inform me that I would be travelling to Liverpool, all expenses paid. The 60,000 entrants had been whittled down to 25.

However, my joy was soon replaced with misery when my visa application was denied. But I don't believe in giving up, so I tried again. Hopeful and excited by the prospect of a new adventure, I was crushed when this second application was stamped with yet another decline. Many people tried to discourage me from trying again, but I didn't listen and collated more evidence and information. My third attempt finally proved successful and I was granted a visa to visit the UK.

During my visit to Liverpool, I met leading entrepreneurs, including Sir Richard Branson. I couldn't comprehend why he would be interested in speaking to me. Even though I was the runner-up in the competition, I had succeeded. I had given everything and as a consequence, more opportunities followed.

Returning to Kenya, I was inspired to think outside - and far from - the box. A few months later, I was invited to speak at a conference at the United Nations in Nairobi. I sat in a semi circular conference room at a huge wooden oval desk. The room made me think of a modern indoor coliseum, with microphones.

I gave my speech to 500 delegates from around the world, talking about my organisation and what I wanted to achieve in Kenya. As I spoke, my mouth went dry with nerves. But then I realised that so many people in the audience shared my dream to help others. They too had tasted the bitterness of adversity and never wanted to experience it again.

It was through this conference in Nairobi that I had the opportunity to travel to America to share my story with young people. Working as a volunteer, I travelled from California to Wisconsin and Minnesota, covering 24 states and visiting more than a 100 towns and cities. I was able to learn new skills from some amazing people, becoming more confident as a result. I also learnt how to really knuckle down because as volunteers we worked more than 12 hours a day.

My final destination was more than eight hours away by coach. All I could do was curl up in my seat and look out of the huge windows in awe. I was excited as I gazed in amazement at the huge skyscrapers that arrowed up into the sky. The sun beamed down and glistened off the mountains, and I was happy. Happy from simply absorbing my surroundings and listening to the different accents and the sound of soda bottles being opened. As I inhaled the smell of hot food, I felt grateful to be alive.

My gratitude soon turned to nerves as we approached the final stop. This was the visit I had wanted to make for many years. So at 6am on May 21 2013, I stepped off the coach, turned around and saw a face from a photograph I recognised. Aileen!

With a huge hug and a broad smile, I could not thank Aileen enough for giving me a chance. As we sat and talked in McDonalds, I realised that everyone can make a difference. It was an emotional experience to see her sitting opposite me – she was no longer an imagined person behind a series of emails. It was her gift of contribution that had enabled me, in turn, to give to others.

I took this experience back to Kenya and used it to fuel my work, particularly in schools. Only a few years earlier, I'd been sat at the same desks as the children I spoke to. I'd felt alone, just as they did, and I'd spent my time wondering what would come next.

When I talk to students in different schools in Kenya, I see the same fears that clung to me.

Often, all the children can see are bricked up walls. Even the wooden classrooms are surrounded by corrugated iron, with no windows. The main sound they hear is the unrelenting buzzing of flies. Nevertheless, I am able to share my experiences with the children. I see them lift their heads, listening with curiosity as they wake from their usual drowsy state. By letting them look through my eyes, I show them what life can be like. I am someone who has seen the world they live in.

Children are starting to believe in themselves and see potential opportunities. They are able to learn from the people I've met and the connections I've made during trips to the UK and other parts of Europe and America.

It was during those trips that I had time to really reflect on my own adversities. They have taught me many lessons, but I came through because of my faith. When I was a child, I prayed for answers, and by taking action I found people like Aileen and

Darleen who were ready to give me a chance. I decided that I wanted to be one of those people. I wanted to help others.

In the last three years, Change Mind, Change Future has helped inspire 5000 children, from different slums and orphanages in Kenya, to believe that they too can achieve their dreams. Everyone has dreams, even those who live on the streets. Focus on the positive and become who you want to be. If you have faith you can change the world. If I can do it, you can too.

There was a special connection between Calvin and me because we were both working to achieve the same objective; to help young people improve their educational opportunities. In fact, I had been crafting an idea to help a school abroad, but I didn't know where to start.

Exploring possibilities in South Africa, red tape had held the process up, and I wanted to be free from any potential bureaucracy. What I really wanted was to continue along the path of fulfilment, which I was achieving through helping others. I was skint but happy. For so long, financial motivation had dominated my life, and while it is important (as we all have bills to pay), the joy I had experienced from helping others on this journey was an emotion I had not encountered before - and I was not done yet. Maybe Calvin could help?

I wanted to avoid the horror stories; the cases where money or goods sent in good faith never arrive at their intended destination. Corruption and greed dominated many areas, but in Calvin I had found someone I could trust. He was on the front line making a difference, so who better to inspire than him?

I dreamt of supporting a school for children living in the slums, to let them know that they can achieve. Calvin was proof that this could be done. I wanted to make sure that these kids were educated so they could read for themselves how other people have overcome adversity.

Then I thought about trying to involve you, the reader - asking you to leave your own legacy by writing a quote to go up in one of the classrooms. I wanted the children to be surrounded by inspiration. I thought about naming the rooms after the people in this book. That way, the kids would be constantly reminded that they can do it too.

Through Calvin, I have the opportunity to push my dream forward. The coincidence of him working in education makes my purpose easier to pursue, because we are both working towards the common goal of inspiring others.

Ali Jagger – Rollercoaster

I came to arrange my next meeting through pure chance – but then chance was playing a crucial part in my journey.

Sitting on a mahogany chair at home, I rubbed my temple in an attempt to stimulate ideas. My head was pounding with preoccupation. I had completed 13 stories and had another 27 to find. When I thought of it like that, it dampened my spirits somewhat, but one thing was for sure, the book was swelling quickly in terms of page numbers.

It was a cold Friday afternoon in early December. The cloak of darkness began to descend at 4.15pm, but light shone on my search for inspiration. I browsed the internet and saw my name mentioned on Twitter. Georgie Moore, who was helping me with my editing, had nominated my name, along with a number of others. This is a trend that happens on Twitter on Fridays, and it's about showing appreciation for people you have met, or with whom you are working.

A clutch of other names were also included and I clicked on one randomly and saw the title 'Networking Mums'. Navigating to a Facebook page, I saw photographs of a huge audience of women who had gathered together to promote their businesses. 'Yes!' the voice in my head said.

I rang the creator of Networking Mums, Zoe Humphries, the following Monday. I'd been expecting to hear a local accent, but her gentle Scottish lilt was evident on the phone, as was her passion and determination to make things better, and to inspire. I couldn't wait to meet her.

Later that week, I munched on a piece of toast and gazed out of the long windows of a Turkish restaurant called Eaton Place.

Arabic music played in the background, giving it a gentle ambience. As I absorbed the atmosphere, I also wondered what Zoe would be like.

Soon after that, she called to announce her arrival and I walked outside to meet her. She was running across Woolton Road in her high heels and I saw a beaming smile and dyed ruby red hair. Intelligent and well read, Zoe had dark eyes and olive skin. A mother of three in her mid 30s, she led a hectic life trying to juggle many activities.

We chatted away and Zoe spoke of a football team she had mentioned on the phone prior to our meeting. What was brilliant about it was its name: 'Deaf Leopards'.

It was beautiful to hear of two women who had set up a football team for their deaf children. I love stories like this because they're such an inspiration, and I just had to donate some money for the team to buy some balls and bibs.

Zoe also had fundraising on her mind. Her aim was to set up a free networking event to help inspire and teach women how to set and achieve goals. To do so she needed £500, and that was way out of my league. But I wanted to help. I could think of only one man who might agree to fund the event; it was the same man who had helped me on many occasions when I had nothing or wanted to attend a course - Alan McCarthy.

Zoe told me of her desire to help me find equally amazing people to interview, and true to her word she provided an introduction, via email, to a woman named Ali Jagger. Ten days or so later, I was on my way to Rodney Street to meet her.

Rodney Street is one of those addresses that everyone in Liverpool knows. It boasts beautiful, Georgian buildings complete with their original windows. They reminded me of houses I'd seen in Notting Hill and parts of Chelsea and Fulham, but with a slightly lower price tag.

The street itself is a hub for business. Nearly all of the four story buildings have been converted into business premises, and they are just walking distance from the main heart of the city's bars and restaurants.

I pressed the intercom and Ali let me in. As I entered her building, I heard voices at the top of the steep wooden staircase. The staircase was really narrow, which meant I had to position myself like a crab and walk up it sideways. At the top, I heard a soft Scottish accident I recognised. It belonged to Zoe.

I had no idea that she going to be there; this was yet another chance encounter. Beaming with excitement she said:

'I got it today'.

Initially I thought, *got what*? Then I realised and a wave of satisfaction washed over me as I learned that Alan McCarthy had agreed to support Zoe with the £500 she had requested. I sat down on the couch with her and she showed me her vision board on her laptop. At the centre of it was a picture of £500 and the reason why she wanted to deliver the event.

It was a theory I had discussed in schools. If you share your goals with people, and if you ACT, you never know who might be able to help. Obviously, you have to use your common sense and be wary. Never share your invention or solution with competitors, or people you don't trust. Do everything you can to secure your ideas to avoid disappointment or the heartache of being used.

Zoe's good news had given me a great sense of fulfilment, and after she left I introduced myself properly to Ali. Her enthusiasm struck me first. She seemed so alive and happy, and she had every reason to be. Her business was thriving and she was sharing her story while training thousands of people across Europe.

Ali is tall. She's easily 5'10", maybe even taller. She was wearing leggings, trendy boots and a grey jogging top, and she beamed bright with life. Slim in stature, with blonde shoulder length hair and a fringe that covered her forehead, she could have easily been mistaken for a Swedish athlete.

We sat and talked for an hour about life, personal development and the importance of giving back. Ali had an idea there and then to help young unemployed people, and she acted upon it. It would prove to be an event, a memory that will live long within me. (I will discuss this some more later on.)

Time flew that afternoon and as we'd been distracted by general chit chat, we agreed to meet again a few days later in the quaint seaside town of West Kirby, which is on the opposite side of the River Mersey from Liverpool.

I have always loved the train journeys over there. On this particular Sunday, there was not a soul in sight and gazing out of the train window was a real pleasure. I felt like I was looking at a Monet painting; the views over open marshlands glowed in the morning sunshine. It felt good to be away from densely populated housing estates and see some wildlife for a change. The view lasted for a couple of minutes until the train shuddered and vibrated as it pulled slowly into West Kirby train station. Walking into the cold sunshine, Ali was already waiting to pick me up, and she began telling me about her extraordinary life.

Ali Jagger

I grew up in the 1960s and home was a redbrick terrace in Tranmere, Cheshire, which I shared with my parents and younger sister. The local area was industrial, a densely populated part of North West England, close to the docklands of Birkenhead.

My mother was an alcoholic – no doubt about that. Chaos reigned most of the time, or else she was in bed sleeping off a hangover. My sister and I thought this was normal, as it was all we'd ever known. But for most of my childhood I was supremely angry at her for choosing alcohol over us every single time.

Coming home from school and putting the key into the brass lock was a nightmare because I never knew what I'd find. But again, to me that was just my life. I may not have understood what was going on, but I knew it wasn't good.

The thud of walking up the stairs each day after school made my tummy turn over. I'm experiencing the exact same feeling as I recall this now. I was aware that every step I took on the carpet was invading the personal space of the demons that infested my mother's mind. The creak of the bathroom door exposed the horror. Sometimes I'd encounter razor blades, sliced wrists and a polythene bag. Another suicide attempt – snapshots of a woman controlled by alcohol.

My father loved her so much and continued to do everything to help her, even though she would disappear for days on end. Sometimes she would appear at the school gates, staggering from side to side in an attempt to collect my sister and me. Holding my hand, she would fall to the ground and I had nowhere to hide my embarrassment.

Hoisting her up exposed her grazed knees, the pain of her injuries nullified by alcohol. Instead of rushing to help, the other parents would rush to the security of the exit. They wanted to avoid any drama and were careful not to let their children witness the sorry side effects of addiction. Some days my mother would be so drunk that she would fall over a small garden wall, and it was me who had to perform the role of a parent.

At home, my grandmother would care for my sister and me while my father worked. The whereabouts of my mother was more unpredictable. She was sometimes gone for days and sometimes in bed. I hated trudging up those stairs when I knew she was in.

One afternoon after school, the trepidation of what I might see played games in the pit of my stomach. Reaching the top of the staircase, I moved in the direction of my mother's room and pushed the door, but it wouldn't open. I pushed again harder and saw my mother lying still on the carpet behind it. Tablets were sprinkled all around her. She was dead.

Through the years of pain that followed, my emotions were mixed. Even as I reflect now, and put myself back in the shoes of the child at the top of the stairs, I remember my immediate thoughts were of extreme sadness and relief. It's hard to describe, as for many years I blocked every aspect of the torment from my mind. The only positive thought I had was that my mother could now rest in peace, free from addiction.

The family never spoke of what happened and life continued in the loving protection of our father. My sister and I continued our school life at Prenton Pram Pushers, an alternative name for Prenton High School. It was called this because by 16, the female pupils were usually pregnant. I survived and was one of a handful of students who went on to college to complete a course in communication studies. It sounded cool, but I didn't know anything; there were no role models or advice on offer at my school. The best you could hope for was a pat on the head, which was the equivalent of being told to piss off. Well, that's how it felt to me.

I longed to do something different after college and so I did. Armed and dangerous with my new qualifications, I boldly applied for a job in London as a secretary. Inside, I was as nervous as hell. Me, a 19 year old girl from the north. Could I really get a job? I soon found out and the answer – it was YES! I landed a position working for the BBC (British Broadcasting Corporation).

Working and playing hard, I hadn't realised life could be so much fun. Each year my confidence grew as endless opportunities presented themselves, and a stream of promotions followed. My very first production job was working on a follow up to the Young Ones with Ben Elton, Rik Mayall and Nigel Planer – and I started hanging out with these guys after shows. I'd worked my way up to the role of PA (Personal Assistant), and this was followed by the title, Assistant Production Manager. A few years later, I was promoted to Production Manager, which included managing budgets and working with celebrities.

Privileged and proud, the harmony of work flowed beautifully with my personal life. I'd made lots of friends in television and there are no other words for it; we were the 'party crowd'. Being absorbed in alcohol felt good; it numbed the pain and extinguished memories from the past. Plus, I was never on my own with the outgoing crowd I hung out with.

The busy lifestyle speeded up and having rented a flat with friends for two years, we realised that we had not stayed in once. Complete madness, but amazing all the same!

Confident and riding high on life, the demand for my services soared. Waking up each day was a dream. Channel 4 was next and culminated with a project for Motown, the iconic music institution. One of my favourite moments was meeting Stevie Wonder. In him, I saw unparalleled beauty and intelligence. As part of my job, I had organised for him to do an interview. I sat with my mouth gaping as he explained how he'd never blamed anyone for being blind. In fact, he saw his blindness as a blessing. *Wow*! I thought. What an incredible human being.

My link to music and alcohol continued as I managed the productions on each leg of Soul II Soul's world tour. I visited Japan, America and Australia and was in awe of these incredible artists at the peak of their career. But regardless of my professional achievements, my rock 'n' roll lifestyle and love of alcohol was a habit and work became too much to handle. Rather than swilling a cup of coffee down my throat of a morning, my temptation was to swill the strongest lager or a glass of red wine instead.

Drinking had taken over my senses and I don't know what came over me, but one day I upped and walked away from my BBC career and went AWOL. For over two months, my family didn't know I was hiding in Brighton. That must have been so difficult for them. When I reflect, I think my age had something to do with what happened. I was 37, the same age my mother was when she died, and this played on my mind. Was I going the same way? I was certainly emulating the type of behaviour I remembered from her as child. I know from speaking to other people who have been through similar experiences, that it is common to follow in a parent's footsteps.

The easiest way for me to forget the past was to have a good time. During the day I would sit with a group of friends in a bar, staring into space or watching the tide roll back and forth on the pebbled beaches of Brighton. I had disappeared into alcohol. All I had to do was get up and repeat the party process – I was having a rebellious good time, wasn't I?

But one day I realised that enough was enough. It was time to walk away from the party lifestyle and return to real life. It was time to bring an end to my two-month binge – I had reached my own personal low.

My sister was now working in television too, and she agreed to rescue me from my nightmare. She offered me a home in London, and time to clear my senses and rebuild.

A new job meant a new start. With international travel a distant memory, I worked locally and nationally on TV productions. My return to normality, however, brought an unexpected twist; a cameraman who I worked with became my husband. Within six months of falling in love, we married in Sri Lanka, Ted's original home. Then all the pieces fell together. Ted was offered a job working in the North-West, close to my childhood roots, so it was natural that I returned home.

For our honeymoon, we'd planned an around the world trip, visiting Melbourne first to attend a relative's wedding. It was a fantastic feeling to know that I had expelled the old me. Sitting in the Australian sunshine and meeting new people, life felt stable and good.

Honeymooning, travel and love; this was the polar opposite of my party lifestyle in Brighton. However, the second leg of our journey started in hospital. Instead of alcohol flowing, it was blood. I clutched my stomach in pain. The cramps I was experiencing were proving much more violent than my traditional monthly periods. I discovered I'd had a miscarriage, plunging me from the high life to the low life yet again. I hadn't known I was pregnant, compounding my sadness at such a dreadful experience.

We cut our honeymoon short and returned home. Tiredness dominated my life. As my energy levels dwindled, I sought answers from the medical profession.

A year on, there was still no explanation from my GP. My heavy periods continued and I struggled to breathe when I walked. The decline in my health meant I couldn't work and my new lifestyle consisted of early nights with my legs raised to ease the swelling in my ankles. They had grown so large that I couldn't put my shoes on. Even the act of bending down would leave me exhausted. My body ballooned with water retention and my head was in contact with my pillow so often that it felt like part of the embroidery. Now in my late 30s and unable to move, my daily routine was to wake up at 11am and go back to sleep at midday.

My metabolism morphed uncontrollably, but it was the reaction of the people closest to me that hurt. Although the weight gain was significant, it seemed gradual to me. However, the looks of disgust nourished the negativity that was starting to bloom from within.

'Oh my god, Ali, what have you been doing?' one person asked.

This natural cynicism was present in most people I met. Their body language said it all. It was telling me, 'you can't get that big from being sick'.

I surged from 10 and a half stone to nearly 20 in just over a year, but that wasn't because I'd been raiding the fridge; I didn't have the energy. I didn't have the energy to do anything – I genuinely felt I was dying.

Attending parties was the worst. I would sit watching others having a good time and then I would hear people ask Ted, 'is she OK?' They would tilt their head patronisingly towards me as if I was a newborn baby.

The irony, looking back, is that it was me who used play the role of party animal, but going out became the last thing I wanted to do. How could I? Chained to tiredness, sprawled across a bed - what kind of a life was that? I existed in a mental fog where the colours of everyday objects all seemed grey. Whatever motivation I had to investigate this illness waned. I tried to research it, only to slump into a daydreaming mess at the keyboard. Alternatively, I'd drift into a haze for what seemed like five minutes, but was actually an hour. Home alone as Ted worked away, at times my mind was lost.

Luckily Ted was at home when I collapsed in the bathroom one day. He found me with my swollen cheeks resting on the cold tiles. Just a few days earlier, I had been taken into hospital suffering with extremely heavy periods, but the consultant had no answers and sent me home.

Ted strapped me into his Toyota Celica and rushed me to hospital as I drifted in and out of consciousness. With the car door left wide open, he ran to get help and I wondered if this was the end. Next thing I knew, a paramedic was hauling me into a wheelchair. This was followed by forceful shouts: 'Move! Move!' Hoards of medical staff joined the pursuit along the corridors into A&E, and that's the last thing I remember. Waking up groggy, I realised I was lucky to be alive. I discovered that a blood transfusion to replace five of my eight pints of blood had kept me in this world.

Numerous blood tests were taken and I waited for the results, all the while existing in a living hell. I thought the gravity of my illness would push forward the investigation into what was wrong with me. Someone please must know! Willing my ordeal to be over, doctors pursued their theory that my health problems were a consequence of the miscarriage. The next step was a hysterectomy. And when you are desperate, you trust. But in the end, I flatly refused to have my womb removed.

Lying in a hospital bed I thought, *just fucking get me out of here. Does anybody in this hospital know what is going on*? If I could have put on the white jacket and hung the stethoscope around my neck, I felt I would have been more qualified than the medical professionals around me - such was my frustration.

A new GP revealed the results of some blood tests. I had a TSH (Thyroid Stimulating Hormone) count of 150 when it should have been 15. After 18 months and a 10 stone weight gain, I was relieved to learn that I had an underactive thyroid. *Just give me the pills*, I thought.

But as time went on, fury rose from the pit of my stomach. I'd encountered so much pain and spent so much time visiting doctors and gynaecologists. Even to the near extreme of signing papers to have my womb removed.

Taking the prescribed medication brought a rainbow of colour back to my life. *Thank God, the weight will drop off and I will be back on my feet,* I thought. No such luck! The doctor informed me that taking the tablets would aid my recovery and stabalise my metabolism, but it would not rid me of the excess weight. Oh well, thank you for another piece of great news!

The simple decisions I'd taken for granted in the past, such as going for a swim, now became a major obstacle. Standing before the mirror in the changing room, I felt embarrassed as flesh sagged from my every part of my body. The illness had not only stolen 18 months of my life, it had caused much greater damage by mutilating my self-esteem. The reflection staring back at me revealed a body that was not mine. I wanted to scream to the world 'this is not the true Alison!' I looked like one of the fat men from the French and Saunders series – ironic as I'd worked on two series at the BBC with Dawn and Jennifer dressed in those costumes!

Embarrassed and lost, my rehabilitation started in the supermarket. I felt like I was from another world. People whizzed by collecting fruit and vegetables while I stood like a tortoise without a shell, alien and exposed, leaning against a trolley for support.

But shopping acted as therapy, reintroducing me to society and suppressing my loneliness. As the internal cogs within my body started to turn, my mind began to function. I trawled through the job centre website and applied for roles online in an attempt to regain some independence.

I wanted something part time, something steady to galvanise my will and confidence, but rejections followed. None of my previous experience seemed to matter. Now long-term unemployed, I wondered if maybe I was a risk. Even an administration job, managing diaries and booking hotels, was met with yet another rejection.

For years I had travelled around the globe with some of the biggest bands in the world. I had worked my way up to become one of the highest paid production managers at the BBC.

However, my skills now counted for nothing. Some employers thought I was not suitable for conducting basic tasks like ordering toilet rolls and medical equipment. I knew because I applied for jobs like this and was turned down.

I knew my TV career was over. I didn't have the energy or confidence to pursue that path. But my road to recovery properly started as an office worker at a tearoom. I was on minimum wage but the money didn't matter. Just to be valued and to contribute my typing skills sparked my comeback from the abyss. My friend asked me to type up her notes from her coaching qualification and as I did this I thought, *yeah, there's something in this*.

I gave some personal development CDs a chance and was immediately captured and fascinated by the ideas that flowed through my speakers.

'Wages are good but profits are better.'

'Work harder on yourself than you do on your job.'

I realised from listening to those success principals, which were eloquently stated by motivational speaker Jim Rohn, that I would love to have a business and to set myself goals.

No longer housebound and motivated by learning, I attended educational courses, some of which had a profound effect on me. I was still caught in a quagmire of trying to lose weight so I began consuming Herbalife shakes. I wanted to look in the mirror and feel proud, to close this chapter of heartache. To my delight and surprise, I managed to transform my body through a combination of exercise, gritted teeth and good nutrition. A year on and I had achieved my goal of returning to my natural weight of 10 and a half stone.

On the morning I discovered I'd reached my target weight, I sat down and wrote my story to sell to the press. I was determined that no other woman would suffer with a misdiagnosed underactive thyroid. Perhaps there was a way I could turn this negative story into something really positive, and if I could help some other women along the way, then even better!

The Daily Mail bought the story and I called the TV show *This Morning* on the day it appeared, asking to be put through to a producer. The one I spoke to said:

'Oh my God, I'm just reading about you in the Daily Mail.'

'Are you going to have me on then?' I replied

'Sure,' she said.

And that was that - I was about to go live on TV.

Following my appearance, my inbox was flooded with emails. Women told me about having their wombs removed when there was nothing wrong with them. And this was simply due to a lack of education among some medical staff. I was outraged because I could empathise with these women. I began coaching and using my experience to encourage many women through the most desolate of times. Because of the response to my story, *This Morning* reran my interview at the end of the year. According to Dr Chris, the show's regular medic, we were 'making waves in the NHS (National Health Service)', which was exactly what I wanted!

Propelled by passion, I removed my old photos, cleared out the tents I used to wear and became determined to create my own business. Even though my health challenges were over, I was now facing the heartbreak of divorce after 12 years of marriage.

Although I was angry and felt massively let down, I said no to negativity. I'd decided to become a weight loss coach, teaching people about nutrition. There was no doubt that there would be difficulties along the way, but I didn't care. This was my dream.

Attending my first Herbalife event, I walked into a room of happy clapping and high fives. I met highly charged people tattooed in Herbalife branding. They all seemed in love with life and were embracing positivity. *What the hell is this?* I thought.

It wasn't long before I understood why these people were so happy. They were working with their friends, changing lives, earning money and going on holiday. It was everything I wanted.

Visualising and creating vision boards, I focused on my goals (one of which was to earn more than my ex-husband) and formed positive habits regarding health, exercise and learning. Taking action, I pushed through my fears. I didn't care that I didn't have any selling or financial experience, and I didn't care what people said or did. I might not have been sure where to start, but I knew I would find a way to keep going, no matter what.

My growth coincided with my search for answers. One of the questions asked by a facilitator on a training course was: what challenges would you like to resolve? My answer was instantaneous. The horrific memories of my mother's death.

I'd avoided her suicide for 30 years, preferring to keep the anger and unanswered questions suppressed. But now I stood tall and sought answers from my dad. By doing this I learned that I was in control, but, more beautifully, I also learned forgiveness. It was time to forgive my mum and to forgive my own mistakes. It was time to understand rather than judge. With this forgiveness came peace of mind. I now wear a necklace to remind me of my mother, and if I am honest, I know that she is with me on this incredible journey.

For us to understand our true potential and face our challenges, we must step into the unknown and find the answers to our questions. I did this through learning personal development methods, which helped me to chip away at the beliefs that I held deep within me and to see the bright light of possibility.

In the three and a half years since listening to personal development CDs and taking action to recover, I have built an incredible Herbalife career, and a life that I love. Although it's not about the money (although I did fulfil the goal of earning more than my ex), I enjoy the freedom that money allows. This is the freedom to go, do and be what I want.

I have learnt not to accept second best. For far too long I was persuaded to ignore my true voice, which I now realise always has the answers. My advice to you is to listen and trust yourself, and also to ask yourself what is the worst that can happen? If you fail, go again and use your learning to make you better. Tasting adversity only made me hungrier for success because I was determined to get better and make my mark!

We all undoubtedly face challenges, but it is the decisions we make that determine our destination. Life is an adventure and you get just one shot, so it's important to get out there and do it. I love the fact that I now do Stand Up Paddle boarding (SUP) and my next goal is to train as a SUP instructor aged nearly 50 – why the hell not?

On top of this, I'm paid to regularly travel to other parts of Europe to share my personal and business story. My life now is exactly like the one I pictured in my mind and on my vision board. I've demonstrated that dreams can come true.

Once I became excited about life, I started living it. The beauty of this is that I did it in my mid-40s, proving that it's never too late.

Affirmations help change your thoughts. I started by repeating ones each day, in the morning and evening. Write out some that are pertinent to you, or see the examples below.

When suffering through bereavement and illness, it can feel like you are to blame and your thoughts can betray you. I used to think: *I am worthless, I am fat and I am useless.* When you think this way you feel awful. So in order to feel good, replace the negativity that is playing on your mind with positive beliefs.

Repeat and repeat, even when the voice in your mind says, 'yeah, right!' Your job is to drown that voice out and change the way you think. Here are some affirmations that worked for me:

- I am a capable person; my future will be brighter and stronger than my challenges.

- I have one life and it's my own adventure to create.

- I am proud to be me – I'm not perfect but hey, who is?

- I am proud of speaking in front of so many people.

- I am proud each day because I am a stronger character.

- I am a good person and always learning.

- I am strong because I can ask for help and let people into my life.

Confidence and self-esteem

We all have things that we don't like about ourselves. However, instead of dwelling on these, think about what you do like about yourself. What can you be grateful for or admire in yourself?

Here are some examples for you to consider:

- I am grateful for my persistence because this is the key to achieving what I want for my life.

- I am grateful for my parents' support and for them being with me on my own life adventure.

- I am grateful for reading about positive people overcoming adversity, because every single person is MUCH stronger than they will ever know.

- I am grateful for every single event that has brought me to where I am today.

- I am grateful for my desire to change, improve and help others.

- I am grateful to be alive and for growing as a person every single day.

Write out five grateful statements like the ones above. You can and will overcome the challenges you face, and you will live the life you want. If I can do it, you can too.

Ali's story was upsetting, and yet at the same time I found it inspiring and uplifting. I was proud of how she had overcome so many challenges to become so positive. I also admired how she was able to forgive. This sounds easy in principal, but it's essential to move on from the past - although in my opinion it takes a special kind of person to be able to do this. I actually feel that forgiveness is the mother of all traits. When I think of cases in the news, particularly murder or other brutal incidents, I know it must be hard to forgive. Time, without question, is a significant ingredient in helping to develop such a quality.

Could I forgive? Yes, but my past relationship still grated, along with some of the other incidents that had happened in the year. I still had my moments where I wondered what had happened and wished things could be different. But each day and each story helped me to strive towards gratitude and forgiveness. Since I'd begun focusing on the positive, I'd found that life was getting better - and I was about to receive more evidence that this was true.

I returned to Rodney Street just a couple of weeks later. Ali wanted me to give something back by telling people from the local community about her legacy fund to help young people. I was both excited and nervous to be doing this.

Travelling into Liverpool city centre by train, I mulled over what I wanted to say. I was still caught in a daydream as I wandered across the main zebra crossing towards the bus station and into St John's Shopping Centre, where I was promptly stopped in my tracks.

'Antony, do you remember me?'

A young man was standing in front of me, his hair slightly longer than I remembered.

'Thanks for all your help, Antony,' he said. 'I am now training to be a dentist.'

Whoa! What an amazing young man. Lewis had taken a course with us a year earlier. This business had 'failed' remember, but here was an example of how it had been a success. Lewis had been unemployed and now he was on the road to fulfilling his potential.

Glowing with pride, I marched more confidently towards my destination. I decided on a speech entitled: The story of Tim Reddish OBE, Chairman of the British Paralympic Association. It had worked in school, so why not here?

When the time came to deliver my talk, I stood before a gathering of around 20 people. As I spoke, I could see that the power of the story was moving some members of the audience. I felt confident that I was showing them what people are capable of doing.

Excited by the evening and having met some new people, I could have floated home. It must have been gone 9pm. *What an amazing day,* I thought. With Christmas just a couple of weeks away, I considered going for a drink to celebrate the evening.

Just after the presentation, I spoke to Simon O'Brien, a TV presenter who was also at Ali's event. I realised that we shared a mutual friend, Martin Lappin. I had not spoken to Martin for over a year, so on the spur of the moment I decided to send him a text. To my surprise, he was out having a drink. After exchanging a few messages, I got into a taxi and headed off to meet him, but nothing could have prepared me for what was about to happen...

Pulling up in a taxi on Lark Lane triggered memories from the previous year. Martin was in Que Pasa, the bar where it had all gone so terribly wrong with my girlfriend on the evening of December 21 2012.

Peering through the glass of its huge wooden door, I could see Martin sitting at the same table my ex and I had been seated at a year earlier. I couldn't believe it!

A grey haired man, who I guessed was in his 40s, was sat where my girlfriend had been on that fateful night. When I entered the bar, Martin moved over so I could take a seat next to him. He asked what I'd been doing since I saw him last. I explained everything and how it had led me to write this book.

'You should speak to him,' he said, nodding at his grey-haired friend, who was called Pete.

'Why, what's your story?' I asked.

'Did you hear about the coach accident last year?' Pete replied.

I immediately knew what he was talking about. In September 2012, three people had been killed in the accident. In fact, I'd met one of the victims, Michael Molloy, just a few weeks before the tragedy happened. Michael was a talented musician and he and his friend Alex often played in the local bars. I loved listening to them do Ray Charles's *Hit The Road Jack*.

An inquest heard how a 20 year old tyre was still being used on the coach, a fact that shocked me.

Pete went on to tell me that his son Zach had been sitting next to Michael. He was propelled through the windscreen of the coach and glass had entered his spine, leaving him paralysed from the waist down. I was still reeling from the shock of this information when Pete explained how Zach was swimming as part of his rehabilitation.

I listened intently, aware that just 45-minutes earlier, I had told the story of the most senior person in the British Paralympic Association. He's a swimmer, gold medallist and an inspiration, and this was yet another incredible coincidence. I immediately told my companions about my speech, and asked Pete whether he would like to speak to Tim. I knew it was a special moment. I am not usually keen for a photograph, but I wanted to capture this synchronicity and remind myself that life does move on and good can come from adversity.

(From left to right: Peter, Martin and Antony.)

The decision to go for a pint that night was one of the best I could have made.

After speaking to Tim, Zach is now being fast tracked through his swimming assessments and is working with senior swimming coaches. I have no doubt he will achieve his goals, whatever they may be.

For me this closed a loop. The catalogue of coincidences that had taken place during one day were difficult to comprehend, but they were truly amazing. I'd bumped into Lewis, heard about his achievements and taken solace from knowing that my business could have succeeded with the right funding. And then, through Ali's event, I'd got into contact with Tim again and met Pete. I'd sat in the seat where it had all gone wrong almost a year earlier and made a difference to someone's life. What a day! It gave me a feeling of complete exhilaration. This was exactly the type of day to signal that I was on the right track.

When I got home, after having a few beers, I wrote the below paragraph, but totally forget about it until sometime later. It came from an accumulation of thoughts gleaned from people who feature in this book. They had suffered relationship problems far worse than my own. It's funny how they had all prospered once those particular relationships had ended.

Here it is:

Focus on the type of person you want. Don't dwell on someone who cheats or values nothing from your past. Never sway in the direction of the so-called love that has wronged you. If you paint a picture in your mind of who you want, and the qualities they possess, faith will steer your ship in their direction - and it will be greater than anything you imagined. Don't settle for the person who wishes to break you, settle only for the person who makes you! There's great truth in the wise words of those who have trodden the path before you.

Jasvinder Sanghera – Shame

Following that incredible night in the pub, the good vibes continued to flow. After many months of trying, I finally secured a date to meet and interview Jasvinder Sanghera at her office in Leeds. I'd heard a snippet of Jasvinder's story, which ignited anger within me. The most basic of liberties - freedom - was not possible for many Asian women.

Jasvinder's heritage stems from India, although her roots are fixed firmly in Derby, where my friend Lynette, who had pointed me in her direction, also lives. Lynette had helped me through the worst of times. She had made me understand that running away to Australia would not be the answer to my problems. The confidence she had in me was invaluable to this book, as was Jasvinder's input.

Leaving Liverpool, I arrived at Leeds train station at 9am on a frosty December morning. Arriving during rush hour, people bumped and bustled for space, marching around like an army of ants. I was lucky. I could sit and observe them as I scoured the electronic notice boards for the next train to Bramley.

Arriving there on time and on track, my next step was to find Javinder's office. I randomly looked down at my shoes. Oh no, they were odd! Fortunately, they were the same colour, but the shape and stitching were a little different. I lowered my laptop bag onto the top of my mismatching shoes to hide my embarrassing mistake.

Seeing the funny side, I walked up a steep hill from the train station and planned what I was going to say to Jasvinder. Little doubts crept in. Would she agree to appear in my book? Why would she want to speak to me?

When I arrived at the business complex where her office was, I rang her buzzer, tapping my foot nervously while I waited for an answer. My shoes, however, were still hidden under the safety of my laptop bag.

My immediate impression of Jasvinder was that she was calm, gentle and focused. We sat together inside a small corporate meeting room and chatted about education for a while before she revealed a shocking story that brought us both to tears.

Jasvinder Sanghera

Imagine waking up to the horror of never being able to see your family again...This is what happened to me. All I wanted was the freedom to attend school and learn and play with my friends. However, seeing the man of my nightmares in a Polaroid photograph meant that my life was to take a savage twist. I had been promised to him since I was eight years old. Now I was 14, and it was time for me to be married. The man I was to spend the rest of my life with looked short and ugly. He wasn't a person I wanted to meet, let alone marry.

I was the second youngest of seven children. I'd seen with my own eyes how my older sisters' lives had been transformed beyond recognition - particularly when they were taken from school. School was the only place where we had any freedom of thought, and it was a far cry from our life at home where we were expected to abandon education in order to become teenage brides, marrying men who lived thousands of miles away in India.

At home, my only freedom came from watching Charlie's Angels on a Saturday afternoon. However, the TV series represented a white woman's world and my mother hated it. Her biggest fear was that my sisters and I would grow up and

224

behave like prostitutes – as she believed the white women were doing.

Growing up in a close-knit community of Asians in Derby was tough. Strict rules from the Punjab were enforced in the terraced houses we lived in. It wasn't uncommon for a family with seven kids to cram into a three-bed property. Hilly streets sloped up and down at (almost) 45° angles. On the corners, women gathered to gossip, their eyes and ears alive to every piece of information - the ultimate dishonour for any Asian is to heap shame on their family.

A trunk of beautifully coloured saris sat by the front door. This was a sign that one of my sisters was to be packed off to a new and unknown world. When one left, another returned from a so-called honeymoon. It didn't matter which sister it was, as every case was the same. They would all sit with their heads bowed and stare at the dark carpet in our living room while they complained about their unhappiness; their arranged life without love in which they were married only to be abused. Any pleas or submissive cries for help would fall on deaf ears as my mother would tell them to go back to their husbands and continue their duties. My sisters were all told not to cause disgrace to the family name.

Meanwhile, I wanted to study. But when I arrived home from school with my sisters, our mother taught us how to cook, clean and uphold the pretence of being a doting wife. We were in a training camp. I call this grooming.

There were no activities or fun, simply preparation to travel and become a bride. Once our lessons were over, we moved on to our next task, which was to work so that we could earn enough money to pay for our stranger husband to come to the UK. It provoked me to rebel, and rebelling is something that you just didn't do. We were taught never to go against the family, and we were made well aware of the consequences if we did. I was about to discover them first-hand.

My abdication from the rules meant I was locked away in my room. Aged just 15 years old, I was without hope. I didn't want to go to India, I just wanted to be home with my family and complete my education. However, home was turning into a prison camp. My sisters, the closest people to me, kept watch at the door. They acted as prison guards, preaching a brainwashing moral code that they too despised.

'Why do you think you are different? You are going through with this, Jas,' they would snap.

Then my mother chipped in.

'Jasvinder, you are going to break your father's heart. Do you want to be responsible for that?'

Those brutal stabbing sentences, and my loss of freedom and fear of the future caused endless tears. I sat on my bed imprisoned by my family.

I was, of course, unable to date boys or wear the western clothes I wanted. Each sunset was another step closer to marrying a man I didn't know – I hadn't even been told what his name was.

To try and end the hopelessness, I attempted suicide. I took pills, but my body rejected them. My sister's solution to me trying to end my own life was to give me a strong cup of coffee. My desperate act couldn't eclipse the shame I'd cause if I didn't marry this man. The only way out for me now was to run.

My mother had found temporary work for me in a local factory. This is where I met Avtar, a friend with a similar free spirit: only she was willing to take more risks than me. Through Avtar, I met Jassey, her brother. He was six years older and I felt an instant attraction to him. During our initial courtship, Avtar would tell me where to meet him so that we would not be caught. I would rush to get dressed for work with no intention of actually going. One of my sisters sensed what was going on but decided not to ask any questions. She didn't want to be lied to and also knew that there would be profound consequences for her if she revealed my secret.

At home, the pressure was building. Sat at the top of the stairs one day, I overheard my mother making arrangements for my marriage. She had bought my wedding dress and the only thing I knew about it was the colour...red. My sisters bubbled with excitement and my mother beamed with pride. She wanted to celebrate the success of her daughters - there were only two left to marry off!

Maybe there was a glimmer of hope. Somehow, some way, my parents would come to their senses. Wrong again! I told my mother about Jassey in a desperate bid to convince her that I could make her proud. She thrust her face into mine and I could feel the heat of her breath as she screamed in my face. Once again, the dungeon awaited me. Appealing to my father made no difference, his deep sigh meant that I had to go along with it. Mothers rule the Asian upbringing and he would never go against her. He followed me up the stairs and I listened to the clunks and banging as he fixed a lock to the door.

The seething from my mother continued as she visualised the women gossiping. 'Don't protect that prostitute,' she'd scream at my sisters.

Leaving home now became a necessity. Pulling my carefully packed suitcase of clothes out from under my bed, I felt devastated as I wrote a note to my family. I loved them so much, and desperately wanted to remain at home, but I couldn't marry this man.

I had come home from school to find the house surprisingly quiet. My father, who worked nights, was asleep in his room and my mother was at work. My heart pounded as I quietly let myself out and walked as quickly as I could away from the house. I was desperate to be free from the invisible eyes that lurked on every street corner. On instinct, I made my way to Jassey's workplace, but he was not expecting me. All I could do was sit on a wall and wait for him to come out.

'We have to leave,' I said to him when he did. The panic was evident in my voice. There was no turning back and I begged him to take me away. Jassey did what I asked. He left everything: his job, his family and his future.

We decided to head north - as far away as possible - in Jassey's purple Ford Escort. I was wedged in the footwell all the way to Newcastle, huddled with my knees tight into in my chest. We slept in that car for weeks and I just wanted to be at home. Every memory brought me to tears. Why did life have to be like this? I was still only 15.

Looking out of the car window some evenings, the haze from the street lights was my only company. We got washed in public toilets as we struggled to find somewhere to live. Some nights I slept on a park bench just to stretch my coiled limbs.

Eventually, we rented a bedsit and while Jassey searched for work, I lived like a hermit. I was depressed and missed my family. I especially missed the trips to the allotment with my dad. I lived in the past and spent a lot of time going over my childhood memories. But one day, a rapping noise at the front door interrupted my trip down memory lane. It was the police.

Jassey was home after yet another day of wearing down his shoes trying to find work. I heard him trying to stall the policeman but I decided to come out from the shadows. I was no longer able to hide. As my eyes squinted in the light, a tall, well-built policeman, the size of the doorframe, stood before me.

'I don't want to go back,' I pleaded.

To my astonishment, the officer understood. In a deep, authoritative voice he replied, 'I see this all the time and I won't send you back or tell your parents where you are, but I do expect you to call them so they know you are safe.'

Without his foresight, my life could have changed drastically. Doing what he asked, I rang home from the safety of a telephone box a few miles from where we lived. The horror and anguish in my voice was met with anger from my sister.

'Do you realise what you have done?' she said. 'People spit in our mother's face in the street.'

Each time I rang home, the phone was jammed down. I would hear the voice of my father, but as soon as I spoke all he allowed me to hear was a dead dial tone. I was crying out for the love of my family and couldn't stop thinking of my mother's words when I first spoke to her.

'You are dead in our eyes. You will amount to nothing; nothing, do you hear me? I hope you give birth to a prostitute, then you will know how it feels to give birth to you.'

For over two years, I lived without any contact from my family. I remember feeling like a dead person walking. I was missing them all terribly and felt so guilty. I suffered mentally from speaking out, because in my culture you do not speak out against your parents. I'm not the only one. Every year, women disappear and are married off. If they dare shame their families, they could even be murdered. A damaged Asian girl, who causes the family shame, is better off dead.

Parallel to pursuing contact with my family, the struggle to find work continued. As time progressed, Jassey and I moved to Leeds to seek new opportunities and get married. I wanted to prove that I was not a prostitute like my mother had accused me of being.

We built a market stall business across West Yorkshire and I fell pregnant with a daughter. During this period, I regained contact with my sister Robina; she was home after divorcing her husband in Germany. We'd always been close and as kids we had shared the same room and walked to school together.

Robina toed the family line but she also tried to rebuild the bridges between my mother and I when I gave birth. Having a baby increased my longing to be at home in Derby, so Robina convinced my mother to visit me. I'd hoped for a conversation, but instead she sat on the edge of my hospital bed with her back to me and remained silent.

Silent suffering was also expected of Robina. She married again and was forced to endure yet more abuse. Asian husbands know they can get away with it because their bride's family will always insist that they go back to them. When the going got tough, a community leader - a person Asian people look towards for guidance - is called to mediate. They are seen as gods and this particular community leader's advice was that Robina should stay with her husband. Why? Because we are chained to an invisible wall built over generations; this is a wall of honour, which, despite causing unhappiness, we continue to be a slave to.

I was at the market one day when I received a message to call home. My mother answered and it was one of the few times I'd spoke to her since leaving home.

'It's your sister, Robina,' she said. 'She's dead.'

To this day, the thought of seeing charcoal stains on the carpet after her death still turns my stomach. Robina had poured paraffin over her herself and lit a match. Over 50 per cent of her body was burned. It was a horrific end to such a beautiful person. She hadn't been able to face getting another divorce, therefore death was better than letting her mother and father down, and dragging the family name through the mud.

The funeral became a turning point in my life. I became aware of it despite the plans being made in secret. I was not invited, but I went anyway. While there, I saw the community leader who had told my sister to return to her husband. He pranced around like a peacock, his chest puffed out and his ego inflated as people bowed to him. He'd given advice that had led to my sister's death, yet people still followed his pathetic guidance. I erupted when I saw a Robina's four year old son, my nephew, running around, unaware that his mother had gone.

When I walked into the living room of my mother and father's house, other people walked out. For the first time in my life, rage erupted through every pore and cell in my body. There was no way I was going to continue feeling guilty for wanting to be free.

'You are the ones who are responsible for this,' I screamed. With that I launched into a blistering tirade, which was fuelled by the loss of my sister and all my pent up feelings from the past.

Following Robina's death, Jassey and I moved back home to Derby. Why should I be ostracised? It would be my parents' problem if I caused them shame by walking the streets of my home city. I didn't care who I upset. My mother didn't want to hear my pleas and neither did my sisters, so I accepted that I couldn't change them.

This was my turning point from victim to survivor; my honour was their shame.

Now older and wiser, concerns of a different nature presented themselves. My relationship was crumbling with Jassey. We'd been welded together for a long time. This was no Romeo and Juliet story, we had begun leading separate lives and I had an affair. After separating from Jassey, and while still vulnerable, I met Raj in the petrol station where he worked. Our meetings became more frequent and eventually we married and had two children. But it wasn't a happy union and I suffered the abuse I'd feared.

Aged 27, I read my first ever book. This was late in life by any standards, but my education in my formative years had been quashed. Being a mother, wife and running a business didn't allow time for me to even think about my own aspirations.

By now, however, my desire to learn had firmly taken hold and I dreamt of one day gaining my independence. At the other end of the spectrum, being married again led me along another path. This was one of domination, and it made my life a living hell.

Seeing education as a means of escape for my children and me,

I started studying for my A-levels. But Raj took all the same classes and became my shadow. We lived with his parents, which meant being tied to ancient ways of thinking and living under his mother's rule.

Raj's parents made it difficult for me to study and enjoy any free time. When my eldest daughter and I returned home a little late from a friend's wedding (that I had begged to attend), we were welcomed by scowls and hissing. I was in trouble. Raj's mother stood behind her son, her arms fixed around my youngest daughter. She had bolts of anger in her eyes and looked at me like I was garbage. I wrestled with her as I tried to release my daughter from her claws. The twitch of a neighbour's front door opening was the trigger for Raj's mother to back down. With my daughter free, I packed our things and held back my tears as I drove to escape the madness. This tug of war could not go on any longer, and although we bought our own place and tried to make it a home, our rundown house required renovation. Paint screamed to be stripped from the walls and the gaps in the floorboards were so big we could have fallen down them. But I persisted, trying my best to balance home, two young children and a university degree (which I'd started after completing my A-levels).

One morning, I was busy making sure that the kids were fed and watered when the phone rang.

'Your husband is having an affair,' announced the caller.

I could almost feel the slimy pleasure that the woman had taken in uttering those words. By this time I was pregnant with my third child. My heart broken, I cupped my visible bump. This masquerade of a marriage had to end. Raj denied involvement, but the look of guilt on his face was as clear as the voice I'd heard on the phone.

Following the divorce, my life became all about education and helping others. My vision was to make a difference, to never see another woman end up like Robina, and to break my own silence. I set up my charity, 'Karma Nirvana', in 1993 while still at university and worked tirelessly to broadcast my message. I knew it would take tremendous courage for someone to call and seek help. Communities would not come forward as they are entrenched in ancient beliefs. Forced marriages have become a modern form of slavery. Young Asian girls can be beaten, threatened and, in many cases, killed.

How many dreams are stolen - in countries around the world - behind closed doors? Hundreds live without the freedom to be able to make choices that many take for granted. Many young Asian men and women walk in fear, scared to reach out as they preserve their family rituals with their hands tied behind their backs. This was evident when I began the helpline. The enormity of my challenge was met with deafening silence as the phone failed to ring. For the first four years I didn't receive one call. Faith, commitment and a vision of what I wanted for the future kept my soul's ambition alive. I wanted to cry, and some days I did. People told me to give it up, but there was no way I would do such a thing. The only way was forward.

The first part of my day involved a maze of bus routes. Carrying heavy files over my shoulder and holding my baby under my arm, I'd watch my other children as they stood patiently waiting for the next stop so I could take them to daycare. I then raced to university. By the time I got there, I was exhausted and sweating, but free. Lecturers advised me to postpone submitting my dissertation until the following year. They could see my pale complexion, and could tell that I was barely able to function.

However, university offered the perfect platform to spread my message. I started to present my story and people were horrified. But exposing what happened in tight-knit Asian communities was fraught with danger. I was on my way home from London one day when I received a call warning me that I was in danger. The flashing blue lights in the distance near Derby train station proved this, and when I arrived there, the place was in complete chaos. Police and other specialist officers equipped with torches and long metal rods with mirrors were searching for bombs - threats had been made against my life.

At home, money was so tight we lived on cereal. I was naturally beleaguered and tired some days, but my internal furnace kept me going; I was determined to save lives.

At the age of 28, while still studying at university, I enrolled on a counselling course - but it was me who needed counselling. To be listened to without judgement as I vented the hurt and frustration buried deep within was a liberating experience. Fused together, my passion and pain became my strongest asset.

The counselling was like an exorcism from the guilt and rejection I had suffered since I was child. Once I made the decision not to be a victim anymore, I gave birth to belief. Filled with surging confidence, I led the march forward, pounding the pavement in order to encourage the community to attend my events.

From starting the charity at home, and after waiting four years for our first response, we now receive 1000 calls per month (which is double the calls from the previous year). Callers are supported by 20 full-time staff members and volunteers, all of whom have first-hand experience of the consequences of resisting an arranged marriage. Our refuges and safe houses give people salvation; they know they can escape and have somewhere to go where they can be free.

Before the 2010 election, I lobbied the government and shadow cabinet to do more to protect the lives of people in Britain. When I spoke to the Conservative party, I took victims along with me. These were people who had suffered and were initially too afraid to report the crimes against them to the police. This lack of reporting, and the severity of what was happening, moved the party and David Cameron. By then I'd written a book about my experiences, which I called *Shame*. I asked David Cameron to read it, and to make a change to protect both men and women. Even though the consultation with various groups was a long arduous process, I continued banging the drum for freedom, as I believe it's the public who ultimately have the power to make a difference.

I continued to get my message out there by hitting the streets and asking people to fill in postcards with messages of support and a statement about why a new law had to be introduced. As a result, huge sacks of cards were delivered to Downing Street.

After the election, I urged the Conservative party, who were now in government, to get some perspective on what was happening within the Asian community. I have fought this battle for more than 20 years now and a significant milestone has finally been reached. As of June of 2014, it is a criminal act to be forced into a marriage in the UK.

Feelings of peace, relief and victory engulfed me when I heard this news, but still the work continues. My own experiences, and the tragic death of my sister, provoked a passion within me. Young people should not be caught up in a situation where they live in fear. Life is to be lived, and to live looking over your shoulder in constant fear is not acceptable.

Without question, there will always be people and circumstances that test the strength of your will. However, if it is stronger than the fears you encounter then you can and will inspire others. Nirvana - which means enlightenment - has been achieved by lifting people from the depths of fear and into a world of inspiration and possibility. I love nothing more than listening to stories of courage, as they provide the measuring stick for us to know that we are making a difference to people's lives.

Recently, evidence of our work greeted me in Canada. While waiting for my passport to be returned at an airport in Ottawa, the lady behind the screen asked:

'Are you Jasvinder Sangehera?'

'Yes,' I replied.

'You gave me the courage and belief to leave my husband,' she said. I read your book and you inspired me. I am now free to live with my children.'

As I continued my work presenting around the UK, a member of one audience came over to say thank you. Nearly a decade earlier, she'd been one of the first teenagers that Karma Nirvana had helped release from the clutches of fear. As she described what had happened since we last met, we both welled up.

'I'm a social worker now, Jasvinder,' she said. 'You saved my life.'

Perhaps you are wondering what happened to my parents. Well, sometime after Robina's death, I started to see my mum in secret. We held our liaisons in the dark to avoid the shame. After that, her health declined rapidly and she passed away to cancer. I was at her side as she said her last words, which were, 'Robina, I come to you now.'

My father took care of Robina's son, Sunny. I saw Dad too and tried to rebuild our relationship. My only disappointment is that he would not attend my graduation ceremony. He was still bound by the fear of shame. After his death, and as I collected his belongings, I found a framed picture of me in my cap and gown behind his bedroom door.

Seeing the photo reminded me that we are the ones who ultimately decide. Do you want to live in fear or have a life rich from fulfillment? Stay true to your aspirations. They are the freedoms that come with birth, and they are available to each human being. Know that help is available. If I can do it, you can too!

I walked down the hill towards Bramley train station more slowly than I'd walked up it. Stunned and mesmerised by Jasvinder's story, what shone through was her belief and persistence. It's almost unbelievable that she had to wait four years for the first call to the helpline she created, and it's really inspiring how she kept driving forward a change in the law in order to protect others.

Her book *Shame* is a no holds barred account of her life. She signed a copy for me with the words:

'To Antony, I hope my journey inspires you.'

It did. Her story was an accumulation of what I had learned so far. Her passion had proved greater than her fears and her persistence had shown that you are never too old to start learning or believing in yourself. Jasvinder reminded me that we all have doubts and we all shed tears, no matter how strong we are. More importantly, I learned from her how important it is to concentrate on <u>what you believe</u>, not on what others think.

Listening to Jasvinder's story had been like placing an ice cube in boiling water; the remaining doubts about sharing my story melted away instantly.

Previously, I had thought about how I was going to write my own personal story. How would I tell it? Did I have the courage to share the details? After speaking to Susan just a few weeks earlier, I knew that her idea to include my journey was a good one. But this wouldn't stop the twinge of fear. I was nervous about exposing my life and frailties; the fact that I'd been dumped with no answers, had a failing business and financial challenges.

I knew that mustering the courage to tell my story was going to be hard. If I'm honest, I was worried about what other people would think. But, after listening to Jasvinder reveal all about her upbringing, her family, her sister and her relationships, I knew it could be done and that I was going to do it.

On the way home, I sat on the train and realised I'd made another small error. I'd accidentally got on the slow train that stopped at every station between Leeds and Manchester. This meant an extra hour of travel, but never mind, I thought positive and opened a can of beer. *Why not?* I thought. It's nearly Christmas. The passengers around me seemed to have the same idea.

During the Christmas break, I cherished the time to plan, think and plot my next phase. I decided to limit the 40 stories to 20.

Originally, the stories were isolated and were only going to be around four pages each. However, they had all swelled to beyond 10. It felt right. My book was evolving and growing naturally, in the same way that I was. Without the pressure of searching for more people to interview, I had time to write the content.

During January, February and March of 2014, I spent most of my time retracing my steps. I arranged follow up meetings with my interviewees, asking further questions to ensure that I had the correct facts, and bounced ideas back and forth in my mind.

However, I still wasn't halfway through the book and these months proved to be the most difficult. I needed to find more stories yet work with the school was intensifying. The administration of marking papers for 700 students was rumbling away as my room became a storage facility.

My writing project was always at the forefront of my mind, though. I would sit in solitude with my work when I could, and was desperate to take another step forward. The trouble was, while I loved being in school, talking all day kills the amount of time you have to make progress. When I came home, I'd lean my head against the magnolia wall to try and think. I had done this so much, while balancing my laptop on my lap, that a patch was starting to form where the paint had worn away. Many times I'd slip into sleep, or into a meditation by accident, only to discover that this was when I was at my most creative - words would jump into my mind; sentences that shocked me with their beauty. I'd always thought of myself as crap at English, but with stories as inspiring as these, nothing was going to stop me.

Time was precious. I had no real social life or a relationship. Life was just incessant thinking, writing, printing and rewriting. It had to be this way to really progress.

As you know, everyone has commitments: work, family, sports, friends, and so on. There are only a limited number of hours in the day, and this is why I needed to make a sacrifice and choose the book over the many temptations that came my way.

Don't get me wrong; sometimes I struggled. It was far from easy, especially because I was on my own. I'd often experience a drought of ideas and will. There were times when I thought of the past, there were times of sadness and frustration and times when I thought, *what am I doing?*

On occasion, I felt frustrated, and this is when I reflected on what I had learned, particularly regarding the benefits of focusing on the positive solution, which I'd gleaned from Clarence's story. When I reflected on the journeys of the people featured in this book, I realised that everyone is human. There are challenges when striving for any goal or overcoming any adversity - it's life. There are also good points, too.

In particular, on February 14 2014 - the day of love - it was confirmed that my goal of supporting a school in Kenya could be realised. The Moonlight School in Dagoretti, Nairobi, was to become the hub and it was going to be called IF I CAN DO IT, YOU CAN TOO – THE SCHOOL! Calvin had been true to his word and introduced me to the Head Teacher, Aluda Samson. Thus, my vision of creating opportunities for young people was born.

Each month, I have helped where I can to provide a little money and support for the school. To see the difference just a little help can make is immensely fulfilling. It's incredible to watch students waving books and saying thank you via a video message. And I want you to know that by buying and reading this book, you are contributing, too. I am donating 20% of the proceeds I make from sales to the school.

Happy and with purpose, it was time to get back on track. After trying to balance so many activities in the first part of the year, a clearing opened for me to continue interviewing people, and here Zoe Humphries helped again. This time I was off to see Rita Hunter.

Rita Hunter – Don't fear it, fight it

On a drizzly March morning, I walked into the Marriott Hotel in Liverpool city centre, puzzled as to why it was so dark. I slid into a dark maroon leather couch and watched updates on Sky News. It was around 9am and grim, grey clouds reflected on the large windows to my right.

Turning from the TV, I observed men with suitcases taking long gulps of coffee. They all looked glazed and glum. No doubt they were about to go to their first appointment of the day or head off on a long drive somewhere. *Thank God I am not part of that lifestyle anymore*, I thought.

Just a few seconds later, Rita walked in through the bar area and I saw her scanning the room trying to find me. I'd first met Rita around Christmas time 2013, but had only heard a snippet of her story. I remember her first words to me: 'Why me?' She said this in a gentle way, as if she felt unworthy of sharing her tale after hearing about the other stories that were to feature in the book. But I knew then that she possessed an incredible spirit for life.

Standing at just over 5 ft tall, and with blonde hair, Rita's broad smile lit up the room. She was also immaculately dressed and oozed professionalism. But underneath the bonnet of Rita's character lied strength and a natural Scouse (Liverpool) humour. She told me about growing up in the Dovecot area of Liverpool, in Adcote Road, and some of the experiences she'd had on the local council estates. She was so genuine and funny. The 'Why me?' was about to be answered…

Rita Hunter

The optimism of New Year's Day always affected me - new year, new start. On this particular one, I balanced making cups of tea with cooking the breakfast, careful to avoid the crackling hot oil that popped in the frying pan.

My dreary eyes stared into space, but my trance-like state was interrupted by soft footsteps creeping down the staircase. A shadow hovered in the doorway behind me. Turning around, I saw my dad, a proud man who never wanted to worry anyone. He was a man's man and worked hard as a steel erector, toiling away in all weathers. This was a time before health and safety regulations, when many would risk their lives walking along planks of wood to get from one place to the next. Dad's claim to fame during his career was tightening the metal wires that secured the Liver Birds, the symbols of Liverpool, to their position overlooking the waterfront.

But now Dad had some shocking news.

'Your mother is terminally ill and does not have long to live,' he said.

Cancer is a vicious disease, we all know that, but back in the 1980s so many questions occupied my mind. Where does this disease come from? Where is the cure?

In my family, cancer was unrelenting, and although it affects people everywhere, it felt personal. The disease seems to feed off the negative spirit and the natural sadness of the slave it has chosen. This time, it had chosen my mother.

I was 26 and that fateful New Year's Day in 1981, would lead to a time in my life that I will never forget. My mum was such a kind and gentle soul, and she always saw the good in people. She'd worked in a number of factories during the second world war and I was always suspicious of those places. What did they generate? How did they affect people who worked there?

Later in her life, she took on the role of the neighbourhood matriarch. People would flock from the street where we lived to seek her calming and soothing advice, always over a cup of tea. I admired her tough character and how she braved the physical and emotional pain of her illness. She was so tough that she carried on through stage one of her cancer without going to the doctors. She thought that an aspirin and a cup of tea could solve anything.

Whenever she bent over, she would hold her back in pain and I caught glimpses of the red rashes on her neck and legs. The lumps and bumps were trying to burst through her skin, like gremlins trying to break free. She had kept them hidden to try and protect us - that was Mum. However, as the pain intensified, she became confined to the home. The cold reality was that she was being ravaged by cervical cancer.

Inheriting her strength and being the oldest came with a degree of responsibility. Looking out for the family while holding down a job as a travel agent was stressful at times. The journey to work, from Liverpool to Southport, took 40 minutes and it was my chance to escape. I would pull over on the Formby Bypass and release my emotions. Looking in the tiny rectangular mirror attached to my sun visor, I'd see my tears become polluted with foundation and mascara. All I could do was pull myself together and be strong, like my mum.

There was a certain irony in my job. I'd pack people off to exotic destinations while rain crashed against the shop window. One day, when my car was in the garage, it felt like oceans were pouring down from the heavens. Running from train to bus and from bus to home, I squelched when I walked and cold water ran down my neck. *Thank God I'm home*! I thought when I opened the front door.

Entering the kitchen was a relief. Mum was looking out of the window as if mesmerised.

'Look at the state of me, I'm drowned,' I said 'What a horrible day!'

I'll never forget Mum's reply.

'I would love to walk in the rain,' she said.

Her statement sent a shiver down my spine. Experiences that many feel are an inconvenience are actually a pleasure to some. From that moment on, I made a conscious decision never to complain about the small stuff again.

Continuing our struggle, the darkness of 1981 was drawing to a close. As the leaves fell from the trees, hope fell from my heart. It was now October – the month my mum passed away aged just 54.

The loss of someone so close left a void in all our lives. Our home became a strange place. It was almost ghostly because such an important person had passed on. We'd shared so many special memories and sometimes I walked into the kitchen expecting Mum to be there. On several occasions, I almost called out her name. I used to phone her every day from the office, forgetting that she was no longer there to pick up.

Responsibility fell on me to help Dad and my younger siblings, but we were a strong bunch - you have to be to face cancer and its effects; although I must admit I was not expecting its return just a decade on.

My younger sister Pauline was naturally shy and barely 5ft feet tall. Like our mother, she loved nothing more than a cup of tea. She adored her children, wore her heart on her sleeve and always put others before herself.

In 1991, she became cancer's next victim. I vividly recall sitting outside on a bench with her in Huyton Village, near our home. The day was so cold that our breath was visible in the air. By this point Pauline was in a wheelchair and wrapped in blankets. Her wafer thin skin was so fine that a paper cut could have hit bone. It was the first time she had wanted to discuss her cancer, and her words would come to haunt me, as our mother's had.

'Rita, I don't want to die, I want to live,' she sobbed.

I was heartbroken. However, the cancer didn't care and it spread. My sister died, aged just 34, leaving behind four beautiful children. Through my pain and sadness, it is those children who have made me proud. They have gone on to flourish in their respective careers, despite losing their mother so young in their lives.

After Pauline's death, I tried to continue with my life. My experiences had taught me how precious and precarious our existence is.

At this point I was married to Charlie and our only son James was a year old. It had been hard running Pauline back and forth to Clatterbridge Hospital while James was so young, but I'd done it willingly.

Following any bereavement, it takes a long time to return to normality, and maybe there isn't such a thing as normality, just a more settled routine.

I loved being a mum, and always will, and I loved my work, but I wasn't thinking of trying to go any further in my career. I didn't possess any big ambitions and chose to work hard while having a laugh with the girls. A few years after Pauline's death, the regional manager of the company I worked for, Tim Smith, decided to move on.

'You should apply for the post,' he told me.

He was encouraging, supportive and adamant that I was right for the job. This injection of faith encouraged me to apply.

To my surprise, I got the job and was now in charge of 24 shops around the country. A few years later, and now with a different employer, I was spending most of my life on the motorway driving the length and breadth of the UK. By this time, I was a director in charge of all the company's shops. I couldn't believe this was me!

I now had a corporate lifestyle, which involved long hours, a sore bum from driving and service station lunches. In the winter, I woke up in the dark and drove home in the dark, but I loved my job. Then one morning, I woke up and experienced a strange discomfort in my legs. They were red raw and sore to the touch, as if I had been sunbathing without sun cream. I was also sore down there and I instinctively thought that I had thrush.

Living in the talons of cancer had taught me many lessons. I had watched my mother and sister's pain and their battle to get on with life. They didn't visit the doctor's right away, preferring to ignore their symptoms until the last minute. My attitude was different. I knew deep down that I needed to see a doctor.

I was nervous as I sat in reception waiting to be called in to see the gynaecologist. The creaking of the door revealed a male doctor, who welcomed me into his room. I felt slightly embarrassed and thought, *why are they always good looking*?

Forgive me - this is my humour. I have to look on the bright side of life.

This trait would be a necessity as it took two weeks to find out the results of the tests I underwent. Waiting made me feel so helpless. I endured many sleepless nights, when memories from the past knocked at the door again. I was a similar age to my mother when she was diagnosed.

There is something about hospital waiting rooms. The wait allows you to stew in your own thoughts. Charlie came with me and was at my side throughout, but he was agitated and worried. He's 6'2", with a heavy build, but there was nothing he could do to help me when the doctor's door opened.

'What's the prognosis?' I asked straight away.

The doctor got straight to the point and told me that I had vulva cancer. I'd never heard of it, but hearing the world cancer again made me burst into tears.

Charlie was upset and frustrated. He was in the fire service and it's in his DNA to be protective. I understood his frustrations because cancer takes you into a whole new realm; it's nothing like saving someone from a burning building. He couldn't provide any answers and this ate away at him.

I had to be strong and I asked Mr Kingston, my gynaecologist, to explain what the treatment would be. He drew a diagram and told me that the cancer was in one of the vulva lips. He said that while it hadn't reached the other lip or the clitoris, they would do a mapping exercise to make sure it hadn't spread.

'I'm confused,' I said. 'I thought the clitoris was a figment of a woman's imagination.'

The nurse burst out laughing, but Mr Kingston looked aghast.

'That's just her way of coping, Doctor,' Charlie explained. 'With humour.'

I thought about the promise I'd made to myself all those years earlier not to worry about the small stuff. Well, I tried to apply the same principal here. The next step was an operation to remove part of my vagina. I felt like an alien as a multitude of tubes flowed into my body. I'm an independent woman who loves my social life, but I was laid up in a hospital bed with a mind that raced at the same speed as a normal working day. Nurses washed and bathed me, and as the water spiralled down the plughole, I felt my identity flush down alongside it.

Rather than feeling sorry for myself, I focused on getting out of hospital and recuperating at home. I spent over six weeks recovering from the operation and couldn't wait to get back to work again. I'd been given a promising prognosis so I concentrated on putting my ordeal behind me and getting on with life. I soon slipped back into my old routine: delivering results, meeting targets and enjoying life as best I could.

At home, Charlie and I were like two saucepans of water that were reaching boiling point and about to spill over. I rented a flat around the corner from our home in order to give us some space. James flitted between our two places but Charlie and I both agreed not to tell him about the cancer - we didn't want to worry him as he was a teenager and his education was important. Although he was concerned by my move, I blamed it on my thyroids and not feeling too good.

I was still living in the flat 18 months on. It was April 2007 and I opened the curtains ready for a new day. Spring was in the air and the scent of flowers and the sight of sunshine had put me in a buoyant mood. However, this left me instantaneously when I looked down at my legs and saw that the red blotches had reappeared. Please God, not again, it can't be. I rang Charlie straight away, thinking, perhaps he was right to worry so much. Maybe I was kidding myself that I could escape cancer.

I drove to the hospital immediately and another biopsy was taken there and then. By the time I received the results, I knew in my heart that the cancer had returned. I underwent another operation to remove part of my vagina, which left me feeling mutilated. This illness wanted me, and although the cancer was removed, it felt like a cockroach that wouldn't die. Just six months later, this horrible, disgusting disease returned for a third time.

Meanwhile at work, a board meeting in Yorkshire would mark the end of my career. I stood up to present and the usual squabbling between colleagues began. I felt sick and was battling to stay in control of my emotions. Mistakes were happening and there are strict rules in the travel industry. The disagreement was over a poster. It was out of date, but the people on the board didn't comprehend the magnitude of the error. As I tried to explain that you couldn't market posters with out of date offers on them, I became exasperated. *Bollocks to this*, I thought, and quit right there and then. Closing the lid of my laptop, I also closed the lid on my career. Yes, it was nice to have a company car and phone but cancer had me realise that <u>life really is too short</u>.

Once I'd made the decision, I felt a huge sense of relief. I'd driven along many motorways, wasted too much time sacrificing my life for my job. I was scared but I thought quitting was the right thing to do. However, as soon as I got home, I felt apprehensive about my decision. How was I going to pay the bills? I was renting a flat by myself after all. Charlie would think I'd gone mad.

At home, I found a piece of paper and a pen and wrote a list of what I enjoyed doing. The first things I put down were:

1. Having a chat over a cup of tea and discussing holidays.

2. Meeting new people.

I had spent many years behind the scenes number crunching and working towards targets. But my strength was my ability to talk to people and build relationships. As I continued to write, the ink on my sheet of paper was constructing a jigsaw: a vision of how my life was going to be. It was my job to pull the pieces together and once I'd done this, I bought a travel agency franchise.

Buying into another model meant I could receive support. It was commission based, so I only earned if I sold a holiday, with 40% going to the franchise owner. Oh no, what was I doing? I had given up a great salary, a car and the security of a job. However, I knew within my heart of hearts that I wanted to stay true to my vision on the piece of paper, and I trusted myself. I may not have had a database, but I did have self-belief. I wrote down the names of everyone I knew and sent them a personal letter with five business cards. The letter advised them that I was now running my own business and that I needed their help to make it work. I asked them to spread the message and to give the cards to people who might require my expertise.

I was in my early 50s, but I had a newfound determination to fight. I was adamant that life was going to be better. I was in control and taking tentative steps towards freedom. Even though I had not served a customer for many years and had to retrain, I did it with a smile on my face. That was until cancer returned for a fourth time. Seriously, I couldn't believe my luck.

I underwent another stint in hospital and another part of my vagina was removed. It was time to change. After talking to Charlie we decided that I needed to leave the apartment and move back to the family home. I was sad to leave my beautiful place behind, but I was equally happy to return home.

Aged 55, while still fighting and winning against cancer, I set up on my own, free from the franchise. Charlie thought the cancer had got inside my head. In his logical and ordered brain, I was mad and he fried in his own frustration. Well, what else was I going to do? I was not about to sit at home and waste away watching Jeremy Kyle and Loose Women.

It was exiting to start a business at my age, but it was also a challenge. Charlie and his friend Steve transformed my garage into work premises and I splattered paint on the walls and surrounded myself with memories from the past, hanging up black and white photographs of my parents. I furnished the room with two pine desks, one for my son James, who became part of the business.

It was during the creation of my business that I began to read personal development books. I loved the bestselling self-help book *The Secret* by Rhonda Byrne as it allowed me to see life from a new perspective. I knew I had a positive outlook, but that was about to be tested yet again.

I woke up one morning in terrible pain. The area around my clitoris was swollen and very painful. My upbeat nature had been decimated. It crossed my mind that this could be the end. Barely able walk, going to the toilet felt like giving birth, only this time with sharp glass thrown in, too. I went straight to the hospital, and there was no waiting for an appointment card. The biopsy was carried out immediately by Dr Kirwin, a tall doctor in his mid-40s. He acted quickly. This type of cancer is very aggressive and spreads quickly, which is why there was no time to waste.

The procedure was carried out with no anaesthetic, just a numbing injection. I gritted my teeth so hard that I could have worn away the enamel, and I nearly broke Charlie's hand through squeezing it so hard.

Two weeks later the biopsy confirmed that the cancer had returned once again.

'I am so sorry Rita, we will have to remove your clitoris,' Dr Kirwin said.

Now I didn't use it much, but it was nice to know that it was there. Joking at the time took the edge off the news. However, it couldn't prevent the surge of sadness I felt; this was all a bit much for me. Almost immediately after being given the results, I was taken into hospital to have the operation. The following morning I woke up in such incredible pain and feared for my life, my family and my business.

Doubts plagued my every waking moment. I kept wondering whether I was going to live. I had seen what cancer had done to my loved ones, and it was obviously not leaving me alone. To make matters worse, I had to miss out on an all expenses paid trip to Mauritius. I couldn't fly because of the stitches. Any movement made me feel like I was being sliced in two. I realised it was time to tell James what was going on.

Sitting at my desk in preparation for the worst conversation of my life, my friend Margaret rang to see how I was coping. The answer was not well. Crying down the phone to her, I'd lost all hope. All the strength and experience I had accumulated over the years had deserted me. My sister's words on that cold day in 1991 came back to me. This time, though, they were coming from my lips.

'I don't want to die. I don't want to leave my family.'

James was only 16 when the cancer first stuck, and now he was almost 19. It's an age full of choices and yet he was also vulnerable. Charlie and I hadn't wanted to worry him, but this time things were different. It had returned too many times and there was no guarantee that it wouldn't return again.

James' initial reaction was one of anger.

'I am part of this family as well,' he said.

He was right and I was so sorry that we hadn't told him earlier. However, there is never a good time to break such news.

With the help of Christine, my Macmillan nurse, I eventually got back on track. It was hard losing my clitoris because I felt that it was the last bastion of my femininity. I'd had a hysterectomy at 40 due to abnormal cells, so that part of me had long gone.

Charlie had witnessed the horrors of what cancer can do. During his time in the fire service he'd witnessed things the human eye should never have to see, but now he had retired so at least that stressful part of his life was over. However, he looked on the negative side of life and worried constantly that the cancer was going to return. With hindsight, this was natural. 12 months later, it did.

My cancer had returned for a fifth time. My heart sank as I was not expecting it. This time I didn't experience any pain or symptoms, its return was revealed by a routine check-up. Emotionally, this tore me apart.

The cancer was inside so it wasn't visible, but it was in the same area between my legs. The doctors did a mapping exercise to work out how the cancer could potentially spread through my lymph nodes and consequently removed the ones from the upper part of my legs. Rest and recuperation followed and I was lucky in that I didn't lose any customers - they supported me through this new battle.

James held the fort and I returned to work quickly, resuming my role helping people find their dream holidays. James inspires me and brings a new dimension to the business, as well as a new customer base. He understands social media - I don't have a clue!

In the past 18 months, our business has grossed £1m in sales. I report this not to impress, but to show that it can be done. You can follow your dreams, overcome challenges and give up the work that you don't enjoy.

My attitude since the day I resigned is to just go for it. I will find another job if my business doesn't work. Life really is too short to spend most of it worrying about what might happen.

To have my most sensitive body parts sliced off could have killed me, but beyond pain you can take a pen and paper and write the story of how you want to live. There may be many challenges ahead, but it is much easier to face them when you are armed with passion.

On December 18 2013, I received the all clear again and it's been two years since the final operation. There are now months in between check-ups rather than weeks.

I realise how lucky I am when I spend time with James and we sit and have a laugh or I witness his enthusiasm for the business.

To be able to spend all day with your child is a living dream and we really do appreciate our time together. We now have another director on board, Diane Cannon, and together we are working on an expansion plan.

Through my personal journey, I have learnt the importance of acting when your intuition niggles at you to do so. Your health is your wealth and you must seek guidance from a doctor as soon as any concerns arise. The love and help of family and friends is important. Mine rallied round and this really helped, so it's important not to push them away. In addition, you must laugh and do what you love. If I can do it, you can too.

There is so much to admire about Rita. She is so much fun and such an inspiration.

We sat drinking another cup of coffee as she told me about her trips away with the girls, including one to Las Vegas with her friend and business partner, Diane Cannon. Rita laughed as she advised me of Di's unique spin on the saying: What happens in Vegas stays in Vegas. Her mantra is: What happens in Vegas goes on Facebook!

Cancer affects everyone at some point, either directly or indirectly. Hearing about Rita's fight gave me enormous hope. There is no question, however, that there are many cases when cancer spreads to places where it is difficult to operate, which brings limited hope. But what I learned from Rita - and I kick myself because I have made this mistake many times - is not to moan about the small stuff and waste time. She reminded me of the importance to live each day. Something as simple as the rain falling on your head is a joy if you allow it to be. The other message here is:

A couple days later, my mum and dad were moaning about a cup I'd left lying around. I almost pulled the same twisted face I used as a teenager. *Here we go again*! I thought. It's amazing how a little bit of moaning can set you off on the wrong track if you LET IT. Then I replayed Rita's story in my mind and wrote down the following:

1. Bollocks to the small stuff.

What Rita had experienced would test anyone. I was going through the uncertainty of my dad's cancer diagnosis, but Rita had faced this five times. Her story also reminded me so much of my own corporate lifestyle, which had involved sitting on the motorway at 6.30am. I was grateful that I had left this behind me. It's important to know that you can do the same. You can say bollocks to it, and look for other options.

I love this line from the film *Pinocchio*:

'Always let your conscious be your guide.'

Rita had used hers when she'd felt that something in her body wasn't right. She'd also understood when enough was enough and it was time to quit her job. Despite the cancer returning, she'd had the strength to build a booming business in her 50s. Well, why not? Her story provides great inspiration and it is a big 'up yours' to cancer.

2. Take a piece of paper and write.

If life is crap, then take a pen and paper and write out what it is you want. Rita's method of doing this validated my own beliefs (covered earlier in this the book), particularly with Andy Bounds. He made a decision to become what he wanted. Tim Reddish also delivered the same advice, stressing the importance of being clear on what it is you want and being responsible for making it happen.

John Haynes – Fly with the Eagles

'Alright my hero,' John said as a fine drizzle of rain fell on our heads. It was 7am on March 25 2014. Metal roller shutters hummed as they clanked into action to reveal 1 Maryland Street yet again.

During the two years I'd known John Haynes, I'd never seen him down. He is abundant with enthusiasm and excitement. He reminds me of the character Kris Kringle (played by Sir Richard Attenborough), in *Miracle on 34th Street*. Imagine him with the same glasses but without the beard. He, like Kris, is a man everyone loves, although one thing he is guarded about is his age. I think people are still trying to guess it, but from his experience and silver hair it's clear that he could have retired a long time ago – if he had so wished.

Sometimes I would receive text messages from him in the early hours, or I'd see Facebook posts he'd written at three and four in the morning. He regularly got up early to go jogging, and would run around parks or along the promenade near his Liverpool home.

I settled into John's long green couch and proceeded to tell him how far I'd progressed since I'd last seen him back in August 2013. We chatted for sometime until he asked:

'Where do you want me to start?'

'From the beginning, growing up,' I replied.

'Whoa, you've got me thinking now, lad,' he said enthusiastically.

After a few seconds and a sip of hot water, John began to tell me about his own journey.

John Haynes

Falling bombs crashed the foundations of the family home and my mum cowered under the stairs, cradling my older siblings. This was their place of safety, and I can only imagine the terror they experienced.

I was a war baby and growing up, I was enthralled by my mother's stories. She was strong; she had to be. It was uncertain whether my father would return from fighting overseas.

Jack Haynes, my father, was born in 1914 and spent four years during the second world war fighting in far and distant lands. He hadn't had an easy start in life. He was sent to a boys' home for stealing a loaf of bread - all because he was starving. His parents were so embarrassed that they didn't attend his court hearing. Aged just 10 years old, my father had to grow up fast. I would need to do the same, and my early years seemed to pass quickly.

The cows in the field adjacent to our house would wake me up of a morning. They'd come right up to my window, the bells that hung around their necks jangling as they performed the role of my alarm clock. They were a reminder that it was time for school.

I was a thicko (stupid) and was reminded of this every day in class. I was no good at maths, English, or any subject.

'Haynes! What are you doing boy?' the teacher would cry with anger.

'Sorry, Sir,' I'd reply fearfully, fully aware of what was coming next.

The apologies didn't matter as the whooshing sound of the cane sliced through the air, cracking and stinging my palm. I tried to contain the pain as my hand throbbed and glowed red. It felt hot enough to melt the ice outside.

I was a stupid child, though, worthy of nothing and there to make the others look good. It caused distress to my family, particularly my mother, and the only option for me was to work.

I left school at 14, with a plan to learn how to become a cabinet maker.

What awaited me was the industrial heartbeat of Kirkby, Merseyside and the Hygena kitchen factory. Setting off at 7am on my bike, I wouldn't return until six in the evening. The work left me exhausted and unmotivated, despite being part of a team of 1,200.

The factory was built on a huge, imposing site and the constant industrial noise didn't bring out the best in me. I had so little confidence that I couldn't even look people in the eye, preferring to mumble my way through sentences.

'What are you saying, Haynesy?'

This is what people would scream through the buzzing sounds of machinery.

I didn't have a clue what I was saying. My thoughts were focused on escape and sampling the taste of ale. Come the evening, the lads and I would venture out into the town, determined to enjoy our youth. The only place I came alive was in the pub.

In the early 1960s, The Beatles saved many people. Their songs would bounce from the underground walls of the Cavern Club.

Condensation and sweat would drip from the low ceilings, landing in my pint of lager. I didn't care. I was free. Buoyed by their lyrics, my friends and I would sing Beatles' songs on the bus all the way home. We weren't the only ones. Other passengers would be screaming at the top of their lungs, too. They were youngsters like us, in love with writing their names in the condensation on the windows. We were so excited that we didn't want the journey to end. On many occasions, we'd walk across to the other side of the street to get a bus back into town, just to sing again. It was freedom from the grind of work, inspiration in times of darkness.

Soon I was back at work though, and after years of performing the same job, the realisation dawned. I was a failure yet again - incapable of working on practical projects.

In fact, the only aspect of work where I excelled was football. I managed the Hygena football team and loved encouraging people to play their best. Sometimes I'd watch through my fingers as the tackles propelled players through the cold air and into a mud pit.

'Don't you dare take me off, Haynesy, or I'll have you.'

That was the cry from Big Dan, and I didn't dare replace him with another player - he was a mad man!

Standing on the sidelines, unaware of the white lines, we fought other local teams, won cups and drank ale from them. After a sprinkling of ice cold water from an intermittent shower we were off again - this time to the pub, still with mud splattered all over us. For the first time in my life, I'd found something I was good at - coaching.

After many years of working for Hygena, I was pulled away from the coalface of the shop floor. I was more of a hindrance than anything. Then a new opportunity arose to become social secretary, with responsibility for organising events that would generate a feel good factor within the company.

Invited into the management office, my next job was to deliver a speech to a canteen crammed full of expectant staff. For almost 18 years, the sea of faces that stood before me had been my family, and they revelled in witnessing me attempt to deliver some crucial news.

'I'm sorry everyone, I've got something important to say,' I began from the elevated position of a wooden stage.

'Stop winding us up and get on with it,' my colleagues cried. 'We're not working weekends without proper pay.'

The hecklers cupped their hands around mouths as they continued with their barrage.

'You don't understand, it's all over,' I said.

'Shut up, Haynes and get on with it, lad,' came the cries from the audience.

The directors sheepishly sloped off the stage, sensing violence.

Then reality dawned on the masses.

'He's not joking,' someone shouted.

I proceeded to advise my friends on where they could collect their redundancy money. The factory was shutting down and we had to leave within 48 hours.

I honestly believe that many people died of a broken heart following that fateful day. Work was our only connection to the past and tears trickled down the wrinkled faces of the men and women who had spent their lives working for Hygena. Some had worked there for almost 40 years, and they were practically stuck to the fabric of the building. Many never worked again.

Football was the glue; the one part of life that held ours spirits together. With no jobs, the community begged us to keep the football team alive. Stupidly, I agreed to pay the rent for the community centre so that we could continue playing, laying down my own redundancy money. I did this only because another large organisation had promised it would take over the fees. A year later it pulled out, leaving me penniless. Uproar ensued and the community couldn't believe the way I'd been treated. With the last penny gone, the pitch became overgrown and our decade of success in football ended. The team folded.

And so a new sort of existence began. Shivering cold, I'd stand in the dole queue in the middle of winter waiting to collect my money. I could feel the anger and frustration in the air as thousands waited to receive what was barely enough to survive on. With most of the city out of work, we shuddered like a group of penguins pinned together, trying to gain heat. Workers with sympathetic faces sat behind the metal guards of the unemployment office, asking the same old questions:

'What's your name and address?'

'Are you working?'

'Are you looking for work?'

Having to stand for hours to be made to feel worthless over and over again was a humiliating experience.

'Oh Mr Haynes, I see that you left school at 14,' a patronising young unemployment officer said to me. In other words, my life was over.

Now in my early 30s, I would sit on the living room floor in my house in complete despair. Upstairs, my wife struggled to cope with the pressure caused by my mistakes. With my head in my hands, I tried to come to terms with the guilt of raising our daughter in poverty.

I'd be reminded of my stupidity every day, with each pounding knock at the door from the bailiffs. Eventually, my parents came to the rescue and paid my bills. Embarrassed by my deficiencies, the only place I could turn to for work was a commission-based role selling life insurance. I'd walk the streets trying to collect premiums from people who had nothing.

My home visits were met with angry scowls. When I had finished collecting money and trying to sell a new policy, I would head back to the office to get paid - but on many occasions I would never make it. Often I'd be robbed, getting punched and kicked to the ground in the process. Desperate times called for desperate measures. People stumbled along, drowning their misery with alcohol, and jumping on any opportunity to get a bit of extra change. Left to pick myself up off the pavement, blood trickling down my only clean white shirt, I then had the task of funding the company's losses with my own money.

My daughter Joanne would experience the harsh times with me. On many occasions she came with me to work, particularly during the school holidays. She was forced to see the negative side of life and witness the cold rejection I faced as another door of a potential customer was slammed in my face.

Joanne was always there through everything, and she had even accompanied me to all the football matches years earlier. She would play with the other kids outside the pub, sipping from a bottle of coke and eating a packet of crisps. She was and is my rock, the reason I kept pushing forward. And I would need all the support I could muster.

One Saturday evening, my head pounded with the smell of emulsion. Having painted all day, I slumped in front of the TV. I was tired and kept wondering, how am I going to free myself from this mess?

My wife was ill in bed and Joanne was asleep. Sat alone, I was suddenly plunged into darkness – the electricity had been cut off. This was my dark night of the soul, the most depressing point in my life.

My job, it seemed, was to get beaten up - sometimes physically but mostly mentally through the rejection I faced. That was until I moved to another company. Now my job was to sell to those who had larger budgets. To do this, I needed some extra training.

'John, what are you doing to improve? How many books have you read?' asked a man, whom I secretly named 'The Business Guru'.

'None,' I admitted.

He looked at me in disgust. 'You mean you do nothing to help yourself earn more?' he growled aggressively.

'No Sir, I'm thick. I'm John Haynes.'

But the Guru had a point. Scrambling enough money together, I purchased one book about sales and another about personal development, which was written by the late motivational speaker, Zig Ziglar. Like an actor reciting his lines, I would stand at front doors nervously repeating what I'd read. This process continued for weeks until my confidence finally began to grow. When I got my first sale, I realised that my hard word had paid off.

The more I earned, the more I learned and purchased books. Instead of dismissing training, I would read for 30 minutes every morning and go over what I'd learned in the evening.

In contrast, my home life deteriorated and my wife and I divorced. Without the routine of family life, and with money in my pockets, it didn't take long for me to start splashing my cash in bars and restaurants. I invited everyone I knew out for a good time and my credit card was always behind the bar. But the stress and strain of years of deprivation and trying to provide was about to catch up with me.

One night I collapsed behind a restaurant. Blood flowed from my nose, mouth and ears, forming a stream of red between the cracks in the stones.

Luckily for me, my friend Alan Phillips saw me lying on the floor like a drunk and scooped me up. He frantically flagged down a cab and took me to hospital.

Waking up, I didn't know what day it was. I asked for the lights to be switched off even though it was 10am and they weren't even on. This only compounded the worried looks on my friends' faces.

'John, are you OK?' they asked in unison.

Still groggy and disoriented, I was diagnosed with a perforated ulcer.

The doctor sat at my bedside to explain the full seriousness of what had happened to me.

'John, you are lucky to be alive,' he said. 'You died three times and how you came through I will never know.'

A scar ran from my chest to my stomach, reminding me how grateful I should be. The doctor told me how stress can cause ulcers. Aged 42, this was the wake up call I needed.

As my income started to rise, my obsession with reading and trying to improve gave me more confidence. One of my former managers, Shay McGrath, had landed a better job with Royal Insurance and got me an interview with the company.

However, my past was still affecting my present.

'Look at your education, John,' the senior manager said to me during the interview. 'Really, we can't have you working here. The Royal is an environment for high flyers and graduates.'

However, I had Shay on my side. Blessed with confidence and oozing charisma, he persuaded the management to give me a chance. I went on to outperform the very best. Even so, I was still labelled a 'scouse (person from Liverpool) thicko'.

Just a couple of years on, the opportunity of a management position presented itself. This was my chance to progress, but I still had to get through the interview process. I knew I'd have to sit through the same stupid comments I'd put up with all my life. When my lack of education came up I fought back this time, snarling:

'I am the only man who can do this, look at my work record, look at what I have achieved – no one knows this area better than me!'

Stunned by my outpouring of anger and passion, I stormed out of the interview room, only to receive a call a few days later from the manager.

'John, you've got the job,' he said.

'There's that thicko, John Haynes, he can't manage the team,' one of my rivals puffed on my first day. Many people had gone for the manager's position and I had marched into a wall of jealousy, in which even my secretary hated me.

This lion's den would put all my skills to the test. My strengths were my ability to motivate and learn by drawing mind-maps of the books I'd read. These weren't skills that were measured in the classroom when I was a child.

I read this quote by Einstein, and it had a profound effect on me.

'Everybody is a genius. But if you judge a fish by its ability to climb a tree, it will live its whole life believing that it is stupid.'

That used to be me, but no longer. I had discovered the theory of multiple intelligences, thereby freeing myself from the past.

We all have different ways of learning and school success was focused on logic, the ability to solve puzzles, or verbal reasoning. Was it any surprise I failed? I was so fearful that I couldn't communicate effectively. In my Hygena days, my coordination was so bad that I used to accidentally glue my hands together. I simply didn't possess manufacturing skills.

My ability lies in motivating people and in organisation, which is why I performed so well in football management.

This newfound awareness helped me to shine, to inspire and to achieve. Significant promotions with greater responsibility followed and I became the sales manager for the whole of Scotland.

Settled for the first time, balance was restored in my personal life. I met my partner, the beautiful Linda, through work and we moved in together. One of our first work engagements was to attend an event at Blenheim Palace, the birthplace of Winston Churchill. Surrounded by silver and gold, the finest china and huge imposing portraits, I felt uneasy and was miles outside my comfort zone.

Linda and I stood on the steps and watched as the leading directors waved like royalty from chauffeur driven cars. People filed into the banqueting hall and the buzz of chatter came to an abrupt end when the managing director stood up to address his audience, bellowing with purpose and authority.

'This company is 150 years old,' he said. 'It's time to grow and develop, and to upgrade our principals. We have hired people with the best education and overlooked others. We want people who can also achieve results and we need to change. With that in mind, we are announcing our new regional sales director, John Haynes!'

Pinned to my chair in shock, gasps rung out through the hall as the news dawned on the educated elite.

'The scouse thicko? Our new boss,' a voice from the audience squealed. Yes it was me – and I was now in charge of 1,500 people!

Staying true to my learning habits, I read books on negotiation and understood the concept of win-win. I watched on as directors abandoned their habits of continuous improvement, thinking they had reached the summit. Alternatively, I took a different approach. Now more confident than ever, I negotiated terms with the board regarding my own bonus. My salary was a lot less compared to others with greater potential for commission. The next step was to persuade the management to pay me a percentage of everyone's sales in the group. I even stated:

'If I don't get the results, you don't have to pay my bonus.'

'Are you sure, Haynes?' They glanced at each other with bemused looks on their faces.

'Absolutely!' I beamed. I was no longer the fool.

My position involved growing teams around the country, helping people who were experiencing challenges, sending flowers to those who were down and rewarding those who performed well. Results accelerated, as did the stock of the company.

'I heard the directors talking about you the other day, John,' one of my secretaries whispered one day, as if the directors were hiding in the cupboard. 'They were questioning why you are the highest paid person in the company.'

Persistence proved the trait necessary to overcome adverse times. The experiences I'd gone through with my health, divorce and lack of education would make most people resign themselves to a life of misery. I was no different. But the turning point came when I realised I had skills, it's just that they weren't the traditional ones measured by the success of an exam.

Adversity served as a test. Suffering bumps and bruises, both emotional and physical, has allowed me to steer others clear of danger. I didn't realise the significance of my journey and what

I'd learned until I took redundancy after a decade at the peak of my organisation.

I'd made enough money to go off and enjoy myself. However, it wasn't long before I got bored with the beach. The company approached me with a consultancy position coaching its teams. For me, this was a reward for the commitment I'd shown to improving myself. It was rather ironic, too. The reject that was useless and unfit to work had 'achieved revenge through achieving massive success' – this was something I'd heard Frank Sinatra quote.

I was overjoyed to be back with my old friends and inspiring and motivating again. The years passed by so quickly and after my contract expired, I was asked to deliver a short presentation.

In the audience was a wily old fox in his 80s. He was a tough Scottish man, a multi-million pound investor, and he seemed to be scouring the audience looking for his next victim. Directors and senior management were terrified. This man was the smiling assassin. If he did so much as grimace in your direction it meant you were gone, sacked. I knew I was safe as I'd moved on, but the lads I worked with whispered in my ear:

'John, he is staring at you. He's been doing it all day.'

Wagging his finger, he beckoned me towards him. His frail figure was hunched over as he sternly exclaimed.

'When an educated person dies with all their knowledge, all their hurts, skills and failures, it's like a library burning down. To be successful you need to have failed many times. Make sure your library never burns down!'

For the past 15 years, this man had watched silently as I developed from nothing to become the director of the sales force. His financial success was dependant on great people and he analysed in detail those who would make a difference. His short personal speech reminded me how I'd grown from the ugly duckling of education into a beautiful swan of skills and possibility. And it was time to share what I'd learned along the way.

As the curtains closed on my corporate career, a new musical production opened called Life Changers, which was inspired by my story and reputation for motivating people. It became the curtain raiser for my own business: The International Coaching Academy.

Travelling far and wide, I deliver qualifications in leadership and coaching in my own unique and humorous style. I started the company in 1998, when I was in my 50s. My goal was to inspire one million people. With operations in countries across the globe, coaching thousands of people, I am confident that we can do this. I live to see the smiles on the faces of the people I teach, and I teach in a style that supports all types of learning - so no one has to experience the demoralising thought that they are useless.

Nowhere has the impact of my coaching work been more profound and special than in Kikambala, Kenya, and it started by accident.

A holiday there with Linda in the late 1990s inadvertently led me along an unexpected path when I was jogging along the bright white beaches. I came to a point that led me off track into a wooded area. Clumsily brushing past plants and snapping twigs, I announced my presence. It was like a scene from *The*

Lion, the Witch and the Wardrobe as I entered a new world.

I came across some villagers draped in red gowns and wearing face paint. I stood there frozen in shock. The only word I knew was 'jambo' - a greeting that means hi. It took some time to find a person who understood English, as my knowledge of the local dialect was so limited.

I stayed longer than anticipated, learning more about their culture, all the while nervous and apprehensive as a sense of direction has never been one my strongest assets. During this time a village elder christened me 'Papa John'. We laughed and talked (with them using broken English) and remain friends to this day, some 15 years on.

Throughout my visits to Kikambala, my focus has been on seeing improvements in education. I know from my own life experiences how important it is to get a good one. Over the years, I've taken armies of Kenyan children and adults along to the beaches to teach them a host of different skills, including English.

The children always seemed happy and had broad smiles on their faces. They would travel for miles to a local school, only to find the classrooms already full to the brim. But soon the lack of education would be the least of their worries.

Who was to know that just a couple of years after my first visit to Kenya, there would be so much violence in the country. President Bill Clinton and Prime Minister Tony Blair declared Kenya a no-go area in the late 90s, but they wouldn't stop me visiting the elders there.

My heart went out to the people of Kenya when I learned what was happening there via TV and radio reports. These told of children having their arms and legs amputated as war raged between different tribes. Luckily my tribe was not at war and they smuggled me in from the airport in the dead of night. Sat in the footwell of the car, I hid wearing a balaclava to conceal my identity. This is without question one of the scariest things I have ever done.

An organised rally was due to take place the following day. As I rattled with fear, more news followed. The elders wanted me to go into centre of Mombasa, the second-largest city in Kenya, where tens of thousands of people had gathered to demonstrate. As we neared this destination, booming roars like claps of thunder could be heard for miles around. National politicians urged for calm but also vented their frustration at the lack of support from the West.

'Where are the Americans? Where are the British?' The speaker roared.

Oh no, I'm in trouble here, I thought.

The world's media pointed their cameras and microphones at the stage. I was one of only a handful of white faces in an audience of thousands, so it didn't take long for curious faces to look in my direction.

Cameras, like homing devices, came closer as the elders spoke.

'Papa John, Papa John, they want you speak. Tell world we not bad.'

Oh God, no. No, not me, I thought. I was panicking and thinking of Linda. She would go mad if she found out where I was. No sooner had I tried to quell the commotion with the masses, than a deep voice announced my name.

'John Haynes from Liverpool will now speak.'

My heart was pounding so fast it could have propelled me along the beach without my feet touching the sand. Now I understood what a boxer must experience while walking towards the ring with thousands baying for his blood. In my own case, the audience was baying for words and action.

With one deep breath, I released everything I had.

'You are great people. I have been coming here for years and this is an amazing country, but this madness has to stop. You need to come together as one, to provide the best education and future for your children, to work in harmony with each other and to improve as a nation.'

My speech came from the heart and I could have been beamed up to heaven there and then. An audience of thousands roared louder than it does when a goal is scored at Wembley. A few months on, and after many negotiations, discussions between government agencies, tribes and humanitarian groups began. Steps were taken to begin the journey towards peace.

From the fields of Kirkby to the fields of Kenya, the same principals apply. We all need a little inspiration to pull us through. I hope my story can inspire those who need the belief that they too can achieve. My mantra for life is:

'Fly with the eagles, don't scratch with the turkeys.'

To let your highest dreams soar, be free like an eagle with no resistance. Be in complete control of your direction. Don't scratch with the turkeys. These are the people who are negative, who moan and groan and will try and bring you down and keep you confined in a pen of an enclosed mind. Dream big and always, always remember that if the 'scouse thicko' can do it, you can too!

When John had finished talking, I laughed and smiled in admiration. I used to love listening to John's pre-recorded voicemail as it's completely unique and goes:

'It doesn't matter what problems you have in this world today, John Haynes is there with you, every step of the way.'

He had been there for me and I knew that his door would always be open.

It was good to have a conversation with him that was about his memories and experiences, rather than just work.

Most of our daily lives can be peppered with talk of work and projects. It's very rare to engage in a meaningful conversation with someone where you can get beneath their skin and hear all about their journey.

Many people go to the mountains and hills of the Himalayas to seek out a guru (I don't blame them either). But I was lucky. I hadn't had to travel far to learn about the power of belief.

It's a shame that so many people feel they are not good enough and therefore do not fulfil their potential. I learned that success is a word that's defined by you, not by others.

Too many times I've seen people, particularly young people, told that they can't do this and they can't do that. I reread John's story and thought, *no wonder he felt he was stupid.* He was reminded of it every day and wilted like a rose trying to survive in the blazing sun.

I did some research on the theory of multiple intelligences, which was developed by Howard Gardner, Ph.D. Professor of Education at Harvard University. His work made sense, and I could clearly think of people who feature in this book who are blessed with some of the intelligences that Professor Gardner outlined. Here are some examples of them. What do you fit into?

Bodily-Kinaesthetic

This is basically how the body moves. These are people who possess great coordination and an aptitude for sports or practical and physical jobs, such as building. Instantly this reminded me of Tim Reddish and his achievements within sport.

Musical

This is the ability to dance or sing, and to understand rhythms and timing. No doubt this was Clarence's special gift. When I reflect on my music lessons in school, this intelligence was not an option for me because I thought: *I'm rubbish at this*.

Interpersonal

These are people who can bring others together. They enjoy working in groups and motivating and inspiring. In his story, John Haynes identified this as his skill, but I also thought of Nicola Rowe, with her abilities as a teacher.

Intrapersonal

This is about understanding your own strengths and weaknesses, your emotions and your ability to self-reflect. This is one of my most natural intelligences, and it applies to Elaine Owen too.

Linguistic

Some people are great with words and languages, or have the ability to speak in public. Rick McMunn was great in this area, as was Susan Foster, who writes so beautifully.

Mathematical – Critical thinking

These people are good at maths, logic and following instructions and rules. With his superior accountancy skills, Andy Bounds fits into this category.

So as you can see, we are all different, and we all possess numerous skills. If only this theory was taught in schools. Maybe then students could be supported in understanding their strengths.

Fighting against beliefs is a part of life. John has proved this throughout his journey. Rita Hunter started her business in her 50s, while Clarence Adoo was told to get serious by a teacher when he announced his intention to play music. Ali Jagger spent time on unemployment benefits and started a business in her 40s. Tim Reddish changed career from butcher to swimmer.

Evaluate yourself. Know you are never too young or old to learn and make changes. Understand that the combination of intelligences are special and unique to each and every person. It is up to you to find the blend that makes up your character. And remember - don't scratch with the turkeys that tell you what you should do. Pursue what makes you happy.

Elaine Owen – Desire to inspire

The early evening sunshine glistened on the waterfront in New Brighton, a place I had not visited for many years. It looked good. The town had endured long periods of decline and deprivation, a fate suffered by many British seaside towns in the wake of recessions, bad weather and cheap flights abroad.

But with a splattering of modern buildings, shops and bars, it seemed that this historic seaside town had undergone a positive transformation, although one aspect hadn't changed - the sound of seagulls competing over fish and chips dropped on the floor.

Looking out towards the River Mersey, I waited in Weatherspoons for Alex Melbourne, a man I had met a few years earlier on a project to help young entrepreneurs.

Alex works in education and lives in Indonesia. It was good to see him. He is always on the move, always dressed in a suit. I'd say he resembles Sir Philip Green, who owns Topshop. He has the same hair, build and way of speaking.

I described the book to Alex, and the type of people I was searching for. He slid a business card across the wooden pub table. The name on it read Elaine Owen. It was ironic because when I arranged to meet Elaine, I discovered that she is based in New Brighton, just a couple of streets away from where I'd met Alex.

The home of Elaine's business is Vale House in Vale Park - and what a place. It's a large white Victorian building that sits in the centre of the park. Surrounded by a circle of trees, shrubs and landscaped gardens, it's almost like the hole in a dougnut. The park itself slopes on a 20 degree angle, rolling towards the banks of the River Mersey, with views of the Liverpool skyline.

I felt at home in Vale Park, there is something special about it. It's not huge, but the white Victorian house has a café, nursery and a conference space.

From initially being given Elaine's details in the autumn, it took some time to gain some freedom in our diaries for a longer dialogue.

When I arrived to meet Elaine, I was greeted with a big hug, and I instantly sensed her amazing presence. She was full of experience and knowledge and we chatted for some time until, with a deep breath, I pressed record on my laptop and settled down to listen to her incredible journey.

Elaine Owen

'White wog, white wog!' They were the cries echoing around the playground. Alone and frozen with fear in a new school, I knew those shouts were directed at me. My unusual but natural frizzy afro, along with my pale skin, attracted attention. I knew the name being chanted was a racist one.

I witnessed racism on a number of occasions back in the 1960s and 70s. The black people who were kitchen porters and deck hands on my dad's ship, where he worked as an electrical officer, were treated as second-class citizens. They were very grateful for the menial jobs they were given on board, but the white crew looked upon them with disdain. I also suffered from the same bigoted opinions – and it is those experiences that would come to shape my life.

From an early age, I used any tactic to delay going to school. When I finally got there, I was too timid to mix with the congregation of children who sat on the floor listening to stories. It was all a little overwhelming for me.

But when I got to high school, the innocence of my primary years became a distant memory as I was subjected to a barrage of name-calling.

I knew that if I told on the bullies, the pain would be greater because then I would be known as a 'snitch'. I felt that if my mum found out she would be ashamed of me, as I was not a popular child. If she thought for one moment that people considered me 'a wog', then maybe she would reject me as a second-class citizen.

'Bog brush' (toilet brush) was my new name and it's where I spent most of my time – with my frizzy hair flushed down it. I'd hear only laughter, jokes and the sound of the long chain as it was pulled. Standing frozen, water dripped from my hair. It was so cold that it trickled over my uniform and on to my skin. While the cold may have been temporary, the feelings of worthlessness penetrated much deeper - washing away all my confidence.

My teenage years would yield yet greater abuse. Growing into a larger frame, my inflated chest attracted more negative attention. At 5'3", I was short, yet I had size seven feet. The combination of my features meant I was different and the ruthless bullies would never allow me to forget it. Sunk in a heap at home, I existed in a soulless state...I didn't want to live.

I lived with my mum, grandma and sister. My sister, although younger, had completely different features that made me feel like an alien. She sailed through school as part of the popular crowd.

Dad was away at sea for long periods of time. He was the main breadwinner and I hated it when my mum went away to see him. My attachment to her was my only form of safety. One time when she left for another visit to see Dad, I decided to teach her a lesson so she would never leave me again. With Mum away, Grandma was in charge and her approach to discipline was softer. My new diet of soup without bread commenced (although my grandma didn't notice). The bread she gave me was placed in the bin or hidden in my pockets until I got outside where it was safe to dispose of it. I felt certain that my master plan would work. When Mum returned she would surely notice the difference in me and give me the attention I craved.

The change soon became noticeable. Where there had once been skin and muscle, now there was just bone. When my mum returned after a number of weeks away, I waited for her like an expectant dog. *This will teach you* I thought to myself. She walked up the path and into the house, hugged me and then went straight over to talk with Grandma. It felt like she had looked right through me, as if I was a ghost. She didn't even notice the NEW improved, slimmer version of me. All that effort to attract attention ended in the depressing conclusion that I must not be worthy of love.

Deflated and angry, I stood before the mirror, my eyes now more prominent in their bony sockets. However, some people did notice my efforts to attract more attention. For the first time in my life, girls from the popular crowd in my school year wanted to speak to me! Wow, it seemed as though becoming skinny was the way to finally gain acceptance and it felt good, although it was not my intention. I just wanted to feel loved by my mum and dad. Who was to know that a teenager who had just been accepted by the elite of the schoolyard was about to enter the world of anorexia?

Innocently, I chatted to those who wanted to know my secrets to slimming success. I walked tall and with more confidence.

Skinny was the answer and these positive new experiences fuelled my determination to be thin. How could I possibly eat again? Eating meant being called 'bog brush' and that led to humiliation. Thin meant hope, love, attention and freedom, and this is what I desired.

Standing before a full-length mirror, my reflection revealed a figure that I was still not happy with. I survived on soup, coffee, ice cubes and glasses of water, making sure I was discreet and covert. I was constantly one step ahead of my mum and grandma.

Waking up early, I would leave a dirty bowl in the sink with a couple of cornflakes strategically placed in order to trick them into thinking I'd eaten. With a smile on my face, I knew I was cleverer than my family. Lunchtime was easy; the packed lunch that had been prepared for me was emptied into the bin.

In my search for attention and love, I thought about boys and the clothes I could wear. But the constant scheming and planning left me devoid of energy and will. As this continued to escalate, it was my Grandma (whom I'd considered a pushover) who became alarmed. She pressured my mother to take action and to seek medical attention. My GP referred me to the psychiatric ward of Clatterbridge, our local hospital. The stigma and embarrassment this caused my mother was evident on her face. She walked in front of me, twisting and turning her neck, checking that no one was watching us.

Sitting alone and nervous in an adult psychiatric ward is not something I would recommend for any young teenager. I listened with curiosity as the psychiatrist told me that this was not my fault. I was not to blame, and my mother's behaviour could be described as selfish. Those words were so powerful.

An adult was agreeing with me. I used this piece of evidence like a knife to stab my mother with whenever the opportunity arose. It was my revenge and way of letting her know that I felt she was responsible for doing this to me. I wanted someone to blame, and she was the only person I could vent my anger towards.

Little did I know that my mother's pensive nature was a direct consequence of trying to keep track of my father. His seafaring days and a life of drinking and running up large bar bills caused her untold and poorly hidden stress.

I learned later that my mum would go away to see what Dad was up to. This was her attempt to protect the marriage. She wanted to reduce the risk of him spending all his earnings, leaving her unable to pay the bills.

And her responsibilities didn't stop with operating as a semi-single parent when my dad was away. As well as raising my sister and me, she was caring for her own mother. This was a full time job in itself. No wonder she was preoccupied. It was only in later years, when I became a mother myself and she shared her story, that I understood how amazing my mum was and is. I will always hold her in the highest regard and see her as an inspirational role model. She overcame adversity and single-handedly held a family together.

However, returning to the past, the revelation at Clatterbridge shocked everyone, and my secret was now exposed. My mum and grandma started watching my every move to make sure that I ate. Now forced to sit at the table like a baby in a high chair, I felt disgusting and wanted to free my swollen stomach. I dealt with this by forcing myself to be sick, unknowingly inching closer to the jaws of bulimia.

My party trick in the school playground was to take my fist and lodge it in my hipbone. This wonder delighted the girls and they purred with amazement, awe struck by my ability. So how at 15 could I ever put weight on again? The glimmer of a positive comment from the children at school meant I had to maintain my concentration camp figure. To do so meant pulling the wool over the adults' eyes again. I started wearing thick jumpers, padding the rest of me out with extra socks or tights. The planning was incessant and formed a constant dialogue in my mind.

Intense craving attacks became the norm. One evening, I woke up and crept past Mum's room. All I was focused on was quietly opening the refrigerator door. The internal lights inside stung my eyes as my body vibrated in anticipation. I gorged on food until one haunting demon was fulfilled. But in satisfying one demon, I stirred another.

'What are you doing? Why are you eating? You'll be fat and no one will like you,' the voices in my head jibed.

Feeling disgusted with myself, I would plunge my fingers down my throat. An explosion of violent vomiting erupted as the voices in my mind continued to clash. I worked hard to be as quiet as possible, while ensuring that every last morsel of food was out of my body. Now a bag of bones, but unable to realise it, I would hang my head in the toilet bowl, exhausted. I weighed just under six stone and I quivered with fatigue from the relentless routine of living a loveless life.

At 16, I left school without any real qualifications to speak of, just a diploma in bullying and grades A in anorexia and A* in bulimia. The gates closed on my past, but the wounds were still open in the present. The cravings continued and bulimia governed my every waking and sleeping thought.

My first entry into employment didn't change things. The conversations around me would dance in my temples and I would escape to the toilets to be sick, using all the same tools and tricks to hide my secret from my employers as I did my family. However, the distraction of the job soon shifted my feelings of worthlessness. I'd been given a six-week work experience placement, and this proved to be a real blessing. I'd been given the chance to acquire some basic skills and transform my life.

Escape from my family became another all-consuming thought. In possession of a regular wage, I moved to a bedsit to avoid the watchful gaze of my mum and grandma. I also wanted to be free from the negative memories at home.

My desire to run continued as a new adventure beckoned. Aged 19, I successfully applied for a job in Leeds. On the eve of my escape, I told mum. She didn't think I would actually leave, which fuelled my determination even more. I will show you, I thought. Heading north with my boyfriend, it was tantamount to running away.

Leeds offered hope and my new job was a huge slice of luck. I trained people how to use computerised telephone switchboards and earned £100 per week – a lot of money back in the early 1980s. I also had a portion of my accommodation paid for and I felt like I was dreaming. *How could someone give stupid me a job like this?* I thought. Luckily, my common sense prevailed and I wrote and delivered a very successful training programme, which led to people landing jobs. Everyone seemed to love the way I taught. My grand idea had been to teach by keeping it simple and presenting material in a way I would like, which was fun and practical and very unlike school.

With no experience of training, my naivety helped as I followed company instructions and placed an advert to promote my courses in a newspaper. I became focused only on delivering excellent training to adults, who were often twice my age. Receiving praise and recognition from the learners propelled my confidence. For the first time in my life, I'd received praise that I actually believed in – and I felt good.

The real turning point in overcoming years of harbouring a serious eating disorder and a mental health condition took place just a couple of years later. I'd married during my early time in Leeds, but within nine months I applied for a divorce. Living life trying to paper over the cracks of my past while tied to another person so soon just didn't work.

My mind was still racing, my hormones were volatile and my ability to make decisions was impaired. I needed time to recover, and although craving attacks still occurred, most of the time I was preoccupied with work. This was my release until I was made redundant. I hadn't wanted to relocate to another part of the country, so the only alternative was unemployment.

As my 21st birthday approached, the time when I saw myself as becoming an adult, I made a commitment to beat the wretched illness that had gripped me since I was 11. In the nine months prior to my actual birthday in September, I went on a trial run. I considered what I would do to occupy my mind and how I could change my habit of being sick when I became stressed. The answers were not too far away and I found them at the job centre. Leeds City Council made a pact to employ unemployed people, a sentiment that I thought was amazing. Blown away by this ethos, I walked away with a new job - to train young people at risk of unemployment in office skills.

My first day in the job revealed the wicked reality of life and the harsh environment many of the students had to endure. They were aged between 14 and 17 and some of them lived in complete poverty, cowering in fear of abuse due to the colour of their skin or the way they talked. They had not received a good education and some spoke little English. I found I could relate to many of their experiences. If I rewound my life by just a few short years, I could see that I too had the same hopelessness buried within me.

Stepping out of my shadow and witnessing a world with problems, which I perceived to be greater than my own, had a profound effect; it shook my spirit to the core. My job was to help young people find clarity within chaos, and to give them a chance like the one I had been given through work experience. My spirit came alive when I could help and it gave me a feeling greater than any I had experienced. Up to this point, I had lived a life of hidden loneliness and solitude, in which I was a slave to my thoughts. However, the more care and love I gave, the more my soul seemed to heal, and I progressed from self-obsession to sharing.

This experience of helping shunted my consciousness violently, and I learned that if you are stuck within adversity, in the depths of despair, you can use your own experiences to guide others. When you have responsibility for others it can lift you into a place filled with hope, and my saviour came in the shape of a dog.

It's funny how animals can have such a positive influence on our lives. Although we don't speak the same language, the appreciation is ever present. A few weeks into training the students, they told me about a puppy that had been found abandoned in a hedge. I just knew I had to have her! Owning a dog gave me a newfound purpose to go home each day, as I was responsible for a life other than my own. Now there was something else to focus on in addition to my work.

Living in a new environment gave me the building blocks to form a wall of confidence. All I needed was the cement to hold them together – and this was my decision to recover and convince myself that I wasn't worthless, and that my life had purpose.

From the age of 22, I was no longer plagued by food cravings and their consequences. I stayed strong and worked each day to be free from sickness, keeping my focus fixed on helping others. For too long I'd owned the victim card and had used blame to deflect my own challenges rather than confront them.

My mid and late 20s were a mix of hard work and hard partying, afforded by my high income. But a second divorce left me with a feeling of complete failure and a broken heart, after which time I wobbled dangerously towards negativity. However, stability was once again found through work. I progressed to the position of training manager, which brought new excitement and challenges.

Just a couple of years on, I was faced with another challenge after being made redundant yet again. But instead of viewing this setback as a failure, I saw it as an opportunity. I started a business with a colleague who was also let go from the same firm.

We landed a contract with Vauxhall Motors in Ellesmere Port, Cheshire, and my responsibility was to find work experience and apprenticeships for young school leavers. After this, a new opportunity opened to teach 500 workers how to use computers. For the interview, I had to give a presentation to 10 men. It was an intimidating environment to present in but my passion came across and my company was chosen over some major national training organisations. We were naturally exhilarated over this significant achievement. All the late nights we'd put in had paid off. After this our focus turned to delivering training contracts worth tens of thousands of pounds.

My partner and I grew the business to cope with demand but as success grew, so did my fear of losing the business. At some of my most stressful times, I experienced feelings of inadequacy and of being a fake entrepreneur. After all, I had no business qualifications or any prior experience of running a company. Thankfully, while in recovery from anorexia and bulimia, I had learned techniques which enabled me to 'change my own mind' when these negative emotions threatened.

In correlation with the growth of the business came the news that I was pregnant. I was so happy but also a little overwhelmed. I hid my pregnancy and worked up to the point of labour. I was actually in the labour ward when Margaret Jones, who later became a friend, phoned up to organise a meeting. She wanted to discuss and evaluate our company's training programme. I took the call on my huge mobile phone (one of the original black bricks available for sale back in 1995). As we chatted, Margaret had no idea that my afternoon would be spent giving birth. I chose to blame my hospital visit on a bad back. It's funny when I reflect on this, but it highlights the chaos and the craziness back then. The fear of losing work provoked me to continue. Working in a male dominated environment and winning such large contracts, I didn't want to let people and clients down, and I certainly didn't want people to think that I wasn't capable just because I was pregnant.

As well as supporting small businesses with advice and guidance, Margaret was part of a small group called Women in Business; a network for working women to share ideas, contacts and stories. With a newborn baby to care for and a demanding work schedule, the network became a sanctuary, a place where I could unload my feelings and bask in the understanding and empathy of others. On many occasions, I would rush off from a meeting wearing breast pads to hide the milk dribbling inside my clothes. I'd wake up at 1am to feed and change my baby knowing that within a couple of hours I would have to be up for work. Understandably, I had constant bags under my eyes.

Women in Business made me realise that I wasn't the only one to have thoughts such as: fake entrepreneur and, what if the bubble bursts? Perhaps the safety in numbers helped because subconsciously I still feared falling back into the vacuum of negativity. Aged 37, when I fell pregnant with my third child, I did.

I was at home in the garden catching up with a friend who had moved away. I'd just had my 12 week scan and been told that 'everything is fine'. While in the garden, I had a couple of drinks, which was out of character for me. During my previous two pregnancies, I had avoided alcohol, following all the advice and guidance given to expectant mums to the letter. But standing at the top of the staircase later that day, I tripped over stuff that was lying around and fell from cloud nine into the depths of despair, crunching down the wooden staircase and landing in a heap on the floor. My head filled with horror – 'My baby!' I screamed.

Following the fall, I covered my face with my hands and pulled at my skin in desperation. My partner rightly told me how irresponsible I'd been. How could I have done such a thing?

What if I had hurt my child? What a useless mother I was! For days I remained stuck in a spider's web of emotional shame. Tossing and turning at night, I was unable to free myself from guilt.

In times of crisis, when all else had failed, my grandma would always say, 'just pray', so I did.

Sobbing in bed, unable to escape the torment, I muttered, 'Please God, let my child be OK. Please God, let my child be OK.' I was not expecting a response, but I received one.

'The child will be unharmed but you must change.'

I couldn't believe it! Where had this male voice come from? *Elaine, this must be mental health*, I thought as I looked for alternative answers. However, along with the voice came a surreal feeling of love and serenity, which continued on a number of occasions. In fact, the exact same words were spoken at 3am every morning for a few nights. The voice was different from my internal one – I should know, I'd spent years listening to it.

I didn't dare tell my partner about the voice. I feared he would think I'd gone crackers and that the pregnancy had sent me into meltdown. But I knew who this voice belonged to, and pretty soon I would need him.

When my third child, a son, was born, the umbilical cord tied a noose around his fragile neck. His face turned blue and after hours of labour, he wasn't breathing. My poor partner was naturally an emotional wreck; he didn't know that God had blessed me with his words.

The Elaine of old would have been a complete mess, too, especially with the memory of falling down the stairs still fresh in my mind. But the new Elaine was different. While pandemonium raged in the labour ward, I kept faith in my heart, and it wasn't long before we were able to return home with our bundle of joy.

Through all the torment of eating disorders, divorce and disasters, I have learnt many lessons. These taught me that I could overcome adversity.

At school, my frizzy afro hairstyle drove me to think that I wasn't worthy to grace the corridors, or any other part of the world. My grades provided evidence that my future was destined to be bleak, and this was confirmed by the lack of enthusiasm from my teachers. However, what I've learned in this life is that I have the capability to decide what I want to do.

There is always inspiration, even if you are caught in the most hopeless of situations. The following things helped me:

1. Serving others.

2. Making decisions.

3. Finding inspirational stories.

4. Surrounding myself with great and positive people who understand me.

5. Faith.

There is one other. I've adopted the same philosophy as Leeds City Council, which found me employment after I'd been made redundant. Utilising the fruits of my labour and practising what I preach, I helped to secure the future of a dilapidated old building. My aim was to restore it and use it as a base to provide jobs and training for young people and businesses.

Work on the building is now complete. The place that was once home to pigeons and their mess is now surrounded by landscaped gardens, and has children's swings, a tearoom and a nursery. It is also equipped with conference and training rooms. Most of the team hired to work at the centre were unemployed and have now been given a chance - just like I was more than 30 years ago. Working together, we provide work experience and opportunities for young people - helping them to gain skills that will improve their employment prospects.

Women In Business continues to this day, despite its funding being cut. Ellie, the network coordinator, took it over and I donated my business skills and time to keep it going. It has become the largest free online network for women in business. Along with another woman, Jean, we organise the Merseyside Women of the Year Awards, which attracts an audience of four to five hundred people. The funds raised are donated to help charities succeed.

In modern society, we don't always get the time to breathe, share and heal, but the stories we receive as part of the Women of the Year Awards are incredible and inspirational.

Reflecting upon previous awards and winners, I recall the story of occupational therapist, Afroza Ahmed (who won Inspirational Woman of the Year in 2012).

Afroza spends her time with elderly people in the community and has witnessed first-hand the horrific devastation and loneliness of many, including a 90 year old woman living on her own. Frail, profoundly deaf, partially sighted and suffering from dementia, she had taped newspaper to her body as a way of keeping warm. She had no heating in most of her house and had been burning her electric kettle on the gas stove. After Afroza visited her, she decided to help prevent older people from 'dying to keep warm'. She started using her own money to buy safe heaters for the vulnerable elderly.

As Afroza gave her acceptance speech at the awards ceremony, many in the audience started to cry. Until then, nobody had been aware of the extent of the suffering. One amazing lady, Montse Benitez, stood up and there and then announced her intention to donate thousands of pounds to help Afroza set up her own charity.

I'm proud to say that Afroza is continuing her amazing work and is saving lives. She proved that through the darkness, there is light.

Inspirational stories such as this one provide evidence to show that if you search for support it's waiting with open arms to help you succeed.

Like a snake shedding its skin, I was able to let go of the past, knowing that my experiences at school and lack of academic skills haven't mattered in the long run. There was a place for me despite my appearance, feelings, illness or the mistakes I've made. I've thrived and become a success. If I can do it, you can too.

Elaine glowed with passion as she spoke and possesses an amazing infectious laugh, which made we want to laugh with her.

Deeply intuitive and spiritual, she trusts her feelings and is a fantastic assessor of people and situations. I sat amazed as she relived the past and spoke with zeal about the future.

I was intrigued by her conversation with God. In the past, she was not a great believer and didn't follow any religion, but there is no question that Elaine's faith is strong now, as is mine.

Her story gave a different perspective on mental health issues and eating disorders. Addictions, whether they surround food, alcohol or gambling (and so on), poison the mind. I'd seen this with Ben Donnelly in the first story. I can see how they lost control. I understood how the voice played in Elaine's mind when she looked in the mirror. She was a bag of bones, but it told her to be thinner.

Once your thoughts are poisoned by addiction it can become a hellish journey; a suffocation - akin to sinking into quicksand - that engulfs the mind, body and spirit. Our thoughts govern our lives, and it's only in the last couple of years that I've begun to fully understand this.

Elaine's advice regarding how she freed herself summed up many of the journeys I've covered so far. For the advice to work, you need to apply the principles. Decide and commit today, because you can do it.

Shirley Hand and Teresa Fitzgerald
Don't Judge Me, Understand Me

Shirley and Teresa are a partnership, and they are bonded together by experience. They are a double act and full of humour. I see them as the Cagney and Lacey of their profession.

Shirley is shorter, around 5 ft tall, and great fun. There isn't a bad bone in her body. With her long black hair and deep, dark brown eyes, she looks more Greek than British. Blonde Teresa possesses the same character and humour, though she looks more Scandinavian and stands at nearly 6ft tall.

I was so keen to discover the story behind their exceptional work. What's so brilliant is that they don't realise how amazing they are, they're just extremely genuine. My mum has the same quality, and Teresa and Shirley are mums to many.

We first met in 2008. Their journey began parallel to mine in education. Six years on, it was April 2014 and I'd not seen them for a while, but in my quest for inspiration they came surging to the forefront of my mind.

I went to meet them just a few days after making an initial call to Teresa. They are based in an old primary school, which is now named WECC (West Everton Community Centre) in Liverpool. Here, the magnolia walls are decorated with A4 sized photographs of parents and children in the community having fun.

The building is in the heart of Everton. But being in an area that's considered very deprived doesn't matter to those who call it home. Far more important to Shirley and Teresa is the area's community spirit and humour. I turned up to meet them early one day and they hadn't arrived yet. A member of staff employed by the centre said:

'They're not in lad, they've been on the ale all night.'

They hadn't, but this summed up the humour of the people who worked there. I could tell this was a place where a lot of time was spent taking the mickey, but in a non-threatening way.

Shirley and Teresa's room is huge. It's an old classroom that could easily fit 50 people in it. Its most prominent feature is the flipchart paper that covers every available space on the walls. Written on them, in the neatest handwriting I've ever seen, are inspirational ideas and teaching techniques. A yellow cup with a smiley face on it contained a cup of tea that had been prepared for my arrival. I drank it as Shirley, who had come to sit with me, began her story.

Shirley Hand and Teresa Fitzgerald

'Can I see your qualifications, please? What makes you qualified to teach people with supposed ADHD?'

The lady behind the desk was obviously being dismissive, and she'd preceded the question with a patronising lecture.

'We have life skills,' I replied.

I knew where this conversation was heading.

'I suggest you go and study for a degree and earn some qualifications,' the lady barked.

'No, we get results!' I said firmly.

My husband and I have been together since we were 13 years old. We raised our five children with strong, loving family values and as they grew up, we felt part of a huge jigsaw of people who all fitted together perfectly. Only something was different with our middle child.

One Christmas dinner lasted just 10 minutes. We'd decided to retreat to a hotel and relax, preferring to spend quality time together rather than being distracted by the labour of cooking the dinner, especially as there were so many to cater for.

We sat in a large restaurant surrounded by others families. They sang Christmas carols, the older men sporting their brand new woolly jumpers and everyone wearing their colourful cracker hats. It felt nice, but soon silence and shock would slice through the festive atmosphere. Jordan, my son, then aged eight, left his seat and started climbing on the tables like a monkey.

The sound of glasses shattering echoed through the room. Drinks splashed over people's clothes. Jordan was fast and by now he'd discovered where the roast potatoes, boats of gravy and the Christmas turkey sat. He continued his rampage, smashing plates and throwing salt. We chased him but he was running wild. He launched the turkey like an American football across the hall and it smashed on to the floor. People sat in their seats stunned. My face burned with embarrassment as I apologised. It took time for my husband Michael and me to calm Jordan down and escape to the safety of home with our heads bowed. On the way out, Jordan pushed over a man dressed as Father Christmas. It was such a disastrous day, and we blamed ourselves for it.

With our values of love and understanding, what was going wrong? We questioned everything and lost much sleep searching for answers.

The stress began to impact our family life. I managed a pub and restaurant, but my mobile phone was constantly ringing.

Jordan's uncontrollable behaviour led to many suspensions from school, meaning I would have to leave work and collect him.

Some days he would throw things, other times he'd indulge in his own rituals. In order to feel comfortable, he'd have to brush his hand against every chair in the classroom. If this ritual was disturbed, he'd go into meltdown.

He also couldn't cope with moving classrooms between lessons. The corridors were like subways, with herds of children moving in different directions. Their shouts and the sound of the school bell pumped noise along the narrow walkways, throwing Jordan into a mental spin. To comfort himself, he would take a felt pen and start drawing on the walls. The teachers were horrified at his behaviour, but no amount of discipline or talking would make him stop.

When I asked why he was behaving this way, he admitted that he was confused. He didn't know whether to smile at people or how long to look at them when saying hello. He didn't know the difference between a glance and a stare. All this confusion played at tremendous speed in his mind and his solution was to turn to the wall and draw, to escape and hide.

Hearing the word psychologist, I didn't want to believe that there was anything wrong with my boy. *He'll grow out of it*, I thought. We'll find the solution to his problems as a family. In my opinion, learning difficulties were just an excuse. I thought it laughable how a psychologist could just blurt out a few questions and reach a conclusion. I just couldn't accept it and concluded that it was all nonsense. Even when I sat down with a psychologist, I tried to sugar coat the extremities of Jordan's behaviour.

'In that case, I don't know why you are here,' the psychologist said.

However, at times, Jordan's behaviour was unbearable. Some days, when collecting him from school, he'd run in the opposite direction to the traffic. He would weave through the busy lanes as if unaware of the danger. Motorists beeped their horns as I helplessly gave chase, hysterically screaming and shouting for Jordan to come back. All I could think was, it's my fault. Where have I gone wrong?

Disgruntled drivers hurled insults as they wound down their windows, but I kept going. I was no match for an athletic boy and he would only stop when he could no longer see me in the distance. I'd have to hide in bushes in a side street so that he would come looking for me. It was his attachment to me - the fact that when he turned around he couldn't see where I was - that brought him back in the end.

Almost every night was the same. My husband I would sit on our bed perplexed and broken. How could we have failed our son? Our other children excelled in school and teachers commented how successful and bright they were, but our unit of love was being eaten away.

Jordan would get into fights with his older brothers and run away. On many occasions, neighbours would call to tell us where he was hiding. One of those places was in a back garden that belonged to Teresa, whom I'd met through a mutual friend many years earlier. I knew she had faced similar challenges with her son Daniel, and these became our common bond.

We lived in 'Kenny', which is short for the Kensington area of Liverpool. As I drew the curtains before going to bed at night, I used to look across the street at Teresa's house. She was so close that sometimes we would wave to each other through the window before going to bed. Our connection was strong and so powerful because of what we were going through with our children.

When Teresa told me about her childhood and about her sons, Billy and Daniel, I was shocked. However, it helped to know that I wasn't alone and that there were answers. As our stories are so intricately entwined, it's important to include Teresa's here.

Teresa's story

As an exhausted single parent, I knew the stress that Shirley was under. Although there is a 12 year age gap between Billy and Daniel, both were diagnosed with varying degrees of Asperger's syndrome and ADHD.

My eldest son Billy was diagnosed with learning difficulties at the age of just four. Back in the mid 1980s, he was a timid child who didn't know the difference between night and day. He struggled with maths and English and was considered 'slow'. In fact, a child psychologist coldly made a devastating prediction for his future.

'Your son will only be able to recognise some road signs,' he said, 'and he'll need constant support'.

It was heartbreaking to think that after such a short assessment, someone can come up with such a devastating prognosis. Like any mother whose child is criticised, you fight. I decided that we would find a way, despite his difficulties.

Billy's vulnerable personality caused him to drift into the background at school. Alone and isolated, his chance of getting a good education dissipated. It was as if he was invisible behind the rotten wooden desk he sat at.

In a one size fits all education system, teachers didn't realise the full extent of Billy's challenges. Even though ADHD existed, very few people were aware of it. I certainly hadn't heard of it. Even today, many learning difficulties are frowned upon or considered made up.

In Daniel's case, each day was a battle with the bullies. One day, he came home from school with his lip swollen and one of his eyes shut tight - it pulsated purple from the beating he had taken. Unsurprisingly, he would run away from school sometimes. Alternatively, he'd behave in such an out of control manner that he'd be handed three and four day suspensions. I investigated ways to help him, but I feared social services. I was scared that Daniel would be taken away like I was...

My mother died when I was young, leaving my father devastated. He turned to drink as a means of burying his grief, but to me this was normal; I was too young to understand what was happening. I often didn't attend school and would remain in the house, huddled in a dark corner on a mattress with no sheets. There was never any food in the house apart from bags of sugar. Dad worked in the local Tate & Lyle factory and tiny grains of sugar were constantly sprinkled over the lino of the kitchen floor.

When I did go to school, I was ridiculed. I was the scruff, the child everyone laughed at. Teachers would comb my hair, yanking out the lice that nested on my head. It pains me to speak of this now as my early memories can reduce me to tears. I can still recall walking along the street in winter and freezing because I was wearing my summer sandals.

It didn't take long for my situation to come to the attention of the authorities. I was just eight when people came to take me away. Again, I didn't understand what was going on. I remember my dad standing on the pavement and looking through the car window as I was driven away. I was screaming, banging and bruising my fists against the window. I had no idea where I was going – I just knew that I wanted to be at home.

This was my first encounter with social services, and they took me to stay in a huge Victorian house. The sisters (nuns) dressed in navy and white clothes, which draped down to their ankles. Only their faces were visible.

Dragged up the stairs, I was told to get into a freestanding Victorian bath. It was beautiful and white and everywhere was so clean. Steam from the warm water rose until evaporating close to the high ceiling. When the time came to jump out of the water, there was a black ring of scum all the way around the bath. This is how I felt on the inside, like scum. I was unworthy and terribly sad.

The nuns, Sister Ann and Sister Teresa, were traditional and authoritarian in their approach to parenting. They hacked away at my hair and provided me with some clothes to wear. Then Sister Ann gave me a guided tour of the grand mansion that was now my home. It was situated in the leafy suburb of Woolton, Liverpool. It had sandpits and ropes with tyres dangling from them. Being there was an adventure, but I longed to be with my dad. I knew he would be spending much of his time alone.

When I reflect on dinnertimes there, I think of the film *Pretty Woman*. I was the same as Julia Roberts, confused over where to start with the countless knives, forks and spoons that surrounded my plate. But I was a child and I loved the hot food and the smell and taste of custard poured over warm chocolate sponge. Like Oliver Twist, I wanted more.

I began to settle and make friends, but the same people who had taken me from my house came to take the other children in the home away. Each day, the bustling mansion became more and more desolate. After 18 months of being there, the nuns informed me that I could no longer stay. The home was closing down. It was a bittersweet feeling. I'd grown to like it there, but I still just wanted to be with my dad.

Going home was not an option. Like a lamb to the slaughter, I was carted off into foster care, where I was at the mercy of kids and adults who didn't always have my best interests at heart. I'd been left emotionally scarred by my experience of care, and I didn't want the same for Daniel. No matter how stressful or how bad the situation with him got, I wasn't about to lose him.

And so my life as an adult became preoccupied with the search for answers. Why did Daniel behave the way he did? Why did he shout and scream? Just like Shirley, I struggled to hold down my job, but I had to fight hard to get any support. My only saviour was a solicitor who fought the local authorities on behalf of many parents.

Belligerent and determined, I wanted Daniel to have a mainstream education, but, more importantly, I needed support. Managing a child who faces the extreme challenges Daniel does is a 24-hour job.

Erratic and unpredictable, Danny would launch verbal tirades while standing at the top of the stairs. As he shouted abuse at me, all I could do was look him in the eye and respond, 'I love you Danny'. Those were the words that seemed to slice through the venom he spat.

Fighting aggression with aggression is easy. I'd done it so many times. However, disciplining with love is not to be confused with weakness. Restoring order was tough and there could be no backing down from a decision to reinforce the rules. Equally though, I'd look for the positives. Sifting through my son's character, I'd filter out the negative in search of a positive nugget of talent that I could praise. In Danny's case, he loved music, so I used this as a basis to manage his behaviour. If he behaved well then he was rewarded and we would go to the cinema or to see live music. If he didn't behave there would be no reward, no matter how disruptive he became, I stuck to my decision and never gave in, no matter how much I wanted to. Most of the time he couldn't tell the difference between good and bad behaviour so this strategy worked by training his mental muscles, allowing him to make this vital distinction.

For just a few hours a week, I'd have some respite from the intensity of caring for Danny, which allowed me time to study and learn. I created a group for children and parents in which we could share coping techniques. But I saw many marriages and relationships crumble under the weight and intensity of ADHD. At group meetings, members were able to vent their frustrations in an understanding environment.

While I worked on the support group, Shirley and I remained thirsty for knowledge, but the courses we attended weren't designed for our circumstances. Shirley encountered a similar problem with Jordan. He attended a specific course designed for his needs, only to be told not to come back because his behaviour was so extreme.

It was frustrating, so in the end, and after many discussions, we decided to create a course of our own. After years of experience with trying and using different strategies, we felt the time was right. We had both realised that the only way of gaining answers to our questions was to write our own.

In our first two years together we focused on helping adults. My belief was that ADHD is hereditary. Therefore, if you could help the parents, they in turn could help their children. Gradually, our group grew larger. It didn't cross our minds that we could earn money from our courses, we ran them purely on a voluntary basis. But then someone suggested that we should apply for funding and become a social enterprise.

We knew nothing about business and instead relied on donations. A community organisation called WECC (West Everton Community Centre) gave us a room to have meetings in and provided us with printing facilities. We knew nothing about accounts, logos or funding. We didn't even have pens or pads in which to make notes. However, we made a start, calling ourselves 'Ladders of Life'. Our mantra became: Don't judge me, understand me. That's what we both believed.

Our primary goal was to help people and to learn everything we could. But we were judged when we asked questions at major conferences or spoke about our experiences. We were frowned upon by professors, who either yawned or rolled their eyes when we spoke.

When we presented our idea that there is a correlation between parent's and children's behaviour, we were made to feel insignificant. We will admit to feeling inferior then, and we used to choke on the number of letters after people's names. However, our results were proving harder to ignore.

There were so many people in the community with challenges at home, especially with their children - and we found many adults pleading for information. While studying the research papers and listening to people speak in different parts of the country, I stayed committed to my hunch that ADHD is hereditary. We had spoken with many families and they shared the common traits of this condition. Between 20 and 50% of the prison population have been diagnosed with ADHD. Some 80% of adults don't realise that they have it. But that's not to say the experience of ADHD can't be a positive one. Many business people, professionals and athletes have been diagnosed with it. However, left undiagnosed, people run a greater risk of walking along the wrong path, particularly when there have been challenges at school, which can lead to crime.

Our room, in a converted primary school, is famous for the A1 sized flipchart paper that decorates the walls with sayings, symptoms and solutions. They also act as a weeping wall of realisation. So many adults stand before the paper and understand for the first time that they are not to blame.

Furthermore, in 2010, it was scientifically proven that ADHD is indeed hereditary. What's funny is that now the people who turned us away, who rolled their eyes during our presentations, have suddenly started knocking at our door.

Our courses began attracting attention. People who'd served prison sentences, or who had been finding it difficult to function in their daily lives, were finding work. Individuals who had been expelled from school were going on to find jobs as counsellors. Those who had been scared to speak presented in front of large audiences.

One man, Stephen Kenny, wept in front of the paper that hung from the walls. For 42 years, he had been labelled a disgrace and was told that he would amount to nothing. Unable to distinguish right from wrong, he'd spent nearly all his life using alcohol and drugs to numb the pain. His addiction led to a life of crime and years confined within the cold concrete walls and metal bars of a prison cell.

When he read the walls he said, 'Why didn't somebody tell me? Why was this information not available to me?'

It would have been easy for Stephen to be angry. He could have carried on displaying his old negative, demonstrative ways. But he didn't. He worked hard to gain access to university and was motivated by his will to investigate his condition. He later earned a degree in counselling and now works for us at Ladders of Life.

Ibby came to us in his late teens while entangled in gang violence. His school record told of a 'class clown without the ability to learn'. His family was naturally worried. The community they lived in had poured scorn upon them, blaming them for failing to control Ibby's behaviour.

When they came to see us they were facing up to serious charges and the threat of being ostracised from the community. Ibby signed up to one of our courses and progressed well. To help, we also wrote a letter to his solicitor, describing ADHD and it's symptoms. We promised that we would take responsibility and support his family through this period in their lives. The solicitor was hesitant at first, thinking that a reference to ADHD would not be looked upon favourably. Hardened by our experiences, it was another example of judging before understanding. We persuaded him otherwise, and to our surprise the judge delivered a verdict of compassion. We were now trusted to guide him along the path of redemption.

Although Ibby started our course with an arrogant attitude, he left it as an ambassador. His story inspired employers at our graduate celebration day and he received sponsorship to the tune of £1,200 to complete a counselling course and help others entangled in gang violence.

ADHD, and other learning and neurological conditions, do not discriminate. They affect people from different backgrounds, countries and ethnicities. We want to make it clear to professional people, as well as those attending university, that they can attend our courses. We campaign for support for all.

In 2010, we travelled to Downing Street with the purpose of lobbying for qualified medical professionals to support and diagnose sufferers of ADHD and Asperger's syndrome. To our delight, we won and a doctor has been appointed to specialise in this field, covering both conditions.

Swimming through shite is sometimes a necessity. It is often a prerequisite to achieving a purpose. But a sense of achievement tastes so much sweeter when you have earned it. We are proud to have helped people caught up in crime avoid prison. Likewise, we are proud to have helped nurses and business professionals understand that being diagnosed with ADHD and Asperger's syndrome is not their fault. Support is everything, and to emerge from years of trauma with the knowledge that you are a good person who can live and take your place in society is amazing.

Billy was one of the first to attend our course. Although his negative experiences at school affected him for many years, he has discovered more about his condition and developed strategies to manage it. He has gained qualifications in maths and English, has his own home and is in a relationship. He uses ADHD and Asperger's syndrome to his advantage. The accuracy of his work and the speed with which he can do it has won him the title of Employee of the Year. This is an amazing achievement for someone deemed unworthy of recognising road signs!

Daniel has now completed all his music and drama qualifications and is applying to the prestigious Royal College of Music in London.

Jordan has channelled his energy into construction and demolition. He's gained qualifications, excelled fast and has a loving family.

This whole experience has taught us the importance of remaining true to your heart and going ahead with all the conviction you can. We absorbed every bullet that was fired at us, and we learned quickly that many people talk and don't take action, and that they also let you down. We knew we didn't want to be like that. We continued silently and we have helped thousands of people seek guidance. Our training courses have helped people understand they are not alien, stupid or separate from others.

Many of the policy makers - the people with funding - who once held their noses in the air, came back with their tails between their legs when it was confirmed by science that ADHD is hereditary. It was not some myth or a new label to poke people with. We, 'two birds from Kenny', were vindicated with the first adult ADHD course of its kind in the world. And if we can do it, you can too.

If I'm honest, I've raised my eyebrows in the past at the mention of ADHD, Asperger's syndrome and others learning difficulties. When I met Shirley and Teresa some six years ago, I admired their passion but thought that some kids are just naughty. I was not sure if such conditions even existed. So when I heard that ADHD had been proven to be hereditary, I smiled and thought, *well done to you.*

It's so easy to judge, but it takes compassion and patience to understand. When I think back, I've spent a lot more time judging people rather than understanding them. Where's the benefit in that? The answer is that there isn't one. It was a complete waste of time and produced nothing but negative energy. Walking down the street, it's easy to judge people by their appearance, hair colour, the way they talk or where they come from. Maybe this is a lesson for many people who are reading this now with crumbs of humble pie falling from their mouths. But what's amazing and inspirational is that you can overcome negativity and past experiences and go on to achieve.

And with that sentiment, two aspects of Shirley and Teresa's story inspired me. The first is the knowing that you can start. You can follow your feelings, test your ideas and make a difference. It's important to know that you can change, improve and grow.

The second is their mantra, which is as clear as a church bell:

'Don't judge me, understand me'.

I'd learnt so much and it was time to do something with that; to train my brain and make it focus on understanding. Repetition is always the key, I've found, so I am working hard on this - and it's working.

There is just one step to follow. When you meet someone or hear an idea, repeat the Ladders of Life mantra: 'Don't judge, understand.'

Repeat it three times in your mind before making a comment, and focus on understanding the concept or person before passing judgement. Inevitably, we all need to make decisions on people and circumstances, but do so only when you have the facts. Keeping an open mind means understanding first. I've always been quick to do the opposite, but I decided I wanted to change.

Perhaps it's a mantra that many of the warring factions in the world could use, maybe religions too. Or is that too Utopian? I think not, because it's positive. Any stride towards understanding is better than nothing. What do you think?

Amanda & Reanne Racktoo –
Through a Mother's Eyes

Now in August 2014, I'd gotten the first inkling of my next story on a sultry evening a year earlier.

On the same long green couches of the International Coaching Academy, where I'd found out about Eileen O'Connor's story, I heard about another incredible tale.

When I broadcast my request for stories, I met a man named Andy Colhart. He was busy creating and implementing worthwhile projects to help local communities.

He lived in Woolton Village like me, yet I'd never seen him before. In fact, he lived in a road where I'd spent hours playing football as a teenager.

He told me of the uniqueness of the story and how it would take time to understand, but also to write. It did present some challenges at first that made me think (more on these later) and this delayed the progression of the story. There was, however, someone who could help. I travelled to Bury, Greater Manchester, to meet Amanda Racktoo; she was the only one who could unlock this incredible story.

Amanda is a tough woman, but when I arrived at her home she greeted me with a broad smile. She spoke directly and with pride in a broad Lancastrian accent. As she went over the events of her life, I felt like I was reliving parts of them with her. This was an opportunity for me to witness pure persistence and view a story through a mother's eyes.

Amanda & Reanne Racktoo

Retching on all fours, I clambered across my hospital bed as green liquid poured from my mouth. I felt like I was starring in a horror movie. I thought I was dying.

A hot, painful and putrid abscess protruded from my back and throbbed. The burning was so unrelenting and searing that I felt as though someone could have fried an egg on me.

Crippled with poisoned blood as a result of septicaemia, my mum screamed at me to stay alive, beating the bed in her grief. Between 1991 and 1993 I easily spent a total of six months in hospital.

The cause of the pain was my fallopian tubes. Inevitably, they were removed, along with the cancerous cells that lived in parts of my body. I was a mess, emotionally and physically drained because of this sickness. But I had a reason to live - my son Khigh. He needed me. I could not miss him growing up. I would not leave my two year old without a mother.

Fallopian tubes are a crucial element in the process of life. When you remove them it's like pulling out the roots of a tree. The doctors and nurses sat on the edge of my bed describing the consequences of this. I would be unable to have any more children. I was too sick and it would be too risky. I was devastated, but my first thoughts were, I'm happy to be alive.

I was a single mum to Khigh and was not expecting to have someone special in my life again. My focus was on my health and the upbringing of my child, but falling in love has a way of changing your view of the world. After meeting Andy, I got married for the first time and all we wanted was to raise a family.

IVF (In Vitro Fertilisation) in England in the mid 90s was out of the question as I already had a child. We couldn't afford to pay thousands of pounds to do it privately when there was no guarantee of success.

Andy's life was in the forces and when he was posted overseas, Khigh and I went with him. Within 48 hours of arriving at our new home in Osnabruck, North West Germany, in 1995, I registered at the doctor's. The receptionist then proceeded to ask, 'Do you want to be placed on the waiting list for IVF?'

I was dumfounded. Had I heard right? The woman who'd quietly uttered those words hadn't realised that this was my dream. It appeared that the stipulations that applied in England didn't in Germany.

Since the second world war, Osnabruck has been housing generations of British families. It's a beautiful town where modern buildings interweave with traditional ones, many of which have unusual red-coloured roofs. The streets were tree-lined and open fields lit up the horizon. And when it snowed, the effect was so calming and pure. We lived in standard housing estates similar to those back in my hometown of Bury, Greater Manchester. Here, thousands of expat families formed friendships through the common bond of the armed forces.

The scenery, however, could not protect me from pain. For four months, the routine and discomfort of IVF was sometimes too difficult to bear. Injections interrupted my natural monthly cycle and some hormones were removed while others were injected into my bloodstream to help stimulate egg production. My moods fluctuated wildly, and I'd go from calm and happy to sad and depressed. I felt like I had constant PMT, which as many women and men know, is NOT a good place to be in! But I dreamt of children and prayed for a pregnancy.

318

When the eggs were extracted it hurt like hell. Long metal rods were used to probe inside my body while I remained conscious throughout, watching the procedure on a screen. This was painful but inspiring and thought provoking. Technology had evolved so quickly. All that remained was for the fertilised eggs to be inserted into my womb. This brought hope that the miracle of life would flourish inside me.

My medical treatments had taken place in a number of locations around Germany. After a long drive home from one of them, I received a call. Medical staff summoned me urgently, but it didn't sound good. Looking up and cracking my neck backwards, I saw a British nurse standing at the top of a long and winding staircase. I pleaded and begged for news as my voice echoed up the stairs.

Her expressionless face drove my heart into my stomach. Racing into her office, she informed me, in a very deadpan manner, that I was pregnant...with twins. Her expression changed as we leapt up, screaming, hugging and performing silly jigs around the room. Against all the odds our wish had come true, on Easter Sunday no less.

My babies were due at Christmas and my excitement grew each day. For the first time in my life I felt stable, happy and secure. Andy was also overjoyed but had to spend a lot of time away on training exercises. Luckily, my mum visited often from England to keep me company.

The pregnancy progressed well and while I bathed Khigh, I tried to absorb the dramas of *EastEnders* on TV. Meanwhile, a drama was brewing closer to home. With a sudden knotting in my stomach, water seeped from my body, even though it was still only September. Confused but wary, I rushed to my friend Tracey's house to tell her of my concern.

'Get to hospital now,' she shouted. 'Your waters are breaking!'

No, they can't be, I thought. But I took her advice and Andy flew back to join me at the hospital.

This was not going to be a smooth process. Tests revealed I had strep B, an infection that could lead to meningitis and even death. Such was the panic that I needed an emergency caesarean. I was forced to eat charcoal to prevent vomiting and retching.

Heavily sedated, my stomach was sliced open. I could feel two sets of hands rummaging inside me as the nurses tried to rescue my babies. Rhys was born first and Reanne came along second. All I can remember are Reanne's screams. She was so ill and tiny, weighing in at fewer than two pounds. She was so small that I could have placed her on the palm of my hand. But as soon as the twins were born, they were taken away, so I didn't get the chance to hold them.

The trauma of not knowing how they were doing haunted me as I writhed in agony. Swollen, anxious and worried, I lay helpless, empty and exposed until I finally got to see their tiny teacup faces staring at me through bundles of towels.

I was asked if Reanne could be placed in a new experimental incubator. She was desperately ill, so I had to take the risk and hope that she would pull through. Tests revealed damage to her brain and mild cerebral palsy. She'd suffered three huge brain bleeds and I can't even begin to describe the turmoil as each day unfolded. Although Rhys was progressing well, Reanne suffered more damage - this time to her cortex - and was lucky to make it through. I was informed that if stret B had continued for even another 24 hours, we would have lost both babies.

I'll never forget the doctor. He was 5'5", with a shiny bald head that resembled a bowling ball and round goggle-like glasses. A polite and friendly Grim Reaper, he delivered the news in his monotone voice that Reanne would never be able to walk or talk or have any kind of meaningful life. While I listened to his words, I couldn't accept them, as ultimately he was suggesting that we switch off the life support machine. My response was fierce and clear.

'When she gives up fighting, that's when we give up - and not a second before.'

But it was hard to ignore the specialists. The people who had helped create a new life suddenly wanted to play God and take it away.

What if I do let this happen? I thought. After all, they are the experts. They see the precarious balance between life and death every day. They are only trying to help.

Still driven and determined, I had to prepare for the worst. Thinking about losing my twins made me retch physically and my head was ablaze with thoughts. When I awoke from what little sleep I had, I opened my eyelids to a sickening and helpless feeling - I could lose them.

My mother and I spoke and decided that if there was a funeral, it would be back home in England. This was the reality of the situation, and I couldn't escape it.

Outside, a ferocious storm lashed and howled against the windows and more bad news smashed my heart. Reanne's lumbar puncture had produced a tube of blackened blood, which suggested meningitis, and then there was an outbreak of chicken pox in the baby ward. Reanne faced it all, but still she kept moving forward, surviving on milligrams of green tea – she was unable to consume my milk because she was allergic to it.

Her legs were like those of a rag doll, it was almost as if there were no bones inside her. But she kept fighting and on December 18 1995, after nearly three months in hospital, she beat all the odds to return home.

Only five months later, an unrelated trip to the hospital to visit a friend led us to a chance encounter. Standing in the lift, the jarring of huge metal doors opened to reveal a short, bald headed gentleman with circular goggle-like glasses. Overjoyed to see me, he looked down at the twins' pram. Staring back were two babies who were kicking their legs and responding to my voice.

'Is that Rice and Reeny?' he asked, unable to pronounce their names.

He couldn't believe that Reanne had lived, and that she could respond and move her legs. Sobbing, the tears rolled down his cheeks. I could see that he was happy, but he was also shaken. After all, his grim advice could have led to the deaths of the two gorgeous bundles of joy that now lay before him. But I understood why he'd given that advice - complications at birth are prevalent. Each case is different and the medical professionals who have to advise on such matters do so with the best interests of everyone.

Reanne's life wasn't destined to be easy, we all knew this, but we didn't expect to hear the news that she was blind. She was two when she was diagnosed with Cortical Visual Impairment (CVI) and horizontal and vertical nystagmus. In layman's terms, it looked as though her eyes were rotating in their sockets, like those of chameleon. It was another devastating blow to our confidence, but the operation to help correct the alignment of her eyes was successful. This meant that her eyes were now fixed in a normal position, but she still couldn't see.

My poor little baby had spent so much time in hospital receiving physiotherapy that she could barely move. She couldn't walk and was unable to explore like most toddlers.

After settling in at home, life with the twins became a rigorous routine of physiotherapy. Reanne had to learn how to use her reflexes. As a parent, one of my simplest and most natural expressions was to place one of my fingers in the tiny palm of my children. However, Reanne's reflexes were dormant and her fingers wouldn't grip mine. Intense physiotherapy began on her body and the medical care and patience of the people involved was incredible. Reanne progressed much more than predicted.

Sadly, when the twins were toddlers, and now back in the UK, Andy and I split up. Taking inspiration from my daughter, I had to stand up tall again. Seeing her walking in callipers for the first time was heartbreaking, but it also revealed the fight in my little girl. She walked like a baby gazelle, stumbling and falling down, only to rise again. As I watched her, my tears flowed. I can only liken her to Forest Gump. She loved running and would shout for me to watch her. She may have spent two years tied to metal, plastic and leather braces to help strengthen and straighten her feet, but she didn't have a care in the world. It was such a joy to see all my children play, but as the twins grew my thoughts turned to their education.

School, surely that would be easy? Was it ever! Sometimes, casting my mind back is hard. For nearly three years, I fought the local authority and the people who sat and made decisions without any investigation into the potential consequences of them.

Reanne required special care and attention. Possessing only five per cent of her vision, she also had to try and conjure the strength to walk. She would not have thrived in a mainstream school.

Many parents reading this will know how stressful it is to seek, find and compete for places in schools, but each one we visited - although wanting to help - simply didn't have the infrastructure in place to take Reanne. How could a four year old with such difficulties climb steep staircases or go the toilet? It was ridiculous.

The Labour government used education as their mantra. The problem for me was that the local government didn't want to listen. Each day, politicians would vocalise their support for inclusion so that all children, regardless of their disabilities, would have the chance to grow and develop. It was great to listen to, but somehow it didn't apply to me. People in the local authority office paid lip service to my requests. They said the right things, while letters and phone calls went back and forth with no one taking responsibility.

Rebuffed and challenged over Reanne's disabilities, I would not be denied. There was no way I'd relinquish my energy and power and become a slave to the bureaucrats who couldn't even spell her name right! Visiting some of the suggested schools,

Reanne herself knew that they were not right for her. I could feel the vibration of fear in her tiny body as she clung to my trouser leg. These schools just didn't possess the necessary curriculum to help my child evolve. I spent all day and every day scouring for someone who could give her a chance.

Determination dictated the outcome, and my groundwork paid dividends. I found a school named St Vincent's, which is a specialist establishment for children with sensory impairment. At last I'd found somewhere that could provide the required care.

Walking into the school for the first time, I knew I was in the presence of experts. They exuded warmth, confidence and care. Emphasis was placed on engaging all the senses, particularly taste and touch. For the first time, Reanne left my side. She walked off in her callipers to play with the other children for over an hour while I took in the facilities at the school. Reanne would have two teachers and much of her time would be spent engaging in one-to-one tuition. The first objectives were to help develop her speech and boost her confidence.

Despite my excitement and protests, pleading to the powers that be was like pleading to stone statues, they also lived without hearts. Shrouded in red tape, the long paper trail clogged the decision making process. My local authority would not sanction a move to another school in a different authority. But over my dead body were they going to win.

Exhausted, I carried on my fight to get the best for my child. I raised £650 to hire a respected educational psychologist to spend the day with Reanne and write a report describing her requirements and potential.

It worked, and after a long fight we got the funding so Reanne could begin her education at St Vincent's in Liverpool.

From her very first day there, I've watched her character blossom. She was taught how to work independently with an egg timer, completing tasks for 10 seconds, then 20 and then 30. During this time she learnt to ask questions of herself rather than relying on others. From a young age, Reanne has been encouraged to face her fears. She was scared of fire until St Vincent's asked the fire service to attend the school with one of its fire engines and go over safety procedures with the children. It's an example of the lengths the school will go to in order to help its pupils. I don't feel that I could handle these matters with such aplomb while trying to raise my two other children.

Since the age of five, Reanne has competed in gymnastics and swimming galas. To see the power in her legs propel her off the pool walls is a miracle. Her arms carve through the water, releasing endless supplies of adrenaline in her body, and tears of pride in mine. My lungs burn from screaming her name in encouragement.

Like all kids, Reanne dislikes some subjects and has begun questioning why she has to study others. But I'm grateful for this because it shows she is using her mind and the skills that she was never destined to have.

The special care and attitude to teaching at Reanne's school changed the direction of our lives. St Vincent's has legions of connections, all marching in the same direction to provide an enriched and meaningful education for its pupils. One organisation, named On This Roc, visited the school and offered students a chance to explore climbing. Reanne, then aged just 15, told me about it and I was horrified. My daughter, who is registered blind, bouldering without ropes! The thought scared me to death. Was it even possible? At first, it was difficult to comprehend. But on further investigation, and after understanding the safety procedures, I thought, why not? This is her life, and opportunities such as these should not be scoffed at when we've all fought so hard to be free.

How Reanne even attempts to scale a wall is incredible. Like any new sport or hobby, it took time for her to master. Being blind means she requires a sight guide on the ground to direct her through an earpiece. Imagine climbing vertically up a 20-metre wall in the pitch black of night, guided by someone else.

Her determination was evident and more spectacularly, with each lesson and hour that passed, she proved herself worthy of competing against others.

Indoors, the walls were so high that my neck ached from watching. Sharp points and overhangs protruded from the white walls. To see her clinging on to a coloured piece of rock just two inches long was incredible. Her legs stretched as far as they could and her hands, white with chalk, released little plumes of dust that danced in the air. Her coordination was so precise, and yet she had been climbing for just eight months.

In 2012, Reanne competed in the UK Paraclimbing Series, winning two gold medals and one silver. In 2013, at the same event, she won three bronze medals - only this time she was competing against adult males with much more experience.

Next, we were off to Paris, where my girl competed in the World Championships. The trip allowed me to bask in the sunlight of this great location. I was able to absorb the smells of the local cafes and taste the fresh bread. I witnessed the traffic, and heard the beeps of horns as people tried desperately to manoeuvre around the city. Beaming with pride, I marvelled over my girl's progress – she was about to compete with the best of the best. She finished eighth, but this was remarkable for a girl of just 17. Then it was on to Chamonix, France, where Reanne competed in the European Championships, winning silver.

Reanne dreamed a dream when she started climbing. Not only did she win medals, she hopes to become one of the first visually impaired climbing instructors in the world.

More than the achievements, her story is one of triumph over adversity. As I summarise it now, I understand that the huge obstacles Reanne climbs are a metaphor for life. Jagged, pointed edges sometimes razor through our feelings. Sometimes we fall off the wall; sometimes we need to dig in with our fingernails when all seems lost. More importantly, her story is a reminder that the impossible is possible when you persist.

To see Reanne's legs stretch and to witness her grit her teeth and compete, sums up the ingredients needed to keep going. Persistence is a human quality that can supersede any circumstance. My persistence to protect and get the best for my children - even when this drove me towards breaking point – has made it all the more sweeter now our dreams have come true.

I've been close to the end myself, gone through the heartache of divorce, battled with the authorities and with doctors who presented me with a decision I would not wish on anyone. Through all of this persistence, the fighting has been worth all the blood, sweat and tears.

Rhys is now applying for Sandhurst and has his heart set on a military career. Reanne has amazed the medical profession and the sporting world. And if they can do it, you can too.

It was a story that made me punch the air and shout 'YES!' It encompassed the greatest of all traits required to overcome any adversity - persistence. Although all the stories had revealed this attribute in abundance, Reanne and Amanda gave it extra significance.

You may be wondering about the difficulties I'd mentioned having with this story earlier. Well, back in September 2013, I'd received permission to chat with Reanne in the company of Andy Colhart - I was initially going to tell the story in her words. However, it became clear a few minutes into the interview that Reanne struggles with her long-term memory. She can only remember certain parts of the recent past.

This is why I had to think, how can I write this?

I got my answer inside a church conversion. To drive past it, you would think it was still in use. However, the inside is no longer a place of worship, but an adrenaline junkie's paradise.

Steep climbing walls were painted in rich bright colours and electric heaters warmed the chill inside. Climbers talked to each other while looking up and preparing for their next ascent. It looked great and I could feel positive energy and excitement coming from everyone, particularly the young people.

It was at this moment that it came to me. I needed to tell this story through a mother's eyes.

Hence I arranged to interview Amanda.

What I've learned from both mother and daughter is that we all face three primary obstacles in life: negativity, adversity and pressure. At some point we have to confront these - and sometimes we face all three at the same time.

The negativity Amanda faced was from the authorities; the people who tried to prevent her from accessing the right treatment for Reanne and Rhys. She has also had to face the adversity of her own health challenges, as well as doctors making predictions about her children's lives - not to mention the financial pressures of trying to support her family.

Ultimately, Amanda, Reanne and the other amazing people who feature in this book succeeded because they had the sense of purpose and strength to overcome adversity and work towards their goals. They have used their adversity to find and fuel a passion that drives them forward each day.

This has proven to me that anything is possible.

The Learning
September 2014

It's hard to believe that this part of my journey has come to an end. It feels strange that I won't be writing as much, but I'm excited by the prospect of sharing the message that inspiration and fulfilment can be found beyond adversity.

One question I ask myself now is this: if I could, would I transport back to before December 2012? My answer is no. But there is no question that it took time to reach this conclusion. At times I did want to go back and wished I had a relationship, money, a business, my own space, a car and my grandmother - so called normality!

When I reflect now though, I realise I have much more. I have a feeling of fulfilment, joy and purpose, and I still don't have the aforementioned relationship, money, a business, my own space and a car. The only unfortunate point is not having my grandmother around.

Like I've said throughout this book, healing from emotional anguish can and does take time, just as it takes time to recover from a finger cut, a broken bone or ligament damage. To heal from a physical injury, you may need a plaster cast or some stitches; in the case of the mind, inspiration is required – evidence that the bad times can be overcome.

Even now, as I lay on my bed with my head resting against the magnolia wall, I see the difference in me. After reading through the first pages of the book and transporting back in time, I realised that my heartbreak and anger has turned into gratitude. I am grateful that I have overcome my own adversity to learn many lessons and meet many people.

Earlier in the book - in Elaine's story - I compared an evolution of the mind to a snake shedding its skin. Now I wondered, is there another way to describe it better? My answer was no. When you see an actual snake slithering off after shedding its skin, you can see that it is focused on its next adventure, not on the dead scales it left behind.

Death, addiction, a sudden accident, betrayal…whatever the adversity, shock pierces the mind first. You ask questions such as: Why me? Is it my fault? Am I to blame? The mind accelerates at such speed that it's hard to sleep, eat or function. Sometimes, death seems a better existence than life – only it's not and never will be, it's just that your senses are drowned in emotion. Through my own experience, and through writing this book, I have learned six valuable lessons. I felt it was important to evaluate the correlations between the stories I've covered, and what I've discovered myself, in an easy to understand way. So, here they are. I hope they can help you and many others.

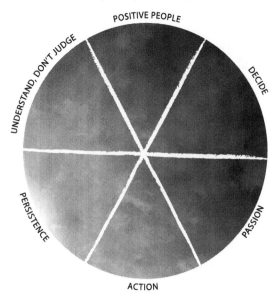

1. Positive People

When you have lost your senses, you need the power of positive people around you. Friends, family and even strangers can help. Positive people are genuinely there to help guide you, and they are interested in your welfare. They don't come running when they detect the scent of money, or any other personal gain; they are there because they want to be.

I think back to the story of Nicola and Adam. The support they received from their families and the people closest to them was crucial in helping them overcome the loss of their child. Likewise, Ben Donnelly needed the positivity of his sister and a relative stranger. They acted as a crutch when his senses were lost in addiction.

It took seven long, agonising years for Tim Reddish to become blind because of a genetic condition. I can't imagine his feelings when this was going on, but the faith and love his wife Val demonstrated, helped him to turn adversity into triumph.

Maybe you think that you can do it on your own, but after writing this book, I feel it's better to cocoon yourself in the radiance of people who wish to help you in your recovery from adversity.

Negativity can cling to your being like cigarette smoke clinging to the fibres of your clothes. If you're down and experiencing the worst time of your life, and the people surrounding you offer no support and keep pumping negativity into your psyche, then it's very difficult to grow.

Use your feelings as a compass to guide you towards those who can help. The person to illustrate the effect of this is Calvin Jodisi. He found a stranger in a newspaper who could help with his education. This came at a time when he thought he knew of no one who'd be able to help him.

'Adversity is like a strong wind. It tears away from us all but the things that cannot be torn, so that we see ourselves as we really are.' (Arthur Golden, author of *Memoirs of a Geisha*)

2. Decide

The second step I've learned on this journey is to decide. I know it sounds simple, and it's probably been said a million times, but deciding to overcome your challenges is an important step. There's no doubt that the initial tsunami of emotion can strike hard, leaving nothing but an emotional hangover. But when the dust has settled you need to make a decision. Are you going to decide to make a stand? Are you going to decide to fight? Are you going to decide to make a positive change?

Decision is the thread that weaves through these stories. Remember Andy Bounds? He made a decision to leave behind a safe, secure job and enter an industry he knew nothing about. He also decided that he no longer wanted to be overweight. Likewise, Emma Hawkins decided to create a business helping people with disabilities after watching a TV documentary. Sai Prasad decided that he would no longer conform to the notion that people with disabilities could not make a worthwhile living. This decision has proved very powerful because it is changing attitudes towards disability in his country, and around the world.

Terry Nelson made a decision to recover from his transplant. He also decided to learn everything he could about running in water and help others recovering from injury.

Only you can bring down the sword and slice through the shackles that are holding you back from whatever adversity you face. Whether you're overcoming challenges, or considering starting a new career, the hardest part is deciding.

With regards to my own story, I decided to write this book, and I decided that I wanted to help a school in Africa. I didn't know how I was going to do these things at first, but making a decision brings your clarity. It signifies that you are in control and, as a result, you can channel your adversity into an outcome of your choosing.

Eileen O'Connor is an example of this. Breast cancer and a road traffic campaign fuelled her decision to discover what caused the illnesses within her village. This is a campaign that has seen her take on the giants of the telecoms industry. The persistence of 12 years of fighting has seen the case brought to the European Commission, which is the executive body of the European Union, responsible for proposing legislation and implementing decisions to protect millions of people.

3. Passion

Passion is inseparable from decision. Just as fish need water to breathe, humans require passion in order to make the decision to grow beyond adversity.

When I think of my own challenges, it would have been easy to seek revenge and broadcast my anger. I wanted to see others (whom I deemed responsible) suffer the way I had. The same thought crossed my mind regarding the people who didn't pay for the work I'd done for them, leaving me with nothing. In my mind, I wanted to blame others for the failure of my business. Indeed, I blamed myself, too. This is why you need to transform your anger into passion, and into something positive.

What I'm trying to say here is that within the depths of emotion, adversity can stoke a fire and light the embers of a passion we never knew we had. With passion, you can conquer anything.

One breathtaking example of this is Clarence Adoo. He was paralysed from the neck down but told doctors:

'What is there to be angry about?'

This still gives me goosebumps now, nearly a year on. He has used his passion for music to show how you can overcome adversity. Seeing him inspire students, conduct orchestras and perform at the Royal Albert Hall provides evidence for my theory that passion can conquer all.

Existing day-to-day, in what can be a mundane reality, means that it's often hard to understand what your purpose is. But sometimes passion can be stirred by a person's words, or the example they set. In many cases, passion is discovered in adversity.

I feel angry when I think of Jasvinder Sanghera's brutal early experiences, which include running away from home and losing her sister. But I also admire her response to overcoming adversity. Despite death threats, she continued to fight for freedom for all - and this was all because of her passion. I was speechless when she told me that it was four years before her charity received its first call. Her urge to continue was fuelled by passion.

The same is true of Ali Jagger. She found a beautiful new desire following a decline in her health, which led to her restarting life in her 40s and setting up a business. Her passion and desire to create has led to a life of freedom – she now travels the world helping others.

Napoleon Hill, author of *Think and Grow Rich* said it best:

'Every adversity, every failure, every heartache carries with it the seed of an equal or greater benefit.'

Maybe, as you read this now, you can see the correlation between passion and overcoming adversity. Passion, love, anger and heartbreak can be channelled into a positive, passionate force.

4. Action

None of this guidance works unless you do. Once you have made the decision, and know why you have the passion, take action. Action is the embodiment of life – it's needed to overcome adversity and fulfil a purpose. Debra Santoro embodies the importance of action. I could understand the depression she felt after waking up to discover that one of her legs had been amputated. But, after listening to her brother, she took action by getting on a motorcycle and exploring the beauty of the US. She took action to pursue a career in accounting and finance, the same plan she had prior to the accident.

The same is true of entrepreneur Elaine Owen. Her memories of fighting bulimia and anorexia live on, but she made the decision that her life would improve. Ultimately, her story is one of action. She took action to start a new life in a new city, later founding a successful business. Likewise, Elaine has taken action to create a community facility which helps hundreds of people by providing them with training, employment and work experience.

Action is the glue that binds all six pieces of learning together. Taking even the smallest step helps to build the confidence required to overcome any challenge, and each step fosters an even greater momentum.

5. Persistence

Persistence is having the strength of will to keep pursuing a course of action that you believe in.

The ability to move forward in the face of a challenge is a necessity. Amanda and Reanne's story epitomises persistence, so if you haven't read it yet, read it now! Amanda fought the education authority to ensure that her daughter got the very best education. She also faced up to her own health challenges and went against doctors' advice, keeping both Rhys and Reanne alive.

Equally, Reanne has to cope with many physical challenges, but the persistence she's shown in her life, and via her competitive climbing, has led to her achieving incredible honours.

Susan Foster's journey has incorporated a lifetime of persistence after she was left with limited movement following a car accident. For years, Susan has fought a lonely battle to prevent cell towers being placed on fire stations - her strength and persistence has helped those people who risk their own lives to assist their fellow Americans.

And the final example is Rita Hunter. Not only has she created a business in her 50s, she has persisted through all the challenges of creating it. She left behind a salary, a secure job, a laptop and all the other trapping of corporate success to start from scratch. What makes her story even more remarkable is that she did this while constantly fighting cancer.

One cancer diagnosis is bad enough - it creates such uncertainty, not only for the person diagnosed, but also for their family and friends. It's the fight, grit and persistence that Rita has demonstrated in overcoming cancer five times that provides inspiration and hope for all.

6. Understand, don't judge

Try to understand situations and people before you make a judgement. This was a powerful piece of learning for me because on many occasions, as I mentioned in Shirley and Teresa's story, I'd done the opposite. But my view of the world has changed because of what I've witnessed. To watch Reanne Racktoo climbing 17-metre walls despite being blind was amazing.

To hear about Shirley and Teresa proving judgemental people wrong certainly opened my heart and mind to the fact that you can overcome adversity and fulfil whatever purpose you desire.

Judgement and negativity are adversities in their own right. They can crush the hopes of many people before they even embark on a mission. The best example of this can be found in John Haynes's story. He was judged all the way through school and was told that he was too stupid to learn and too uncoordinated to work. The judgements continued throughout his younger life - at job interviews and while collecting his unemployment benefits. Ultimately though, through the adversities he faced, John found his passion, which was communicating with people as well as motivating and inspiring them. It took many years for John to dismiss the judgements that other people had placed on him, but once he decided not to listen to those anymore, his destiny was in his own hands.

These days, I would be loathe to say to anyone that they can't achieve. It is up to them to decide, not for others to judge. I believe that it's up to individuals to discover their own passions and to implement the actions necessary to overcome their adversities or pursue their goals. This is what I intend to teach, and it's perfect timing.

On September 8 2014, I travelled to Kenya to get a first glimpse of the school this book will be supporting. My aim was to deliver a message of inspiration to children who face adversity on a daily basis. It was a trip that fulfilled all my values and reminded me that I was on the right track.

It was inspirational to see the desire and hunger of the students to learn. It was also inspiring to teach them what I'd learned on my journey and to share the stories of the incredible people who feature in this book.

And my message was - if I can do it, and if the people in this book can do it, then so can you.

To help support the IF I CAN DO IT, YOU CAN TOO school in Kenya, please go to my website www.antonystagg.com and click on the IF I CAN DO IT, YOU CAN TOO - SCHOOL menu button at the top of the website to see how your contribution will make a significant difference to the children who attend it.

A special thanks to Anne Pontifex, Jimmy Yoxall and the amazing team at St John Bosco High School for contributing so many books to help support the school project in Kenya.

A huge thank you to Mike McNulty and Paul Stirling from Archbishop Beck Catholic College.

14168250R00192

Printed in Great Britain
by Amazon.co.uk, Ltd.,
Marston Gate.